THE COMPLETE GUIDE TO
DIGITAL VIDEO

THE COMPLETE GUIDE TO
DIGITAL VIDEO

Ed Gaskell

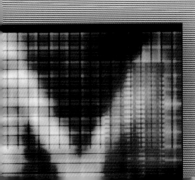

MUSKA&LIPMAN
Publishing

First published in the United States by Muska & Lipman Publishing, a division of Course Technology, in 2003.

For Muska & Lipman Publishing:
Publisher: Stacy L. Hicquet
Senior Marketing Manager:
Sarah O'Donnell
Marketing Manager:
Heather Hurley
Associate Marketing Manager:
Kristin Eisenzopf
Senior Acquisitions Editor:
Kevin Harreld
Manager of Editorial Services:
Heather Talbot
Senior Editor: Mark Garvey
Retail Market Coordinator:
Sarah Dubois

ISBN 1-59200-103-3
Library of Congress Catalog Card
Number: 2003108312

5 4 3 2 1

A CIP catalog record for this book is available from the Library of Congress.

Educational facilities, companies, and organizations interested in multiple copies or licensing of this book should contact the publisher for quantity discount information. Training manuals, CD-ROMs, and portions of this book are also available individually or can be tailored for specific needs.

Muska & Lipman Publishing,
a Division of Course Technology
(www.course.com)
25 Thomson Place
Boston, MA 02210
www.muskalipman.com
publisher@muskalipman.com

This book was conceived, designed, and produced by
THE ILEX PRESS LIMITED
The Barn, College Farm
1 West End, Whittlesford
Cambridge CB2 4LX
England

Sales Office:
The Old Candlemakers
West Street
Lewes
East Sussex BN7 2NZ
England

Publisher: Alastair Campbell
Executive Publisher: Sophie Collins
Creative Director:
Peter Bridgewater
Editorial Director: Steve Luck
Editor: Stuart Andrews
Design Manager: Tony Seddon
Designer: Jonathan Raimes
Cover Art: Jonathan Raimes

Printed in China

00

01
THE THEORY

02
THE KIT

CONTENTS

THE SHOOT

THE EDIT

INTRODUCTION A video timeline

1951

Charles Ginsburg, working for the Ampex Corporation in San Francisco, developed the Video Tape Recorder—the first VTR. It could record live images from broadcast cameras, converting their signal into electrical impulses that could be saved onto spools of magnetic tape. The first VTR was sold five years later for $50,000.

1960s

NASA changed from analog to using digital signaling to map the surface of the moon and to receive information from their spy satellites.

1965

Sony sold the first color consumer VTR. It had a timer facility and a built-in monitor.

1969

Willard Boyle and George Smith sketched out the first CCD… in an hour.

1970
Bell Labs made the first CCD video camera.

1971
Sony sold the first Video CassetteR—the VCR as we know it today. It was the start of U-format VCRs.

1975
Sony introduced the first Betamax videotape.

1976
Matushita (today's Panasonic) introduced VHS as a more compact rival to Betamax.

1981
Sony released the Sony Mavica electronic still camera. It recorded images digitally to a mini-disc. It wasn't a true digital camera—it was a video camera that captured freeze-frames.

...THE DIGITAL VIDEO ADVANTAGE You've probably got a digital video camera if you bought this book. Plenty of people have…and plenty of people don't use them. The path to redundancy is paved with both good inventions and good intentions, but beyond the realms of simply recording a baby's growth, there's a host of reasons to push your toy as far as its technology will allow.

Digital video is cheap—no, it's really cheap. Shooting on the professional DigiBeta format with a camera op, a director, and a sound op will realistically cost you at least $1000 a day—without stock. It's a fact that you can buy a digital video camera for that price and shoot for the rest of your life (obsolescence permitting). The main cost of commercial shooting comes with postproduction. You might be able to strike a deal to get Avid online for $700 a day and then, if you have any effects, you might want to hit a Symphony suite for $900 a day (you're not going to be in the edit for less than this time). Then there are the client changes and the technical changes to consider… To realize your video-making genius can easily run into thousands of dollars, if not tens or hundreds of thousands.

But video can be cheap. Once you've got your camera and a PC to your desired spec, a video card, and a suitable desktop editing system, you're set up to make any number of potentially professional programs.

Digital video is immediate. What sets video apart from any other time-based medium is that you can see what you're getting as you get it. It's as realtime as you can get in its original state. It wasn't so long ago that broadcast news was shot on film that had to be developed and cut before it could reach audiences. Not only had the story often changed by then, but the quality of the film was unpredictable. Was it exposed properly? Was there a hair in the gate? The use of video has catalyzed the news industry. An event is taped and biked back to the news editor, who cuts the story and broadcasts it within an hour. The story can be recut with additions (or, usually, cut down) as running time permits. It's easy.

Because our eyes are now used to seeing video and the variant qualities and quality of it, broadcast television often plays images from digital video cameras, eliminating the need for crews—and again, because we're used to viewing slightly

THE ACCIDENTAL PURIST
Still hanging onto shooting film?
Telecine into a digi-suite for the
ultimate in celluloid manipulation.

introduction

It is a medium that can offer total ownership. If it's you with a camera and you in the edit, the video can, by nature, be yours. It can be the most personal video diary; it can be shown to no one; it can be a celebration or a naked exposure of who you are and be shown to everyone.

degenerative images (i.e., not officially broadcast standard), we have now reached the stage where we can forgive live weblinks from the frontline of warzones, with low resolution, low light, and low sample rate. It's utterly immediate—and that's the point.

Digital video is also portable. No crews, no baggage—just you and the camera. Or just you as a reporter with a camera op in tow. It's the nirvana of discretion. Digital video cameras are now so small that they can go anywhere. Even mobile phones can store the moving image. The surge in guerrilla video-making is largely due to the fact that we don't necessarily have to deal with red tape to attain permission to shoot in private places. Because digital videos are so discreet, the gamble is that you can get at least one take in the can before you're escorted off any premises. For this reason, digital video is perfect for travelogs and has taken over from simply carrying an SLR stills camera, rivaling them in size while taking memories of travel into another dimension.

Digital video is a declaration of independence. Having noted that the digital video camera can negate the need for a crew, it becomes an eye of personal perception—it's literally seeing what you see and how you want to see it. No one, of course, sees in the same way. Our own psychological make-up ensures that the video we shoot is a literal representation of what we see. The edit is the stage at which your project can be twisted, simplified, manipulated, romanticized, however you really see it.

CHEAP SHOT
Video can be cheap because you just don't need the sort of setup shown here. If you were paying for this crew, you'd probably be paying for at least one person you don't really need...

The bottom line is that our society is getting more and more aware of video, used to seeing it, used to artifacts and all the terrible things that video can give to us, but it can also show us things that we'll never see, haven't seen, and wouldn't want to see. Its versatility as a tool is second to none. It can deceive or be truly honest. It can make anyone a director (for better or worse), from wedding videos to cinematic commercial hits.

It's just technology that can be used domestically or professionally, but whichever way you use it, push it. Use the advantages that it offers.

FROM AMATEUR TO PROFESSIONAL So video is a tool. It's something available to us to do with whatever we wish. As a brilliant auteur, you have the wondrous gift of cutting-edge technology in your hand. There are no parameters, just the limitless boundaries of creativity. There is so much space that…actually, you don't know what to do.

The first thing is always to justify production. Is digital video really the best medium for what you want to do? Around the world there are countless numbers of companies which simply assume that because every other company has a corporate video, then they should have one too. Why? Just because you sell the most durable wall anchors in the world doesn't mean that you need to spend lots of money making a video.

The questions that need answering to justify your production include:

Have I the time?
Have I the budget?
Who is this for?
Is there an audience?
Is there a story?

LIVE TO TELEVISION
Some things just demand to be shot. One-off gigs or events have an already established audience consisting of those who were there and those who couldn't be.

Back to the wall anchors. If you have hit upon a constitutional compound that will drive the anchor into flint walls like butter, then are you going to tell the world, the nation, the region? Will you shoot for a Video News Release, for your website or just for the trade? Or is it merely another story for your intranet or staff magazine?

Video is the best way to capture events—but it can also be the worst. For example, if your image doesn't move or if there's no-one to interview, then you may make the shortest and dullest program of all time. Justify your production: is it worth your personal investment?

Of course, if you're an auteur bursting with creativity, there's nothing to stop you from doing whatever it is that you want to do. And if you've got far too much money for your own good and no idea (or ideas), your program will merely join the world's video library of dust-catching vanity projects (or you'll work in Hollywood).

The cheapness and accessibility of broadcast-quality digital video has opened the market for everyone from amateur to professional. And it has also flung open doors for potential audiences, notably via the Internet.

If you have decided that video is the perfect medium to tell your story, enrich your music, or visualize your perspective, there are two further important questions. These are:

What am I trying to say?
How am I trying to say it?

Focusing on these two aspects will ease you into preproduction logically. You'll be identifying the core of your video—its theme, its look, and its purpose. These are the key elements to plan your vision through storyboard, budget, shoot, and edit. Whether you're working high end or low end, keeping focused on what you're doing and why you're doing it will not only keep your production structured, but keep you enthusiastic. It's easy to lose both your way and your cool.

...but if you're editing or vision-mixing overtime, any comprehension of a life outside will be determined by what's on your monitors.

Even if you are out on your own, there are still parameters and you might find them good to work within. Your time and your budget are always the first to consider. If you haven't got that much time available, concentrate on your most important shots, the best investment of time for the most coverage—whatever you need to tell the story efficiently. If your budget is limited, move a scene to a location you're already using, use establishing shots from previous shoots or convince yourself that what isn't seen is scarier than what is...

Professionally, your creative parameters are likely to be less lenient. If you're employed by a client, they'll want you to convey exactly how their company demands to be represented; if you're looking for cinema distribution, you'll probably be working within MPAA guidelines; if you're shooting for the Internet, you'll be using tighter, less motion-driven shots. Many of these are things you may rather not do—but like all good disciplines, they force creativity.

The same goes for the camera in your hand. Shying away from the technology that it contains may be fine for what you want to do, but it won't help you push its potential. And it won't help later in the edit, when you're troubleshooting. Work the left-hand side of your brain as auteur, but try to keep the right side functioning too. And bear in mind that there are numerous architects who design buildings that engineers deem unbuildable...

THE THEORY

01.01

You used to have a digital watch, huh? Why was it digital? Because it didn't have hands?

The confusion even graces the pages of dictionaries: try 'a watch with a digital display', for example. The misuse of the term to somehow distinguish it from analog causes some basic definition problems. The fact that something is electronic rather than mechanical does not mean that it is digital. Even a contemporary mobile phone that has the choice of time displays will differentiate a traditional clock face from that of LCD/LED emulation by using the terms "analog" and "digital."

Keeping with the concept of time, it is essential to understand that the world revolves around four dimensions: height, depth, width, and time. Together, they create something that is recognizable to us, something that is truly analog. Unlike the two dimensions of a painting or the three dimensions of a sculpture, film and video are able to capture all four dimensions from this analog world. It's a copy, a representation, an imitation of life, just as a conversion from source to digital is.

A progressive example from analog to digital is the phonograph. It's definitively analog but contains electronic circuitry to enable the disc to rotate, and the arm to lift, as well as incorporating an amp. To further the complication, the advent of the professional DJ industry now enables part of the circuitry of contemporary phonographs to be digital while still translating analog vibrations from the disc's groove into audible sonic wavelengths.

PART 01. THE THEORY

CHAPTER ONE

WHAT MAKES "DIGITAL" DIGITAL

A turntable or associated hardware may now contain a processor to turn the disc's analog signal into a digital signal that is a truer representation of the disc's audio information; it would encode it, it might even compress it into a specific file format, and then decode it at its destination (the amp or the speaker) back into an audible analog signal.

For this is the crucial point: digital is a way of taking information from one point to another as a truer representation of the original than any analog transmission could.

This is the place to start with digital, differentiating it from its entirely non-identical twin: analog.

ELECTRONIC VS BINARY The difference is actually quite clear, visually. An analog signal can be seen through a vectorscope as a wavelength. Both audio and video analog are sent as waves that are interpreted by analog hardware as vibrations. And the difference between them is best described by comparing the speed of sound and the speed of light—we see things before we hear them purely because the wavelengths of light are far faster than the wavelengths of sound.

THIS IS THE REAL WORLD

In the digital realm, information is contrived to be sent as a matrix of zeros (0) and ones (1), where—quite simply—one is on and zero is off. In audio terms, this means that there is no sound with a 0 but there is sound with a 1. With video, the same applies with an image. One 0 or one 1 is termed a bit.

Where it's not so simple—and this is the reason why digital is so precise in its sound and audio—is that there are eight zeros and ones to a **byte**, which—using the binary system—allows **256** permutations within one byte. Rarely is digital used as one byte these days unless a gadget is very small or doesn't need it. To put this in perspective, the laptop that these words are being typed into has 256 **megabytes** of **RAM** and 20 **gigabytes** of hard disk memory. In real terms, this computer allows information to be stored of 268,435,456 and 21,474,836,480 combinations of zeros and ones respectively.

SINE OF THE TIME

The analog world, represented as a wavelength, is captured and played out by digital at a sample rate that can only roughly represent it. The higher the sample rate, the closer digital gets to representing analog's infinite values.

THE DIGITAL ADVANTAGE

This is where digital comes into its own against analog: a simple array of 0s and 1s fed into a processor can be compressed, stored, and manipulated—something that wavelengths are less capable of doing without distortion.

Because wavelengths are physical in terms of their natural form (they reach the ears and eyes without intervention), they're also subject to interference and electromagnetic distortion. If you can imagine that everything you see has a sound, then you can also imagine how both audio and visual wavelengths are continuously around us, bombarding and interfering with each other.

The same thing happens even when capturing analog sounds and visuals into a computer: wavelengths can be distorted by anything else electrical sending further electronic impulses around it. Think of any television show where a person on their analog phone is calling in within close proximity to their own television set, or taking your microphone too close to the amp down at the local karaoke bar. Digital technology completely eradicates interference like this (known colloquially as "feedback"). It does, however, have its own drawbacks, to be discussed…

Analog signal

Digital signal at 64 kbps

Digital signal at 128 kbps

PLASTER CAST

Left: Analog VHS edited digitally won't cover it up and make it better. More realistically, digital can be so precise as to highlight the weakest parts of a streaky low-res image. Below: The less pixels that can represent the analog image, the worse chance the eye and brain have of reading it.

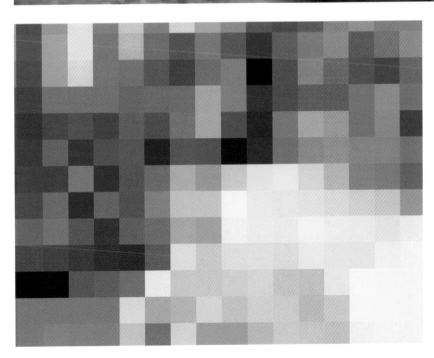

THE IMAGE

If you look up close at any digital image, just like any television set, you will see that it is made up of pixels. The more pixels, the better the ability to represent the source image accurately.

The pixels that construct an image are displayed as a rectangular array, each (in a color image) made up of red, green, or blue. The primary colors not only combine to become any other color in order to truly represent that part of the image, but also use luminance to dictate the intensity or subtlety of resolution.

The pixels themselves can either be square or non-square. Square pixels can usually be found with graphics software and programs, which can lead to stretching and shrinking issues when importing them to your edit. Your solution to this is either to compensate with your edit or effects program (After Effects uses a Shrink To Fit command) or calculate in your artwork (Photoshop would be 720 x 534 pixels). Fortunately, today's software is mindful of the difference and formatting is easy to find on menus.

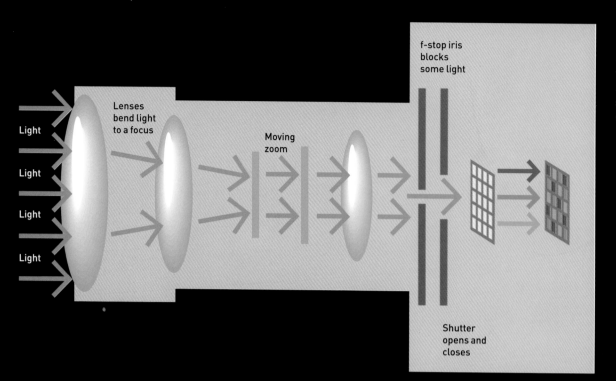

CONSUMER DIGITAL VIDEO CAMERA
Single CCD with a filter matrix for RGB, generally ¼ inch. The 250,000 to 1,500,000 pixels are split evenly between the red, blue, and green colors.

Light

Light

Light

Light

Lenses bend light to a focus

Moving zoom

f-stop iris blocks some light

Shutter opens and closes

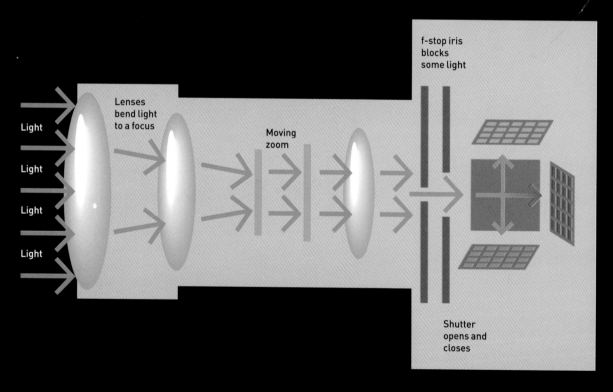

SEMIPRO OR PROFESSIONAL DIGITAL VIDEO CAMERA
A 3-CCD camera with beam splitter sending light to 3 CCDs, each with a color filter to record either red, blue, or green. The CCDs are usually ⅓ inch to ⅔ inch with 300,000+ pixels for each color.

Light

Light

Light

Light

Lenses bend light to a focus

Moving zoom

f-stop iris blocks some light

Shutter opens and closes

MAKING ANALOG DIGITAL: THE CCD
A digital video camera doesn't record images. This is the difference from a film camera, where light from an image exposes various parts of light-sensitive film running past the lens.

A digital video camera records all the information needed to represent that image, that moment in time, for when it is translated back as a visible analog signal. In order to actually capture the information required, the image has to go through various processes. Initially, the image needs to be scanned into the camera.

We see an image with our eyes only because of the way light responds to it by way of reflection, absorption, and diffusion. This is precisely the information that a digital camera needs to represent a captured image. Light consists of the entire spectrum of colors, which can all be constructed from the primary colors: red (R), green (G), and blue (B). For this reason, when the light from an image passes through your digital camera lens (and filters), it hits an **optical beam splitter**, separating the light into RGB characterized by their analog frequency.

The beam splitter works using two **dichroic** surfaces. These either reflect light onward to the correct RGB filter or transmit it to the **Charge-Coupled Device (CCD)**. The CCD is the crucial part of the camera. It is a photosensitive surface made up of thousands of individual semiconductors. Each part of the filtered-off image collects here as an individual pixel. What your CCD then does is turn the amount of light that each pixel is receiving into a small electrical charge directly related to that pixel's color **(chrominance)** and saturation **(luminance)**.

Every charge for every pixel for every scan of your image is then transferred in strict order for storage.

Understandably, this is a great deal of information for one image, let alone a moving image that is constantly being scanned in order for it to be perceived as moving. Indeed, accurate readings when an image is moving can be quite difficult for a CCD, which is why your digital camera probably has an automatic compensating feature: if a pixel is recording values that translate as the blur of your image moving, it will pay attention to the other pixels around it and make logical adjustments to clean up the image in motion.

Likewise, your CCD will usually be responsible for eliminating a certain amount of **pixelation** by analyzing neighboring pixels. Complex algorithms are applied, making sensible adjustments, particularly at color boundaries, where analog cameras have always had problems with streaking. This process is called **interpolation**.

THE ADC The stream of pulses of each scanned image from your CCD are still pulses of analog signal and, as electrical charges, are now presented as voltages. They are very susceptible to interference and so, in order to digitize them and avoid this, they're sent to an Analog-to-Digital Converter (ADC).

An ADC, though, usually has an 8-bit capacity and therefore only 256 values. This means that each electrical charge has to be corrected to ensure that it is within the ADC's limits.

In your digital video camera, there are two ADCs. One controls the luminance and the other the chrominance. Interestingly, luminance is sampled about four times more per second than chrominance because the human eye is more sensitive to brightness than to changes in color. This gives a format its sample ratio where the first number is the sample rate of luminance on the first line of 720 pixels, the second of chrominance on the same line, and the third of chrominance on the second line. Therefore, 4:1:1 means that luminance is being sampled four times for every one color sample on every line, and 4:2:2 means that color is being sampled at half the rate of luminance. 4:2:0 translates as chrominance being sampled only for every other line of pixels.

The way that the ADCs turn your analog RGB signals into a manageable digital signal is for one of them to handle the luminance and sync of your signal (Y) while the other handles red minus Y (R-Y) and blue minus Y (B-Y). The green signal is derived from this information.

The process of turning RGB (ratio 4:4:4) into Y, R-Y, and B-Y (otherwise known as YUV) compresses your luminance and chrominance information in order for them to fit within a limited bandwidth. Whereas an RGB signal requires 24 bits for true representation, a YUV signal requires only 16 bits. The digitized R-Y is known as Cr and B-Y as Cb. Your full digitized color image is therefore known as YCrCb.

The way that the charges are corrected and limited is by each color channel being sent through an amplifier and then to a filter. The filter stops chrominance and luminance from reaching levels where aliasing (pixelation) might be apparent in the image.

The reasons are beginning to become clear why a digital image can never truly represent the subtleties of an analog signal from a natural source to the eye. If an analog signal is represented by a constantly varying sine wave with infinite values, a digital camera can work only within a set amount of numbers—albeit huge numbers. This is why interpolation and anti-aliasing features exist: they compensate for the limited amount of thousands of semiconductors on the CCD.

SAMPLING

Sampling is the essential part of the process for your analog signal to be disciplined as numerical values that digital technology can cope with. The sample rate is the number of samples taken per second from your analog signal to represent it as a digital value. Obviously, the more samples taken every second, the more accurate the representation of the source. Henry Nyquist's original theory was that the sample rate must be at least twice the rate of the source's highest analog frequency for accurate digital coding and decoding.

part 01. the theory

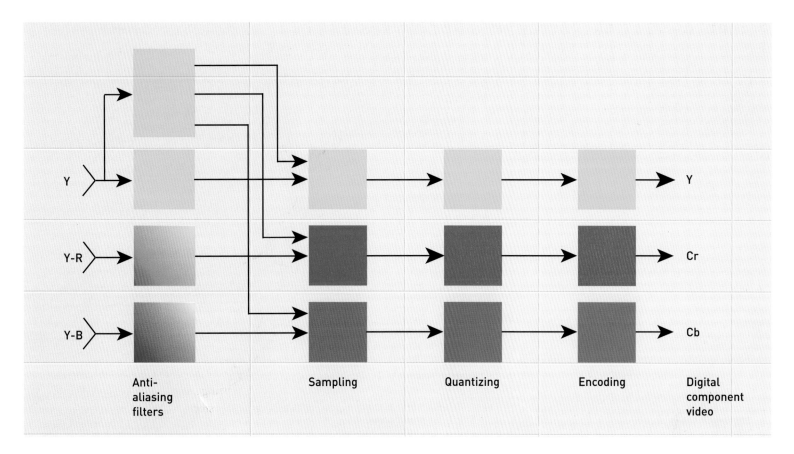

	Anti-aliasing filters	Sampling	Quantizing	Encoding	Digital component video
Y					Y
Y-R					Cr
Y-B					Cb

QUANTIZING

The assignation of one of the 256 binary values to the sampled and amplified analog signal is called quantizing. Your eye can distinguish about two million different colors and an 8-bit camera with three bytes (to allow for R, G, and B) per pixel can represent 256 x 256 x 256 (i.e., about 16.7 million) colors. Because even these numbers use approximations, errors can happen, which manifest as visual interference. This is referred to as quantizing noise.

COMPRESSION

Understandably, the binary numbers coming out of an 8-bit ADC are huge, and the amount of information in the stream is too large to be practically handled by your camera. To cope with this, the data has to be compressed. Compression is a complicated process that removes unnecessary information, prioritizes information in what's left by shuffling data, compresses, then reshuffles the whole thing again, correcting errors, and then recording it as the resulting data to your tape.

THE ADC ODYSSEY

The four-stage process for converting an analog signal into its digital imitation through an ADC is fundamentally just a series of preset mathematics and ordering applied at each step.

BUT WHAT ABOUT AUDIO?

Just like your images, your audio is entering the camera as an analog signal either from your camera mike or your external microphone port. Again, it's being sampled at a rate over twice the frequency of its highest pitch for accuracy and quantizing. You'll probably find that yours is sampling at 48, 44.1, or 32kHz.

Your audio will also be sampled at a bit rate—i.e., how much information can be given for each sample. 16-bit two-channel audio is a good standard of digital audio for the human ear. If you have 16-bit audio, it will take up all the space allocated on your digital video tape. There is only a certain amount of space available for audio, so sampling at 32kHz with 12-bit audio can help to ease up another channel if you want to record any additional audio on the tape.

After all of this, you've got a whole load of 0s and 1s that are the digital representation of your analog world. What you'd probably really like to see, though, is an image...

STANDARDS: PLAYING, RECORDING, AND CONVERSION To see your digitized image requires a DAC, a digital-to-analog converter. Your computer's graphics chip contains such a device to turn the digital images streaming into it to output as a comprehensible image (rather than strings of 0s and 1s).

The way that your analog-to-digital and now digital-to-analog image is represented, just like film, is in frames. Each frame is a still capture that progresses your original seamless analog image at 25 or 30 frames per second. Essentially, it is animation running at a fast enough speed to trick the eye into believing that the sequence is in motion.

The monitor to which you are playing out your digital-to-analog image has options about how it receives that information—by interlaced or progressive scanning. Your computer monitor and your digital video camera use progressive scan, but a non-digital television doesn't, which means that the tape has to have the ability to be read with interlaced scanning. For every frame, then, of your image, you have two half-frames known as fields.

The complication with this, though, is with standards. There are three main standards in the world: NTSC (National Television Standards Committee), as used in North America and Japan; PAL (Phase Alternation Line), used primarily in Europe; and SECAM (*Sequential Couleur avec Memoire*), used in France. NTSC operates at 29.97 frames/59.94 fields per second and scans 525 horizontal lines. PAL and SECAM, on the other hand, both operate at 25 frames/50 fields per second and at a 625 horizontal line scan.

FIELDS OF FIREWIRE
Sampling one still image of your video image is the perfect place to see your two fields at play. Notice that it is close-up movement where the shift in image is more obvious. To get a clean still from your video footage, the filter menu in your edit software should let you de-interlace the picture and decide which field you want (even or odd) to grab.

There is a slight color difference between PAL and SECAM—SECAM will often play in monochrome on PAL equipment—but they both share production equipment. NTSC, however, is incompatible with either and, because of the decrease in the number of horizontal lines, the image has a slightly lower resolution.

Your digital videotape contains auxiliary information about your picture that is also being translated to the screen. One of these things will obviously be the standard that you are using. If you are planning to play your edit in a country without your standard, you'll most likely have to convert it, although switchable decks can be found. If you're ultimately planning a telecine transfer to film, it's always a good idea to shoot with

GET THE PICTURE?
The same shot as seen in standard 4:3 and in true anamorphic. While 16:9 may give you a cinematic sense to your production, it doesn't make much sense to use it unless you anticipate playing out on a 16:9 screen. On 4:3, these are the kind of black bars and smaller image you can be prepared to see.

the PAL or SECAM system using a progressive mode in your digital video camera. This will ensure that you are shooting at 25 frames per second, as near to film's 24 frames per second to be as close to a seamless transfer as possible. An alternative approach would be to look at some of the newest digital video cameras with variable frame rates. Panasonic's Varicams, for example, are capable of a 24-frame rate.

The other important information on your tape will be the aspect ratio that you used for shooting. You are likely to have options in your camera that you will have chosen specifically for the job. If you are likely to end up playing your edit on a television monitor, then you have to consider whether the television itself is likely to be **SDTV** (Standard Definition Television) or **HDTV** (High Definition Television). The standard definition for a television is 4:3. This is the ratio of the number of pixels on the horizontal versus the vertical. High definition's ratio is 16:9—or widescreen, as it has become commonly known. HDTV is becoming much more common and many video-makers are choosing it as their preferred ratio, investing in its predicted future.

The problem with 16:9 is that digital video cameras lie—at least, some of them do. True 16:9 is shot using either 16:9 CCDs, an **anamorphic lens** or an adapter. The image is long and thin, squeezed into a 4:3 frame. It is then unsqueezed to the full 16:9 ratio in your edit.

The 16:9 ratio offered by many digital video cameras, however, is merely cropping; the camera merely takes the top and bottom scanlines and replaces them with black bars. You're losing the top and bottom of your picture. Should you then require your fake widescreen image to fill the frame as 4:3, you'll have to blow it up to get rid of the black bars and lose significant resolution of your image.

You don't have to learn the lesson the hard way for this. If you aren't sure, shoot 4:3. And if you're pretty sure, but not too sure, shoot with your most crucial images in the center or upper part of the screen so that you have a chance to convert it later.

WHAT'S ON THE TAPE Digital video tape itself comes as a quarter-inch width standard. The cassettes come in two sizes: a four-and-a-half-hour cassette or a half-hour mini-cassette. Both types of cassette record at a rate of 25 megabytes per second.

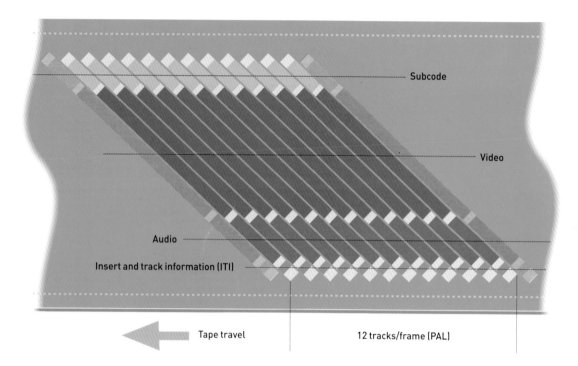

Subcode

Video

Audio

Insert and track information (ITI)

Tape travel

12 tracks/frame (PAL)

Those are the fundamentals, but each company involved in the establishment of the DV standard has tailored their equipment to deal with the system in their own competitive ways. For this reason, tape stock, tape speed, bit rate, compression ratios, and data streams tend to vary slightly. These will be discussed later, but the underlying fact is that whatever you shoot will be put onto the tape in the same way.

Videotape for a VCR has been notable for its degeneration of image. This is because the tape itself is in contact with the play/record heads in an active role. In 1995, IBM revolutionized this system of **helical scanning** with a method where the tape doesn't touch the heads, the only by-product being a slight reduction in the amount of data stored. This is the system that the DV standard uses, and it requires the drum containing the heads to make 9,000 revolutions every minute.

Because this drum is at an angle, helical scanning for your digital video camera distributes each scan diagonally onto your tape. Your binary information **(data tracks)** is transferred to the tape, every frame containing 12 tracks for PAL (ten for NTSC), and 48 scans for each of these tracks. This is where the differences between film frames and digital frames are at their most 'apparent': each track doesn't contain chronological scans of your image. For audio, each of the 12 (or ten) tracks are divided into your two audio channels, all the tracks being used if you have recorded 16-bit audio.

Both audio and video tracks contain further information. For audio, details on the recording time and recording mode are present, and the video tracks have a massive capacity for auxiliary data including the date and time of recording, the focus mode, shutter speed, auto-exposure mode, gain, color setting, and f-stop.

There are two more types of data recorded onto the tape, though. Insert and track information **(ITI)** indicates how all the data has been put onto the tape (including the distance between tracks and whether it was recorded as standard play or long play), and **subcode**, which contains your all-important **timecode** as well as an absolute track number, a unique allocated 23-bit code for each track in your frame.

Timecode is the crucial element in your subcode as it is the numbering system that you will use in your edit. Each frame is given its own individual frame number, which will let you cut your edit to your shots' lowest exact visual component. Timecode is applied while you are shooting on most digital video cameras and will, by default, continue the sequence of number streaming no matter how many times the camera is switched on and off. If you need to differentiate between tapes, change the timecode manually—i.e., 01:00:20:00 for the first tape, 02:00:20:00 for the second tape, etc. (although this facility may not be available on many consumer-level digital video cameras). If you are using lots of tapes for your edit, you will need to ensure that you do this to eliminate your edit software's confusion over identical numbers.

Through all of these four types of data laid on your tape, the application ID of a track **(APT)** runs throughout. The APT defines the internal structure of that part of the tape.

Your tiny cassette is holding all of this information: it's a small miracle. It's still tape, however; something physical with a fragile future. Recording directly to portable hard drives is becoming more fashionable and sometimes more practical. But even with an intangible analog image captured to an untouchable digital memory, there are still ways to sully your perfect recollections…

BURN, BABY, BURN
A tape transfer with burnt-in timecode (BITC) can help to log shots and precise in and out points before entering an expensive suite.

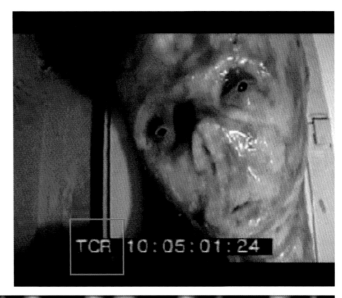

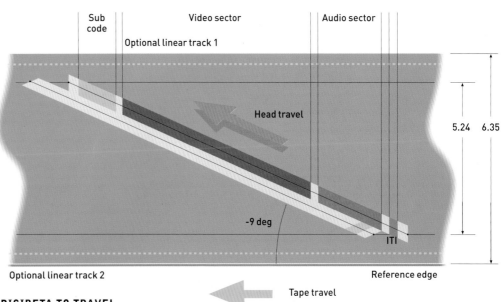

DIGIBETA TO TRAVEL
The same tape is read diagonally by the heads as the tape zips forward. This allows time for the data to be processed as well as for the mechanics of the camera when the tape is running at 9,000 rpm.

THE PRICE OF DIGITAL

There are two sides to every story, as any purist will tell you. And they're not wrong. Digital doesn't mean that your video has magical qualities—indeed, it's an analog world out there and no digital video camera is going to make it a better place.

Because the nature of digital information revolves around pixels, compression, and reproduction, there are usually many things that ensure you won't be looking at a perfect picture. Pixels are rectangular areas of color that you can pick out individually on a monitor in close-up and which destroy any illusion of reality. And even if you haven't got your nose pressed to the screen, you can still fall foul of a noticeable problem picture.

Because your millions of binary codes have lost "unnecessary" information while being compressed (lossy compression), the truth is that they have really reached a compromise in the information that they have retained. Artifacts can be an unsightly product of this, and come in various forms. Mostly, though, you'll bear witness to visible

rectify this, but in reality they're simply disguising the problem, not actually supplementing the lost information.

Monitors also have ways of dealing with the viewing of artifacts. Progressive scanning is normally the way that your digital signal is sampled on a monitor or digital television. This means that every horizontal line on the screen is scanned repetitively in sequence (i.e., for a 50Hz television, the image is re-sampled 50 times per second). The higher the rate of image refreshment, the less you are likely to view artifacts. This does not mean, however, that they don't exist on the original source.

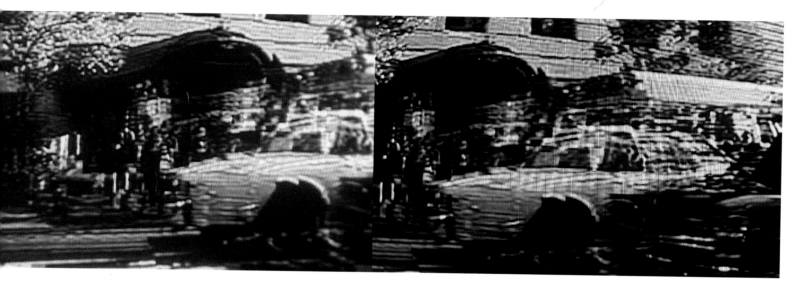

noise occurring around diagonals and contours within your image on screen—and if you are sensitive to information lost during audio compression, it will manifest as a slight buzz on your soundtrack.

As a mass of pixels, your image is created from straight lines and sampled at a high enough rate to comply with the Nyquist Theorem. When they're being sampled at a too-low rate, there is not enough information being received to understand either movement, contours, or diagonals and these become noticeable as aliasing—that familiar "steppy" look. Motion blur and filters attempt to

To add to the dilemma of locating the source of artifacts, the standard definition television (SDTV) uses interlacing as a means of displaying your images. Alternatively to progressive scanning, interlacing scans the image with every other horizontal line at a time, meaning that the picture is scanned twice for every image to be seen. The reason that this is used is that it works to successfully blur motion rather than "animate" an image (i.e., 25 frames per second runs as 50 fields a second).

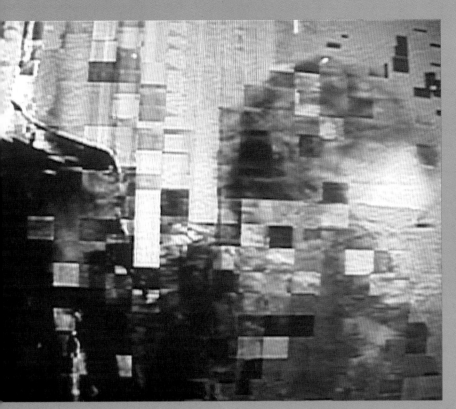

LIBRARY AND CORRUPTION
Even burnt as MPEG-2 on DVD,
your images aren't necessarily
safe from digital corruption.
Digital misreading can look as
unpleasant as this.

Again, if the scan rate is low, a flicker and artifacts can be evident unless a filter is used.

Some televisions now use anti-aliasing filters of their own. Philips' PixelPlus adds another horizontal line for every standard two lines, and doubles the number of horizontal pixels. While this might eliminate a certain amount of aliasing, what it is also doing is clearly highlighting the artifacts from a digital signal. This, coupled with fast sample rates, can also display a purist's nightmare: an original film source that looks uncannily like video.

And there is a more obvious danger to be aware of: your digital codes are also being recorded to a digital video cassette, something tangible—and tangle-able. Clogged recording heads and stretched or chewed tape will affect the code and corrupt the picture. This tends to lead to dropout that can be horribly intrusive. If it is extensive, you will have to find a way around it. Otherwise, dropping the offending frame and interlacing can help you out.

When it comes down to it—unless you are working within the rigidity of commercial standards—it's what you see on the screen that counts. If it's too offensive, change your settings for viewing or editing, choose a different code, or try saving the file as a different format (i.e., with a different compression ratio). Consider that our eyes have filters of their own: we're well used to seeing digital imagery and making our own automatic corrections.

The higher the sample rate, the lower the resolution?

THE KIT

02

Your camera will be where your whole digital video experience begins. If you've got one, it is probably its limitations that have brought you this far: it doesn't edit out the bad bits.

Like every bit of kit on the market, the range of digital video cameras zooms from ultra low-end to unforgivably expensive professional—and, as with your processing equipment, there is no good digital and no bad digital.

Finding a camera that suits your needs is far more to do with budget than anything else. You are less likely to find yourself being cautious given that there aren't necessarily any additional expenses to outlay with a camera. It is also the fact that the competence and confidence of the operator provides most of the versatility for your images to live, so the only real issue is to get value for money.

You can, of course, still go the analog route, although your choice is somewhat limited by today's rabid fervor for anything digital. Analog video cameras will operate using Video8, Hi-8, VHS, S-VHS, and Betacam SP, but there are limits to the quality (hence the advent of digital). VHS tape is capable only of recording 230 horizontal lines, no matter how many lines the camera is capable of resolving. Betacam SP, on the other hand, is still used as broadcast standard due to its resolution. The problem with it, though, is that it is still subject to image degeneration and image tearing (i.e., no one would still record broadcast speed-racing on analog).

Digital video cameras therefore hold the upper hand—especially as your non-linear editing system will be digital too. Within your budget, your choice of digital video camera will either be Digital-8, MICROMV, DV, DVCAM, or DVCPRO. The variations exist because of different companies, not because of any different video encoding.

PART 02. THE KIT

CHAPTER ONE

THE CAMERA

IN YOUR FACE
The power of the size of a lens cannot be underestimated. Sometimes it's an intimidating tool that can silence interviewees...
...and sometimes it's not.

The only real difference is the cost, with Digital-8 and DV offering the more consumer-friendly prices. The more pro you go, the greater the sensitivity of the CCDs and the more versatile the lens interchange—and the more bulky.

Digital-8, MICROMV and mini-DV cameras have advantages of their own—and size is one of them. A digital video camera can get into places that no analog camera ever dreamed of. They can also act as a viewing tool as well as a recording one through the use of their typical LCD screens. The other benefit is that you can simply pick up and record regardless of any settings.

It's this latter advantage that is the key to choosing the right camera. Automatic digital video cameras are all well and good for grabbing Nessie while you can, but it is the manual settings that will give you the images that you want and give your camera a more lasting use: remember, your images are limited only by the operator.

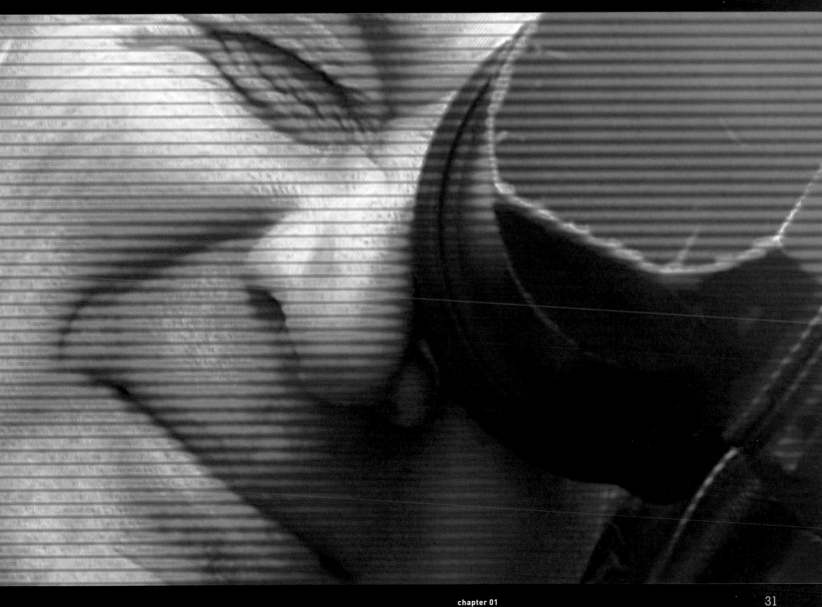

CAMERA FEATURES Once you take your basic demands and budget into account, you can start to narrow down your shortlist of digital video cameras. At this point, you need to take a closer look at the features of your chosen camera to make sure it has everything you need.

Keep in mind at all times the reason you want the camera: if you are aiming to shoot badgers in setts, don't stray from your need to have a night-vision setting; if you know that your budget doesn't afford edit software with flashy effects, make sure your camera is capable of basic image manipulation.

It is the features that the camera offers and the quality of the lens and digital processing that varies the price so much. Lenses will be dealt with separately, and digital processing has been touched on—i.e., try to go for 3 CCD rather than just one; the ability to capture real 16:9; and the variant qualities of inherent anti-aliasing and interpolation. The manual features of the camera that you should be checking out are as follows:

Above: The Canon MV600i is a low-priced digital video camera. Its entry-level price position in the market makes sense of its analog inputs, handy for those who are just coming into the digital market and dragging a whole library of analog tapes behind them.

Left: Overexposure forces a slow shutter speed in order to view an image. The slower that your CCD is gathering the image, the more movement can be seen within the frame. While this can be perceived as misjudgment, it can certainly be worked to esthetic advantage.

VIEWFINDER/LCD SCREEN

The reason high-end cameras tend to still have black-and-white viewfinders is that they work better for exact focus. Many digital video cameras have color viewfinders that don't actually serve much purpose when coupled with an LCD screen, aside from battery preservation. If your camera has a flip-back LCD screen, it will double as a menu to facilitate all of your settings. Both viewfinder and screen should indicate your camera mode (record/VTR and sometimes download), as well as tape and battery remaining, faults, filters, and audio meter—and the following essential manual settings.

SHUTTER SPEED

A digital video camera's shutter speed works differently—unsurprisingly—from that of a film camera. Instead of a change in frame rate, it works by changing the rate at which the CCD gathers an image. A slower shutter speed allows more light and a larger one less light. Besides acting as a visual effect or letting fast action be captured at a more animated, more recognizable image, shutter speeds can quickly eradicate optical problems that you might record, such as evident CRT scans when recording from a television or computer screen.

EXPOSURE

Your exposure is the way that luminance is controlled before reaching the CCD. If you are lucky enough to have a high-end DV camera, it may have the option to read overexposure as zebra stripes. Any underexposure can be resolved using gain. In low-light situations, gain can be applied to amplify your signal. AGC (Automatic Gain Control) is activated if you are working with automatic exposure and your image is underexposed. If you do apply gain, you can expect visual noise in your picture. Some cameras offer the facility of negative gain, which you can use to reduce this noise and reap rewards.

Your video camera has a dynamic range, which is its allowable contrast ratio. If the difference between your highlights and your shadows is out of this range, the camera will enforce its own clipping and lose detail in both areas. This can also be viewed using your zebra stripes. To keep your detail in both is less a matter of using your gain and shutter speed than changing your lighting—although Panasonic's Cine modes and Sony's Dynamic Contrast Control and DynaLatitude (high-end) can supposedly increase the dynamic range by 600% in the highlights.

Above and left: **Your CCD thrives on light and the more there is, the more you can push for the shot you want.** Both shots here are using a shutter speed of 300 fps, but the leeway for exposure in strong sunlight allows for entirely different depths of field.

AUTOBOGUS

Beware the pitfalls of autofocus (above). If you're shooting against spotlights, the chances are that your camera will try and focus on the refractions of light hitting the lens. Sometimes this can be a nightmare... and sometimes it can make your shot.

VISIONS IN BLUE

Intense color saturation can confuse autofocus' ability to find form (above). If the saturation swamps the entire frame—especially here in a room without corners—the lens will hunt without success.

RING PULL BLIND

Pulling focus on a manual setting can be perfectly performed between two parts of the image with a strip of tape, each end attached to the two focal points on your adjuster (below). It should start buckled, then pull gently taut when the ring hits your mark.

FOCUS

Autofocus is the heaven and hell of a digital video camera. The recommendation, of course, is to leave it as manual at all times; the practical side of it, though, if you're picking up and shooting Nessie, is that it's an extremely useful device. When you test your camera, make sure that it doesn't waste time "hunting." Your autofocus should be set to default to the image in the center of the frame. If it's over-sensitive, it will make itself redundant as a feature. The best way to use autofocus and to find out its capabilities is to zoom to your main image, press autofocus, and pull out to see if there's any evidence of hunting.

Your other option will be setting your focus to infinity. This will tell your camera that there is no particular subject to focus on and will stop any inconvenient hunting when used for a wide-angle shot.

WHITE BALANCE

Because light comes in so many temperatures that we take for granted, a brainless digital video camera needs a reference of color in any given location. A white balance offers the camera this measure by focusing on pure white and sampling that version of pure white. For example, white is bluer outside and redder inside. Not taking this sample of white in any given area will alter the chrominance values and turn your pictures untrue—too hot or too cold in color temperature.

Lower-end cameras will rely on TTL (Through The Lens) white balance. This is an automatic reading of the brightest light in the picture as white and doesn't give particularly true results. A manual white balance lets you find an absolute white in your location (paper, a hardhat, or a shirt), focus the camera onto it and sample it at the touch of a button. Programmable auto-exposure settings can help maintain the right white balance, too.

IMAGE STABILIZATION

An automatic feature of mini-DV cameras is Image Stabilization, a device that compensates for jerky camera movement. Every manufacturer has a different name for it (Panasonic has Mega OIS; Sony has Super SteadyShot), but there are two different specific ways that it works to watch out for. Electronic Image Stabilization (EIS) operates by capturing an image larger than your aspect ratio and performing an algorithm on the pixels to compensate. Optical Image Stabilization (OIS) uses a combination of gyros and prisms to steady pixel shift. While EIS is considered to give an inferior result due to digital artifacts, OIS will often keep your image moving at the end of a pan—and both generate a loss of resolution due to the pixels having been processed. Having said this, it's an easy function to dismiss and an incredibly useful one to use.

COLOR TEMPERATURE

Specifically in DVCAM/DVCPRO, color temperature may be adjusted using preset filters. These have largely been brought into use by the quick voxpop where—in Sony's

RANK BALANCE

The same shot without a white balance (above) and with a white balance (below). The blue tinge becomes particularly noticeable with subjects that are essentially white, and recognizable colors (like leaf green here) will develop a slightly unbelievable hue. Unless you want this, or you're shooting day-for-dusk, always use the white balance control.

case—even a Skin Set preset can be used for detail and color warmth. Skin is always a good test of a digital video camera's color temperature settings: it's something we know so well and it's something that is different every time. Mini-DV tends to make adjustments for interiors and exteriors and the best way to try this is a pan from one to the other.

AUDIO CONTROLS

On a digital video camera, you should have the opportunity to change from 12 or 16-bit audio—4 or 2-channel. 16-bit audio will give you CD-quality stereo audio, but if you are using an external microphone as well as the camera mike the 12-bit will take all four channels at a lower sample rate. You should be able to control your input levels to some extent— but remember, the higher-end your camera is, the more you'll be capable of adjusting your audio. Listen for hiss, camera motor sound, and be aware at all times that your AGC is listening for it too…

DIGITAL EFFECTS

With digital technology, you get digital processing—like it or not—and your digital video camera will have ways of manipulating the video signal. A picture effect is one applied to your pixels on the CCD. This can be anything from adding a sepia tint or stretching the picture. A digital effect, on the other hand, is simply digital processing. This changes a whole host of things, such as sample rate, encryption, and compression. Such effects tend to be time-based, such as trails and stills.

Like image stabilization, digital effects degrade the image. A prime example of this is mini-DV's digital zoom option. Although this feature may purport to magnify many more times than your optical zoom— your zoom lens—all it's doing is taking the central portion of your pixels and blowing them up to fill the frame. Your loss of resolution and gain of pixelation makes this a useless device at maximum magnification. Try it and you'll get the picture...or not.

All of these drawbacks only strengthen the mantra to shoot clean. There is little point in buying a camera for its effects in order to save money on your edit software. Buy a camera for its lens and for its chip. You won't be able to get your image back to normality in the edit, and your software should be able to render the same camera effect—and many more besides.

ZOOM DOOM
While a typical digital video camera has a 12x optical zoom that maintains a very natural look (above), its 48x digital zoom can never quite manage to do the sums and maintain any detail (below).

INTERVIEW
Kathryn Fleet, Independent Video-maker

"

My interaction with digital video at work is that I commission people to make short videos as part of intranet and CD-ROM training programs. Because I've worked with film and video for years as a domestic director, the job has filled in the gaps and helps me understand all the processes that it has to go through to get from planning to completion. It works the other way round too—if a director is brought on board at work, I know exactly what they have to go through from my work at home, which helps me prepare them for their job.

The kind of thing that I typically get asked to do outside of the day job are low-level music videos for somebody who is just starting out, is trying to break into the music scene, and who wants to supply a video to go with a track. They provide me with the song and I'll get some ideas together and go out and shoot and edit something to go with it.

Most of the stuff that I do is mostly a mix of 16mm film, super 8, and mini-DV. In the case of using film, I'll develop it myself to end up with a negative. I'll then telecine that using my mini-DV set to invert, which then gives me a positive digital image that I can work with. If I stick to black-and-white, I don't have to go through any expensive lab printing. I just use chemicals from a photography shop and telecine from a projection onto a white door at home. It's cheap, but it works.

I use a Canon XM-1 mini-DV and Pinnacle's DV500 capture card with Premiere. I can do most transitions in realtime, which really helps when I've got the musician breathing down my neck at home wanting to see results. Because it's music video, my clips tend to be short—which is lucky because otherwise I'd have the frustration of a 4Mb limit to my capture. What does get my goat with my setup is that when I export to mini-DV from my timeline, it's glitchy. It's not very reliable for exporting and glitches once every three minutes or so—and I just don't know why. The other limiting thing is that I've only got a CD burner and not a DVD burner and so, as there are problems exporting to mini-DV, I can't export to DVD as an alternative.

I'm therefore exporting a lot of the time to analog, letting me get my videos out reliably to VHS. As part of the problem that I'm trying to solve, if I use FireWire, I'm back getting glitches again.

I'm working on a documentary at the moment, a project with a friend of mine about gay women in Brighton, England, why there is such a migration there, and whether or not it's lived up to their expectations. That's involved a lot of interviews, which I've never done before, and lots of location shooting in the area capturing the spirit of the place. For the interviews, I used a Sony microphone straight into the camera, which switches between 120 and 90 degree angles. As I'm using some of the questions from the interviewer with only the interviewee in shot, the wider angle gives me a better quality sound for both on- and off-screen voices.

We're looking to distribute the finished video on the film festival circuit, and maybe think about satellite—although we're not too sure that our production values are good enough. We're planning on transfer to digibeta for possible broadcast, but mainly aiming it toward the lesbian and gay independent festivals.

"

DIGITAL CAMERA FORMATS If digital is digital is digital (i.e., the basic encoding algorithm is the same), what, then, might be the point in buying a $30,000 camera rather than an $800 one?

The difference between digital tapes relies on the difference in tape microns. A micron is a thousandth of a millimeter and the quantity of microns per tape is increased with the width of the tape, the wider of which allows more tracks. The micron width of a track relates to the micron width of the record head, which are different with Digital-8, MICROMV, Mini-DV, DVCPRO, and DVCAM.

Mini-DV's record heads allows for ten micron tracks with standard play (SP) recording. DVCPRO's record heads are 18 microns wide to be compatible with _" tape, and the broad spread of digital information makes cuts and inserts far more precision-based. The larger track width also allows a control track to be recorded. This CTL (Capstan Tracking Logic) signal allows the correct tracks recorded to be accurately hit by your heads during playback. The manual tracking gauge on a standard VCR gives an indication of how a digital CTL works automatically. Whereas VHS uses a separate recording head for this information, a DVCPRO camera uses the same one to record pulses synchronized with each image. By counting these pulses, the player in your edit can control the servo to lock onto exactly the right part of the tape without much bet-hedging pre-roll.

DVCPRO's use of microns also designates a track to a cue analog audio track. This is relevant for monitoring audio in jog or shuttle modes to increase edit accuracy.

DVCAM uses 15 micron tracks and no CTL track or cue analog audio track. Like Mini-DV, tracking is automatic and therefore less accurate.

Above: **The JVC GR-DV4000 prides itself as the only Mini-DV on the market with an aspherical F1.2 lens to create bright images. With room for an 8Mb memory stick, it leans toward multimedia—although this is probably more useful for the stills aspect of the camera, which has its own USB port for transferring photos.**

Each format records at 9,000 rotations per minute; the speed that the tape runs through the camera depends on the format. Mini-DV tape speed is 17mm per second; DVCPRO 34 mm/sec; and DVCAM 28 mm/sec. These differences—and the difference in the microns of each format's playback heads—mean that the tape between them is incompatible. The higher end you go, the more you have to consider the decks that you use for editing and ensure that they're suitable for your digital camera format.

DVCAM and DVCPRO's tape also give them a robustness. This, coupled with their technique of recording and the physical make-up of their tape, allows multiple recordings on one tape. This is not advised with mini-DV, where multiple passes over the record head are more likely to flake the layer of material that holds the magnetism (which holds your digital signal).

If it feels like a bit of an addendum to discuss Digital-8, it is. Digital-8 is a sop to all the manufacturer and consumer investment in past analog Hi-8 and Video8 formats. Sony and Hitachi still produce a few Digital-8 cameras, but their capabilities are outstripped by stepping up slightly in price to Mini-DV. If you have a library of Hi-8 or Video8 format tapes, you might want to consider it, if only for converting them to digital or shooting on cheaper stock. But you might just want to take them via your ADC into your desktop editing system from your original Hi-8 or Video8—unless it's broken, in which case you might want to buy a one-CCD Digital-8 camera prone to dropout and low-quality images.

SMALLER IS BETTER?

And talking of one CCD, what of MICROMV? There's always something bigger and better around the corner— although, in this case, *smaller* is supposed to be better. Not content with supplying Mini-DV to huge demand (along with every other manufacturer), Sony are flying the flag for MICROMV. This is their smallest digital video format yet.

No one could condemn Sony as unadventurous— indeed, they've been instrumental in making digital video approachable to consumers. And yet, nor is anyone going to say they were content with this, where, in a separate broadcast universe, Sony Mini-DV, Sony monitors, decks, and DVCAM were spotted going about their professional business as usual.

MICROMV camcorders have been introduced to a mid-range consumer market which is being seduced by mobile phones that can record limited data video to be sent to their desktop. MICROMV is a similar hybrid, but balances video with photography plus Internet, email, and basic editing.

MICROMV tapes are 30% more compact in storage space than Mini-DV. Likewise, the cassettes are smaller and unique to Sony. They're expensive, but backed up by a memory stick that acts as a very small, portable hard drive, indicating that tapes may well soon be the Hoover bags of the past. The current capacity of the memory stick is still somewhat limiting—an expensive 1Gb card will allow 24 minutes of MPEG-2 video— but what this does allow is a very user-friendly MPEG-2 conversion to an external hard drive that will make a day's shoot easy enough via the on-board i-Link connection.

As memory card capacities increase, Sony aren't the only ones to realise the market potential of a tapeless society. Although they are only edging there, Pretec's DV-4200 has gone all the way and stores only to a Compact Flash memory card. And forget MPEG-2; they have stuck their necks out and opted for the lower-quality MPEG-4 format.

The level that Sony are aiming at is indicated by their support of MovieShaker, their own low-end edit software that has the capabilities to do away with an editor and human

Above: **70% smaller than conventional DV tape, MICROMV tapes record MPEG2 at a quality that Sony declare to be of equal quality to Mini-DV.**
Below: **The Sony DCR-IP7 introduced the MICROMV camera format, and the incorporation of Bluetooth and MPEG2 to a digital video camera. Despite the size, it still retains the range of manual and automatic features, picture and digital effects that you might expect from a much larger product.**

creativity altogether. The software edits your clips together with random abandon, along with any text that you might input, to a mood (happy, romantic, funny) that you might select. Art, it isn't. However, Sony's recent acquisition of Sonic Foundry's VEGAS editing software could be a sign of a change of direction in its digital video strategy.

What MICROMV does have on its side is a leaning toward Bluetooth as a method of transferring footage. This is something that, while particularly geared toward the consumer mobile-user market, would also be welcomed by the semipro. Another advantage of MICROMV is that recording as MPEG-2 also allows the option of recording as MPEG-4. Coupled with the ability to upload from the camera, it's possible to get anything you shoot onto your website within a few wranglings with the small Internet LCD screen.

Capture and instant MPEG-2 compression may well not be what you want at source—you can't turn it into DV-quality— but used for its size or specific Internet jobs, a MICROMV camera may be a good partner for your real camera.

CAMERA CONNECTIONS Your camera's connectivity determines the amount of versatility that it offers for your future. Your digital video camera offers a bonus function of being able to convert analog to digital, a sideline that you might as well take advantage of and use.

When consumer VHS video cameras first started appearing, they were embraced as a way of updating previously affordable technology—i.e., 8mm home movies via telecine. Now that digital video cameras are available, not only do they have the capability of telecine through the lens, but they can update your VHS into a digital format. This isn't going to change the low resolution of your analog pictures, but what it does offer is a non-degradable longevity straight onto your DV tape and the ability to clean and polish up your pictures (not to mention edit them properly) on your processor. You can have your dropout years back—without the dropout.

If it sounds like you might want to do this or at anytime use analog as your source, your camera should have analog connections—certainly as an input. Your analog source is likely to play out as a composite signal (one visual signal with chrominance and luminance together) and your input to your camera will allow this if you have three RCA sockets. These three inputs will introduce your composite video signal

Above: Functioning as a stand-alone ADC/DAC or through your PC or Mac, Dazzle's Hollywood DV-Bridge takes information from an analog or digital video camera and converts it to your chosen format. Its multi-ports can take most connections for VHS, S-VHS, FireWire and so on without the loss of resolution—and while monitoring progress on a CRT.

and one left and one right channel of audio. If your camera has this type of analog-to-digital conversion available, it may have a separate S-Video connection too—enabling you to capture your bygone VHS shot at a higher resolution.

Worthy of note is that realtime transcoding—using your digital video camera as a simultaneous input/output device (i.e., Analog input straight out via FireWire)—is often impossible due to FireWire's tendency to override other devices.

If you also find that you have a LANC jack input, this offers you the opportunity to use a zoom controller or multiple deck controller should you ever require it…

Enough of analog and past history. Your digital video camera is firmly in the present and looks to a pixel-sharp future. When you are recording with your camera, you may audio a little more sensitive than just using the camera microphone. Make sure that you have at least a jack for one of the many external microphones available. If you are spending a lot of money on your camera, then you should expect to find a left and right XLR for maximum audio quality. In order to monitor your audio, an output for headphones will be essential.

If you have already bought your digital video camera and are frustrated by its connectivity, you don't necessarily have to buy another camera. Think about breakout boxes or converters such as those sold by Dazzle.

Above all, make sure that you have both input and output as FireWire. This is going to make your life easy…

IEEE-1394 One of the connections that you are probably going to be faced with is also one of the revolutions in the modern digital world: FireWire. Originally patented to Apple in the 1980s, it has grown to become a cross-platform digital savior and the jack and protocol (IEEE-1394) an international industry standard.

The recognition of IEEE-1394's success led to most companies working within the digital realm adopting it. While Apple and most others stick with the original "FireWire" tag, Sony has termed it "i-link": it's the same thing. But why has it been such a revolution for desktop video?

There are many answers. The speed at which it transports data is second to no other current technology—and when data is transported, it is a perfect copy of the digital information (i.e., there is no degradation, code, or generation loss). IEEE-1394 is also able to handle more than one thing at once. Even while in use, it can still allow the two devices connected to communicate ideas for sending further configuration information. And while doing this, it can still operate as a power supply to attached devices. The only exception to this is the four-pin (rather than six-pin) FireWire, which can only transfer data.

Because it is a signal-carrying cable, FireWire does tend to lose its data over a certain length. This is why they tend to be short, hardly ever exceeding 4.5 meters. If you do need a longer FireWire—say, from exterior location straight to interior hard drive—then you will need to use a **repeater**, which will amplify the signal for you.

One of the beauties of FireWire is that it may solve a lot of device-recognition problems for you at your desktop edit. Avoiding the conflicts that can be caused with the use of **component video** from **breakout boxes**, FireWire, when it is connected, will usually be assigned to a port of your computer, excluding all other devices. What this does mean, however, is that you may not be able to connect all the devices that you want without a FireWire **daisy chain**, and this may also lead to problems. It has been reported that, in some cases, iMovie can't import footage from a digital video camera if it is part of a daisy chain. If you do find that you are having conflicts, your first stop is to update your FireWire or your device drivers.

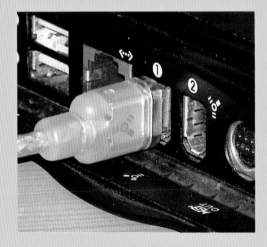

USB/USB2 Since 1996, PCs have supported the Universal Serial Bus (USB). This connection is similar to IEEE-1394, operating as a plug-and-play interface between the computer and other connected devices. USB carries information at 12 megabits per second—decidedly lower than FireWire's 400 megabits per second—but can be found as an output/input on an increasing number of digital video cameras.

So why bother even contemplating using it when FireWire's credentials appear better?

The answer is that the *upgrade* of USB, USB 2.0, prides itself in transmitting information at around 480 megabits per second, 20% faster than FireWire. Coupled with this, because it's backward compatible with the original USB 1.1 (and 2.0 is now standard on any Pentium 4 computer), you won't need to buy a capture card—only software. Like FireWire, USB2 is bi-directional and carries power between devices. Sound like your kind of thing? Here's the but…

Sony's DCR-DVD200 opts for USB2 over i-Link. Recording onto 3" DVD-R or DVD-RW, it takes a digital video camera in an entirely new direction. The disks can be played on most DVD-compatible hardware and each recorded shot has its own thumbnail image to identify it.

While USB2 *will* operate its predecessor's devices, it doesn't make them any faster. It's an entirely different beast altogether. More importantly, the difference between the two rivals is their topology—their signal networking layout. While FireWire can quite happily talk between two devices without a PC (i.e., digital video camera to digital video camera), the USB operates as a master-slave to the computer.

The implications of this are that USB2 will not let you dub from one tape to another without a PC's involvement—a potential hindrance on location and a possible annoyance anywhere else. Most purist shooters would probably rather rely on their camera than on their computers. Its speed is something of an anomaly too. Neither connection fully utilizes their potential bandwidth, and seeing as FireWire runs in realtime without any loss, there is no real reason to look for a faster speed of data transmission.

Aside from this, USB2 is fundamentally cornering a market that FireWire failed to entice: peripherals dealing with potentially complex image information such as scanners and printers. There is a riposte from the FireWire camp in the form of a faster, 800 megabits per second version, but if the standard changes, it will probably be in favor of entirely wireless connections.

Bluetooth is the first real option of wireless networking for the digital video user. An adapter connected to an analog phone line can now receive digital signals from up to 30 feet away. Sony Network Handycams use this as an alternative to USB2. The networking also allows for features such as using the gateway for Internet and email connection, and the camera's LCD as a monitor. This is just another device hybrid such as the video capture mobile phone. Again, watch purists recoil at non-dedication…

BATTERIES

Most digital video cameras will indicate your battery life and how much power you have left available. There are different types of battery with different ways of discharging power. If you are using a NiCad (Nickel Cadmium), the voltage will drop off pretty evenly throughout its use; if you are using a Li-Ion (Lithium Ion), you can expect the voltage to initially drop quickly before slowing up.

Your power usage will be increased with the use of peripherals such as camera lights and mini-DV LED screens and how much of the camera's servo-operated automatic controls you use. Your actual battery life will be dependent on the age of the battery and the conditions in which you recharge it—that is to say, a battery won't charge to full capacity in cold temperatures or in very hot climates. Try to keep an ambient temperature for your battery on charge and never charge a battery that is either too hot or too cold or it may just explode.

Always carry at least one spare battery for even the shortest of shoots, whether you're using a DVCAM hour-long duration battery or a mini-DV 12-hour version. There is nothing more embarrassing or frustrating on a shoot than losing power. Think about using a battery belt if you are shooting all day on mini-DV. If you're using DVCAM, you will be lugging enough gear onto location without an excess of batteries, so make sure that your transportation is near enough to the set for a quick run back...

Above all, save all the power you have. A camera on stand-by is still using power, so switch it off.

Above: JVC's Nickel Metal Hydride batteries offer up to five-and-a-half hours of continuous use before recharging.

Left: Sony's InfoLITHIUM batteries are so called because they are lithium ion batteries that have the capability of exchanging data on battery consumption with their other products.

LENSES The lens is one of the essential elements for choosing the right camera. There are two easy ways to start out checking the quality of your camera: is the standard lens detachable—or does it have a screw-thread around the rim of the standard lens?; and is the lens large enough to let in sufficient light?

Your CCD relies on the control of light and therefore the more light that you can play with, the better. The size of the lens does matter, but the quality of your image is also determined by the way the glass was ground, its density, and the chemicals used to coat it. The same goes for filters.

The standard lens for your camera is likely to be a simple mid-range lens that encompasses a view (as a wide) similar to that of how the human eye sees. These lenses also tend to give the best image quality to mid-range, rather than your foreground or background.

For a better depth of field (i.e., the area of sharpness in front of and behind the subject in focus), a wider angled lens is more appropriate. These are extremely useful, particularly for

WHY DANGLE?
There are often times when only a wide-angle lens will do to get the appropriate amount of depth of field.

mini-DV: if one of its benefits is to fit into cramped locations, a wide angle will let you see more of it. A plus and minus of this type of lens is that the closer the image is to the camera, the more distortion will be apparent. By proxy, they are terrific lenses for exaggerating distance between a near subject and your background.

Your depth of focus also relies on your aperture. A digital video camera will operate with f-stops in the same way—the smaller the number, the more light hitting the CCDs, the greater the depth of field. Difficulties arise when wishing to have a greater depth of field at night or in low lighting where, in fact, you will need a whole load of lights to get the depth you are looking for.

The more confident you become with your camera, the more you will appreciate the benefit of being able to change your depth of field. The flexibility will allow you to train an audience's eye onto your subject matter, to increase the detail of a wide shot with subdued lighting, to make your foreground and background romantically or ominously soft… Your possibilities, techniques, and moods become infinite—especially when used with filters and zooms.

The capability to zoom will come as standard in your digital video camera. We know that the digital zoom is an ultimately useless tool, but your optical zoom can be a powerful one if used properly. With mini-DV, zoom lenses are electronically operational, while those for the higher-end video cameras offer manual controls. The manual control

NATURE CALLS

Flattening the landscape with a telephoto zoom and lots of light can bring an extraordinarily naturalistic look to your shot. Added to this, your subjects can be far enough away to give you much more candid performances.

ANIMAL MAGNET

Lenses naturally attract dust, dirt, and dogs' noses. Get a dedicated lens cloth from an optician or photographic store to keep the lens clean and you won't be losing shots in the edit.

allows for zooming in tight to focus on a subject before pulling out with confidence that it will remain sharp for as long as the camera remains in that position. Because this is usually impossible on mini-DV cameras, it is a good idea to increase the depth of field to give yourself a better chance that focus won't be lost during zooming.

The opposite of a wide-angle lens is a telephoto lens. This is a lens that can focus on detail over considerable distance (definitively at least twice the length of a standard lens). They are very good for fly-on-the-wall, but understandably awful for matching audio with the camera mike. Because you are using a very narrow field of view, your foreground and background will appear flat or foreshortened, while your focal image remains sharp. Telephoto lenses, then, can create effects of their own, and are very useful if you want an impressive pull-focus.

FILTERS Just as there are fundamental aperture difficulties with your extended depth of field in subdued lighting, there are the same problems with getting a short depth of field in bright sunlight. For this reason, most cameras have neutral density filters.

They are neutral because they don't wash away color—and they are dense to stop a certain amount of light hitting the CCD while at your fixed aperture. There are many types of neutral density filters, just as there are many types of other filters. Add-on filters can be used if your digital video camera appropriates it.

If your camera doesn't have a detachable lens, then it might have a conversion lens instead. This is your original molded standard lens with the aforementioned screw-thread rim. Just like a detachable lens, it affords other lenses and filters to be added at will. There are some truly hokey filters out there that both defeat the mantra of shooting clean and make any effects in your edit software redundant. Even some of the staple diet filters of conventional photography are now questionable in use, unless they specifically affect the quality of the light reaching the CCD. These might be polarizing filters (used to eliminate reflections on surfaces and saturate colors) or UV filters (absorbers of cold or harsh ultraviolet light)— even a starburst filter might just squeeze through with these criteria…

Left: JVC's 7x 52mm wide-angle conversion lens fits to a standard camcorder, its large aperture promoting bright images with high contrast and definition.
Below: Canon's still photographic history has left them with a large amount of expertise and backlog when it comes to accessories. An array of Canon's lens converters and filters, plus an MC protector. This protects your digital video camera's lens from scratching during the roughest of shoots.

A neutral density filter can automatically activate at the worst times (above). If you want to keep your sky blue (below), raise your shutter speed and adjust your exposure to suit.

ANAMORPHIC ADAPTERS

One add-on that can be very useful—particularly to disadvantaged mini-DV users—is an anamorphic adapter. Instead of the fake 16:9 inherent in many digital video cameras, this turns your image into a true widescreen picture on your 4:3 ratio CCD. Perfect, you might think. There are four problems, though. The first is that your image is being squeezed vertically onto your 4:3 CCD, which means that when it's unsqueezed, you are likely with some adapters to lose resolution on the horizontal. Choose wisely—some, like the Optex version, purport not to. The second is that you'll need to use a monitor in order to frame your image: your "letterbox" will show on neither your viewfinder nor your LCD screen. The third problem is that, even given available light, your zoom will not fully function to its capacity. And the fourth problem will occur in the edit where—even with your settings set to 16:9—the results are unbefitting to 16:9 broadcast standard. If you really want 16:9, it might be more sensible to opt for a camera with a so-called "wide chip."

MICROPHONES

MICROPHONES All digital video cameras—no matter how low- or high-end—come with a camera microphone. The quality of your camera is directly proportional to the quality of your mike. If you pay for a good camera, you'll get a good mike, and if you don't, you won't.

The internal microphone on a mini-DV has to be reasonably contained and sufficient in strength and direction to pick up anything if you're shooting on the fly. For this reason, the microphone is omnidirectional and sensitive. This is great for capturing things while you can or for warts-and-all video-making. What it is terrible for is getting the sparkling audio that you want to complement your sparkling pictures. Littered among the sound that you want will be the breathing of the camera op, yourself as auteur whispering directions to the camera op, the lens cap swinging against the camera, the sound of your zoom in action, cars, birds, planes, next door's TV…

As an introduction to your camera mike, the reason it is sensitive to any sound is that it's a condenser microphone. This fundamentally means that it has a thinner and lighter diaphragm than its cheaper, rougher sister, the dynamic microphone, and responds quicker and in more detail to soundwaves.

If you care about your production values, you will almost certainly want to invest in an external microphone or two. The good thing is that even for low-end digital video cameras, more and more options are becoming available. If you have such a camera—or even if you're shooting with a higher-end mini-DV—it's the connections that become a brief, major concern. Find an XLR to mini-jack converter and use a good standard of microphone. Make sure that you're not still recording through your camera mike or one channel (or both) will be wasted.

The reason that you should be looking to XLR rather than a direct input into your mini-jack is that recording from a microphone directly into your jack socket tends to give particularly unstable audio. Because it's small, it's sensitive and a bad connection can lead to undesirable crackling and humming on your soundtrack as well as audio overload and being lumbered with a ho-hum AGC. An XLR, on the other hand, provides a balanced audio signal—it doesn't degenerate over cable distance and doesn't create hum. An XLR locks into place and won't yank out so easily, eliminating these problems. Of course, you're still plugging into your mini-jack via the converter, but find a way of securing this—and to your camera—and you're close to laughing (very quietly in the background).

A DIFFERENT WAVELENGTH
Radio mikes tend to be for the desperate. If you are going to use one, steer away from public spaces, where interactive frequencies will make your audio unusable.

Left: The JVC MZ-V3 microphone is a stereo zoom mike tailored for their own digital video cameras. The mike picks up sound corresponding to the picture when the lens zooms in or pulls out.

The converter also acts as a transformer and grounds the connection between your mike or your mixer and the camera. It should have left and right audio channel controls, which will give you a bit more freedom than any controls that your camera might have. Of course, if you've bought pro, you'll probably have XLRs at the back of your digital video camera and will be laughing quicker...

To make sure that you are getting maximum pick-up of the sound that you want, you'll want to choose the right microphone. Avoid mono microphones, as most will record only to one channel even when plugged into a stereo input. Also think about the area you will need to record sound from. The three different directional types of microphone are omnidirectional (all directions), bi-directional (two directions), and unidirectional (one direction). There are some available that are switchable between these, and various types of microphone within each directional type. These will be discussed later...

Whichever microphone you use, make sure that your audio op is monitoring the audio from the record source—even if you're using a mixer, and especially if you're using an XLR converter. This is one of the reasons why camera ops sometimes insist on monitoring their own sound. Avoid the insistence: the two jobs should be extricable as well as working closely together, so use a radio or long cable to enable your sound op to get a feed off your camera.

INTERVIEW
Martyn Lee Wilson, Commercials Director

"

HD At present I find HD very much like DigiBeta in that it's got almost no inherent character of its own—it's pure information and for my taste throws too much emphasis onto filtration in post to give it real character. Early 3D graphics always looked like 3D graphics and the total reliance on post-filtration gives a similarly inorganic look The only big example we've had is the Star Wars movies and that shows the limitations because you seemingly can't move the camera too fast, so there's no fluidity. It's also very flat, like a throwback to the early days of sound with those big, immobile blimps. There's a collaborative working discipline as well as an esthetic discipline that comes with working on film, which seems to be under threat from HD. The emphasis shifts from disciplined technicians to nervous executive committees in post. On the other hand, HD is practically useful in the way that in China, say, there are too many screens for the number of dog-eared prints of a film that are doing the rounds. Piracy grows in this climate because it takes so long to get a print round, but digital media can be sent down a wire and you can open on 2,000 screens at the drop of a hat.

DV I prefer working with DV as a digital medium because it's got a bit of noise, a bit of character of its own that you can latch onto and grade and play with. It's incredibly useful because design and animatic ideas can be sent via broadband, making it quick and cheap. You can also work out grades in Photoshop or After Effects and decide how the whole project is going to look, so DV and desktop video is great for planning. At the end of the day, though, it's just a tool and it depends how you use it—everyone has different things that they want it for. There was a lot of fuss when non-linear editing came out, but I come from a film background and there's really nothing new about cutting in that way.

10P Everybody wants things cheaper and it's widely thought that a digital approach always offers that. As a result there's often pressure to make false economies, less concern for the quality of the crew, with a misguided idea that it's cheaper to fix everything in post. I'm finding that digital is being used for the wrong reasons—because it's cheaper and not because it's the right medium for the job. Money is spent in the wrong places and gets wasted.

EZ The flipside to this is that, because it can be cheaper and more accessible, digital lets people experiment and to realize ideas that otherwise wouldn't get made. I think eventually this will democratize things and we'll get back to the issues of core skills instead of everything being about insider knowledge or specific equipment. Anyone can use a word processor, but not everyone can be Ernest Hemingway—it still comes down to only 15% actually being any good.

PC Because I worked in post-design with Quantel hardware and After Effects, I tend to use animatics quite a lot. They're useful when it comes to clients fresh to the medium. They make it easier to lead clients by the hand and give them a sense of what to expect. I use Photoshop backgrounds and animated figures created in Poser. A lot of the time I can create any graphic elements in preproduction and have them signed off by the time we get to set. This is useful when it comes to the actors knowing which portions of the screen will be covered in graphic text or an animation. It also means that the crew can see everything they need to do in terms of lighting, filters, and coloration.

"

part 02. the kit

CAMERA SUPPORTS

TRIPODS

The school of thought with regard to tripods (also known as sticks, stilts, or legs) and digital video is that only true amateurs or true professionals use them. The amateur is progressing from stills photography and is too unsure of new technology to change their way; the professional has a cumbersome camera and knows they need a truly steady shot for broadcast. In the middle is the amateur who shoots for fun and the student guerrilla who shoots on the fly—and they don't have tripods either.

Tripods *can* be very useful if used properly. While an image stabilizer compensates for jerky camera op movement, a good tripod (and a good camera op) will give you seamless fluidity, or the perfect **static**. When performing a pan or a tilt on a tripod, the control allows better use of a combined zoom or pull focus. Indeed, focus—particularly in **macro**—can be almost impossible *unless* you have a tripod.

Tripods can also be essential. Telecine and chromakey rely on the camera not moving at all. Timelapse and animation need camera control rather than arbitrary movement. A tripod in these cases will allow either to be undertaken as a locked-off static or, by timed or manual movement, during a

LEGS IN THE AIR
Hiring cranes or cherry pickers is expensive. Hiring cranes or cherry pickers when you have to reshoot your wobbly shot is REALLY expensive. Use a tripod.

simple camera move. And if it is a static, keep it that way with sandbags on the spreaders. Animation and timelapse are painful enough without the camera shifting.

That kind of pain, though, pales compared with that of occupational health problems. High-end DVCPRO/DVCAMs tend to be oversized…and heavy. Your camera op won't be the happiest member of a crew if they are performing hand-held or shoulder-mounted shots for a long shoot day. A tripod will not only ease things up in this case, but may also provide shots that help your edit find a rhythm.

Rigs for dollies, **jibs**, and car mounts may also involve you using a tripod—especially if you're starting out making your own. Like any tripod, you will need to make sure that it won't let your camera droop—and let you down—even when you're using the heaviest lens or shooting into strong wind. Weight is always an issue if you're likely to be hauling it around, but if you are buying, try and balance this with durability—you may only have to buy one in your life so it's worth blowing the budget for once.

If you have an image stabilizer built into your digital video camera, it still won't necessarily give you that long, gliding Steadicam shot that you've always wanted to emulate from your favorite Hollywood movie. Such shots are specialized (hence the brand name; Glidecam is the other) because they require a body-rig to work the camera with human ergonomics. Like the stabilizers, though, they compensate for jerkiness to give an "unreal" hand-held camera motion. Steadicams are a combination of gyros and jibs and have now worked their way down from the professional market into mini-DV. They're expensive, though, which has led to a new entrepreneurial market in build-your-own Steadicam…

Your digital images will be useless without a computer to process them. This is where the complications begin.

If you have decided to opt for a Mac editing package, you won't have much of a problem to match the right computer for your work. If you have decided to go along the PC route, the voice of experience tells us that you're in for a ride if you want to get anywhere near high-end within low budget.

If you are buying a package from a store, you can expect to pay over the odds for what you're actually getting. If you want a higher-spec machine from a store, you will be paying much more than you really should be. Beware of anything termed a "family PC." Its secret identity is a non-dedicated waste of money. Your alternative to buying a package (i.e., the whole system and superfluous software besides) in a store is to buy one over the Internet. This is certainly the cheaper method of the two and there is no reason why you shouldn't find many more options at a much better price.

The recommendation, though, is to do neither. There are plenty of other Internet sites out there that offer an alternative to a package—which is for you to opt to build your own computer. It may well be the only part of your PC you need to upgrade anyway. There are two types of build-your-own: the first is to buy each separate component, download a manual, and actually, physically, build your own once they appear. If you're confident and know exactly what you're looking for, this is the cheapest and quickest way to get exactly what you want.

PART 02. THE KIT

CHAPTER TWO

COMPUTER HARDWARE

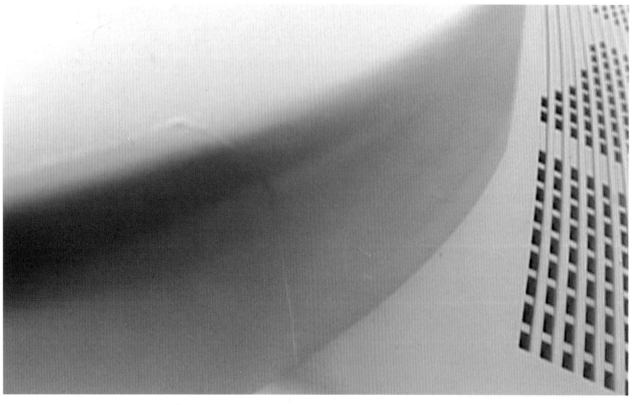

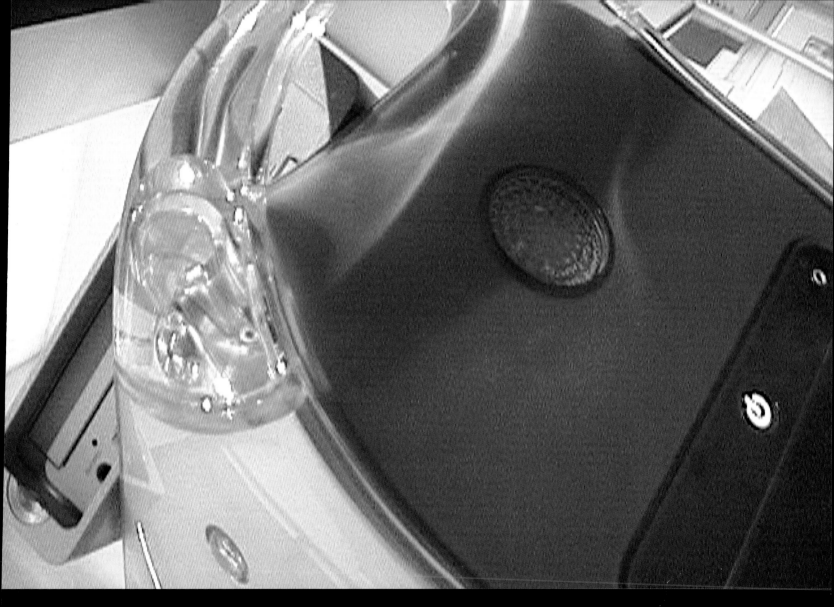

The second type is to find a build-your-own site where you choose the components, and the manufacturer/distributor assembles it and sends it to you. Again, this is very easy and cheaper if you've done your homework. The research, though, is the issue for both of these.

If you've decided on your capture card, edit, effects,

If you do get to a point where you are having problems with, say, devices not being found, make sure you have made a note of exactly what your components, spec, and configuration is. Aside from relying on a manufacturer's technical support, you'll probably want to change a few things around to find out what the lowest common denominator is, and you don't want to be repeating combinations.

One of the vile buzzwords to grace the pages of any IT solutions brochure is **turnkey**. This is a solution where all parts and components for your video-editing system are perfectly configured and guaranteed to work. We're basically back at your first option again—a store or the Internet. You can be slightly more discerning than dismissive, though. There are plenty of specialized outlets which provide a service that will at least not leave you frustrated or penniless. Unless you want a turnkey system you've seen demonstrated (Sony's Vaio range are specifically designed for various fractions of multimedia), there are stores available that will both make a desktop editing system for you, and make it with components that you are satisfied with. Surely not the best of both worlds? Well, it's close—and you will have a frontline to confront if you do have any problems

The problem with the PC is that it is an open architecture—IBM's original blueprint made available for anyone to work with, progress, and transcend. There are so many manufacturers of PCs, components, and all associated hardware and software now, with their own desired specs, that the conflict-free multimedia PC is a rare breed to find. Worse still, once you have one of these beasts, your wont to upgrade one particular component may mean changing another. There are users tearing hair out in every digital video forum across the Internet. Whether it's VIA chipset issues in your motherboard (they tend to freeze images) or your video card capturing with green stripes (a common card/Premiere conflict), conflicts are rife in the desktop video editing market.

Above: **Sony Vaio and CPU.**
Below: **All you need for Final Cut Pro.**

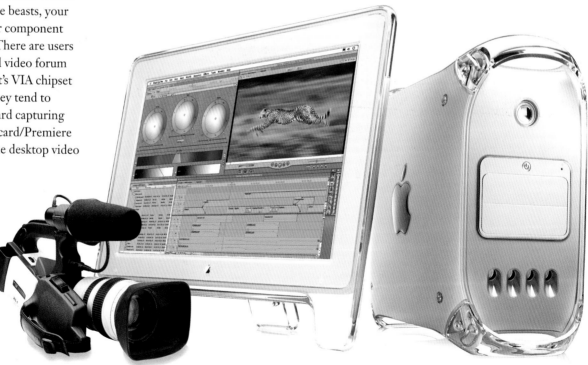

MINIMUM SPEC Whichever route you're taking, the breakdown of your minimum requirements is as follows:

PC CASE
Make sure the motherboard will fit inside, and that you have enough slots for your cards and inputs/outputs at the rear, and room for enough drives at the front—indeed, frontal ports can be quite useful too. Most cases come with a power supply unit included. Make sure yours has enough power for your CPU. Check with the supplier for details.

MOTHERBOARD
Your motherboard needs to support the speed of your processor—and you'll be looking to get the highest speed that your budget can take to process your video images. Most motherboards now handle DDR (Double Data Rate) RAM, which is essential. Ensure that it supports enough slots for memory expansion.

CENTRAL PROCESSING UNIT (CPU)
It's crucial that your combination of motherboard and processor work together for the best possible performance. Your processor is dictated by the motherboard that you choose. AMD's Athlon range tends to be cheaper than Intel's Pentium equivalents, but whichever you choose, select the fastest CPU you can afford. Lower speeds will be tedious when rendering.

MEMORY (RAM)
The more RAM slots your motherboard has, the more scope your computer will have for memory upgrades. When you

BOARD IS COOL
Intel has now sold over a billion processing units and their CPUs have been in use for over 25 years. This is a Pentium 4 motherboard and its intricacies demand fan-cooling to keep the CPU from overheating.

open one of your video applications, your CPU needs memory to run the directions you give the application. As digital video applications are notoriously memory-intensive, make sure that you have plenty of it.

HARD DISK DRIVE (HDD)
Your hard disk is your main storage device, so the bigger the hard disk, the better. Make sure your motherboard can support a fast Ultra-ATA 133 drive with a speed of 7200rpm, and remember that a minute's worth of uncompressed video will utilize 1.5Gb of hard disk space…

CD-ROM/DVD DRIVES
You will need a DVD or CD-ROM drive to install software, and some form of recordable DVD drive is recommended for backing up data and burning finished video. Ensure that anything you buy is write/rewriteable (DVD-R/RW, DVD+R/RW, DVD-RAM, and CD-R/RW), giving you the chance to write/rewrite to used disks.

MONITOR
You are going to spend a lot of time in front of your screen, so try to pick the largest that your budget and space allow. The options extend to both standard CRT screens and LCD. If you haven't much space, you might consider the latter, bearing in mind that they usually work at a lower resolution. If you are lucky enough to have the budget for two monitors (preview and edit screens), pick a graphics card like Matrox's Parhelia that will let you view a full screen "true" image. You might even give yourself the luxury (or broadcast necessity) of a broadcast monitor that will let you monitor legal colors and underscan, allowing you to work within your screen-safe area.

MOUSE AND KEYBOARD
Your motherboard will dictate the connections, whether PS2 or USB. We're all human, and an ergonomic design is essential for long-term use. Try to test some before purchase to see if you are comfortable with the design and layout. A wireless mouse might also help you tidy up your workspace and your mind.

THE VIDEO CAPTURE CARD

You want to record video to your computer and edit it? Then you'll need a video capture card—and it does what it says on the box.

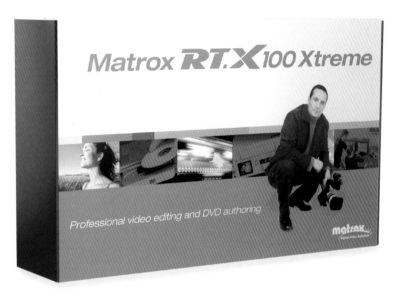

A video capture card allows your digital input—usually from your DV Cam—to be stored as digital information on your hard drive. Like a graphics card, it can also then convert the digital signals of your clips and edit back into analog to be displayed on your monitor as a series of recognizable images.

The card is a piece of hardware that physically slots into the computer and, once there, will protrude inputs and outputs for your player/recorder. One of these connections will unfailingly be an essential FireWire (IEEE-1394) port.

It is becoming increasingly common to find a FireWire port in the back of most computers and unavoidable with those touted as multimedia platforms. It is even likely that you have a video capture card already installed in a PCI slot and that your package came equipped with capture and even simple edit software.

REALITY CHEQUE

If you're expecting to edit realtime, you can expect to pay the price for it. Matrox's RT.X100 Xtreme supplies the market demand for reduced rendering times and faster editing using complex logarithms and preset effects and transitions to do just that.

Today's Macs—specifically the DV, G3, and G4 models—all contain FireWire ports, and their hard disks and graphics power make it easy to begin capturing and editing without you installing either a capture card or edit software.

The market, though, is such that while PCs are still cornering that of general-purpose and office use, they are beginning to realize that many customers wish to balance both home online capabilities and text documents with the versatility of home movie-making as well. For this reason, PCs may contain FireWire ports (look for them on the back of the computer, or a FireWire/i-link logo on the packaging), but may well lack any significant power to satisfy the ambitious auteur.

If you already have a computer, check the back for 1394 connections and further, in the device manager (under Settings > Control Panel > System > Hardware) for the existence of drivers and codecs that will let your card capture properly.

BUYING A CARD

As with all things digital these days, the choice of video capture cards is daunting to a shopper. The Internet is the first place to start to select the right one with the right features at the right price. Many forums now exist that will offer discussions of a video card's compatibility with your computer and any software that you might have in mind. Without automatically dismissing the assistant's knowledge down at the local out-of-town computer superstore, it is the user who will have had first-hand experience of any teething problems, soft/hardware clashes, and out-and-out flaws.

When you buy a video capture card, try to make sure that it is as suitable for your computer and as tailored to your requirements as possible. Your computer's motherboard is the first place that problems may occur. Avoid cross-platform cards and find one that is PC- or Mac-specific.

Something that you are likely to need on your card is an output. This will ensure that your cut program will have the ability to be played back out to another digital or analog recorder. Even if you think you'll merely be burning to the

DVD/CD-R on your computer, there may well come a time when you wish to tape it back onto DV tape. Look to the future…and buy into it…

Another decision that will affect your choice of card will be your anticipation of what you want to capture. If you expect to import from an analog source at some stage, you will need to ensure that your card is capable of it. While the digital image, audio, and power can be transferred via FireWire, analog uses S-Video (separation of luminance and chrominance) or component video cables (separation of video into three signals). Further information on cabling requirements for this can be found under Camera Connections (pages 40–42).

A further option for your card is whether it is promoted to be realtime or not. The frequently found frustration of an average editor is the time taken for rendering in a non-linear system. While the editor may be hot on his or her keys, the computer is not to cross its Ts—the Ts here being transitions and effects, which can sometimes take far longer than just a coffee break to even preview.

A realtime capture card renders as you work, often having many of the more often-used transitions, effects, and filters preset in a "bank." A more detailed explanation of the process can be found later on, but the bottom line is that, although these cards may be expensive, they might just add an extra five years to your life…

Most capture cards are bundled with both installation and edit software. It is important to realize that while the drivers and codecs are essential for your computer to recognize, respect, and animate the new addition, the editing software may well not be what you originally had in mind. With a wonderful video card, you may get a woefully simple edit facility—and anything touted as a Limited Edition is not exclusive: it's only limited in what it can do. Don't clutter up your valuable hard disk with low-end edit facilities unless that's what you're happy using; your chosen edit software is an extra expense, but worth it for a longer, less frustrating, editing life.

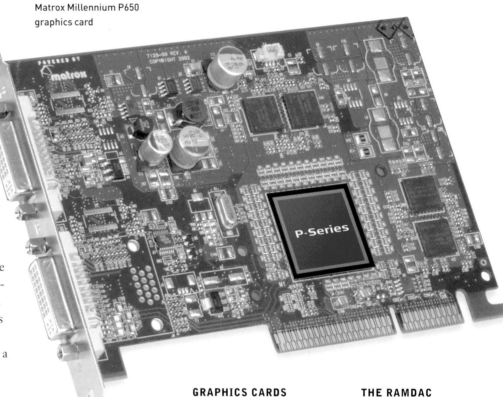

Matrox Millennium P650 graphics card

GRAPHICS CARDS

Sometimes called video cards, you shouldn't get these mixed up with video capture cards. Graphics cards take directions from your computer's CPU, and turn them into a signal that can be output to an analog or digital screen. You don't need to know what everything does, but for the curious:

A GRAPHICS PROCESSOR (GPU)

This processes graphics information and is responsible for turning your digital 0s and 1s into images.

VIDEO MEMORY

Just like your computer, the card has an amount of RAM that stores digital information for processing. More RAM keeps speeds up, particularly in heavy-duty 3D graphics processing.

THE RAMDAC

The Random Access Memory Digital To Analog Converter. This memory bank converts the digital information stored in the Video Memory and converts it into a monitor-friendly analog signal.

THE DISPLAY CONNECTOR

This takes the signal from the card to the monitor. Many cards now have two, letting you work on two screens at once: this is extremely useful if you're working on digital video.

THE ACCELERATED GRAPHICS PORT (AGP) CONNECTOR

This connects the card with your computer's motherboard.

MPEG, DIVX, WINDOWS MEDIA, REALMEDIA, QUICKTIME From the outset, it's probably quite handy to know the file formats that are going to be available to you, both with your captured clips and your finished production. This is an outline of the detail to be found when exporting.

There are two different types of file: streaming and non-streaming. You usually won't require an export to streaming media until you're happy that your production is finished. Streaming media is designed to be watched as it is downloaded. For this reason—and certainly on the Internet—the bitrate is low as a compromise to instant viewing. A low bitrate creates a lossy image. Non-streaming files require the entire media file to be downloaded before viewing becomes available through an application.

Non-streaming formats can have encoders that let you have a streaming version of that same format, and to view each format requires the download of a relevant player, notably Windows Media (MPEG, AVI) or QuickTime (MOV).

MPEG

To you, the Motion Picture Experts Group, the format developer, and to them, ISO/IEC JTC1 SC29 WG11. MPEG meet under the International Standards Organization to decide on bitrates by compression. Different manufacturers deliver appropriate hard and software for this standard: .mpg is the suffix for this type of file as a non-streaming file and .m2v as a streaming file. The standard comes in a variety of incarnations for video use. MP3 (.mp3 suffix) indicates their dedicated audio format, a successor to .mpa and .mp2.

AVI

That's Audio Video Interleaved, cleverly, and one of the formats owned by Microsoft Windows. These are generally perceived to be inferior to .mpegs but they can be useful for transferring large files due to their lower frame rate and—given a good encoder—high compression. Both streaming and non-streaming formats are termed .avi.

MOV

.mov is the movie file extension for QuickTime playback. QuickTime was borne of Apple and the suffix shouldn't be confused with their others (.qt and .moov). .movs are accessible for PCs too and respond as both streaming and non-streaming formats. The format offers impressive media quality.

DIVX

Originally intended as a rival to DVD and MPEG2 as a video rental format, DivX offers nearly the same level of audio/visual quality at a high level of compression. A failure as a commercial format, its strengths have made it a favorite for Internet video piracy.

REAL

Real movies have the suffix of .rm (Real Movie) and it's a common format for downloadable move clips on the Internet. The .rm format is a streaming file format only: cheap, quick, with a desperately low resolution and awful audio.

SKIN YOU'RE IN
As a personality gimmick, both Microsoft and independent designers regularly make available different "skins" for Windows Media Player. Just like clip-on mobile-phone fascias, these can be downloaded and applied to get away from the standard corporate XP screen.

SOUNDCARDS If you buy or have a Mac, you will get a standard proprietary soundcard with it. If you bought a package PC, you'll probably find a Creative Labs' Soundblaster under your devices menu.

Both standard cards operate at 16-bit and 48 KHz sample rate—the same as the audio information on digital videotape and CD quality. As a direct translation and for the purposes of desktop editing, these soundcards are fine. At the risk of being cynical, the sound that they process and deliver is probably due to audio being one of the demonstration fundamentals in a retail outlet.

There are a lot of soundcards that promise bigger and better. For the low-end user, there's no point in spending more money, but anyone else might want to consider it.

Audio for video production is half the battle won. Bad audio can turn a professional program amateur and vice versa. It can also distract an audience from repeated shots, filler shots, your worst shots—and drive a viewer through a video doldrums. A better soundcard—i.e., a more expensive or non-standard issue one—has the potential to do something about this.

SOUND PURCHASE

Soundcards vary a great deal. Do your research and find one that at least promises to deliver. Soundblaster's Audigy 2 Platinum (above and below) is stamped THX-certified and has the capabilities for 5.1 Dolby and 6.1 surround sound. Look for connectivity too. If you're working in tandem with other audio equipment, your aim is to find the easiest way into your PC without diversion.

The difference between 8-bit and 16-bit sound is quite apparent on listening: clipping and lack of dynamic range (measured in decibels—**dB**). If you think of 16-bit video as giving you 64,000 colors, the same goes with audio, allowing it considerable depth—around 96dB. 24-bit 96KHz gives, by ratio, 106dB. The higher the dynamic range, the more your audio has the ability to replicate its analog source.

You're not going to hear the difference, though, unless you're working with high-end studio equipment. Again, it's worth focusing on how you intend to distribute your program. If it is for theatrical distribution, the last thing you want is the hiss of audio compression.

Like digital video, again, the higher the sample rate, the better the audio quality. What 96KHz will give you is a sample rate with frequencies beyond the distinction of the human ear. Audiophiles will tell you that the importance of this is that everything must be preserved as close to your analog source (given an algorithm's tendency to round off numbers and cause errors) until final mixdown with your video. The chances are that you'll burn off or play out your program at 16/48 anyway. If you don't require more than CD-quality 16/48, look out for other factors that will give a better performance from a soundcard.

A soundcard—like a codec—is basically an algorithm. Like codecs, you tend to pay more for better algorithms. The quality of the ADC and DAC in your soundcard may be important to you if you're inputting analog audio straight into your computer. Your soundcard's audio software might swing you too—despite the importance of audio, desktop edit systems are notorious for their audio oversights. There's also the age-old problem of compatibility issues, so try to choose one with strong driver support to make sure that it doesn't conflict with your other applications.

The fundamental issue regarding audio, though, is your peripheral kit. Use an amp and speakers that are worthy of your level of production—and try to make this compatible with the way your program is going to be shown.

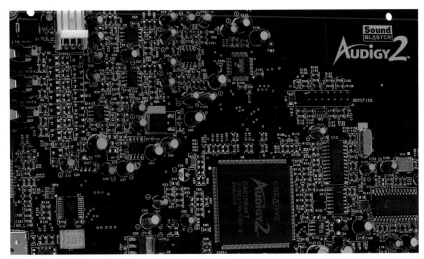

02.03

Just as your focus during production should be the edit, your choice of software should be the primary reason that you purchase your computer. If you already have your Mac or PC and intend to use it for your edit, then this will be one of the factors that dictates your choice. Some edit software is cross-platform. Most is not. If you're opting for PC—aside from checking your computer's specifications—you should check the version of Windows that you're running and that your shortlist of software is compatible with it.

Your choice of edit software is entirely dependent on your computer, your level, your anticipation of use—and your budget. Most beginners admit that they're beginners and find some suitable low-end product to work with;

most intermediate users would like to think that they're professional and aim for high-end without utilizing all that it has to offer; most professionals just get on with their work with mild frustration at a suite's limitations.

There are a lot of frustrations for anyone who works with an edit package, a lot of which are slowly being resolved with the increased use of realtime. Whether or not it's a buzzword to get excited about or a high-tech red herring will be discussed, but for the moment appreciate the choices on offer and the capabilities that they have.

If you've bought a computer geared for multimedia (Sony laptops are famous for this), then you may find low-end edit software preinstalled. This may allow variant forms of capture (i.e., stills from movies, movies from movies) and offer ways of cutting video and audio simply. If you are happy enough to be termed a beginner, then it's a good idea to take

PART 02. THE KIT

CHAPTER THREE

EDIT SOFTWARE

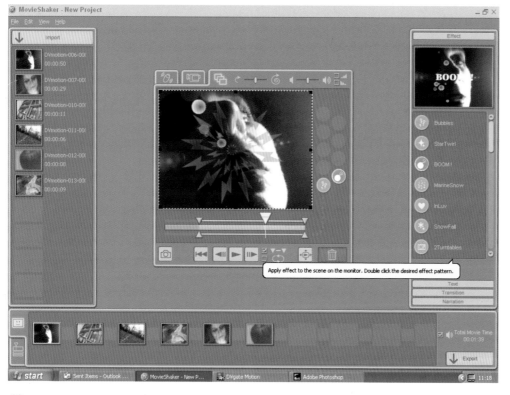

Apply effect to the scene on the monitor. Double click the desired effect pattern.

AUTOMATIC FOR THE PEOPLE

Sony's MovieShaker comes as standard with VAIO laptops and MICROMV models of camera. It's possibly one of the most simple ways to edit (quick, low res) and will even edit for you if you give it a few clips to mess around with.

this to its limits as a "suck-it-and-see." If you decide that editing is for you, then it will also steer you in the right direction as to what you like, what you don't like, and what you really need.

Research your software, ask to see it in action or download a trial version from the Internet: a lot of potential users will instantly be turned off by a poor user interface. If the product appears non-intuitive or complicated, they will instantly be turned off. A straightforward drag-and-drop package can easily do more than you will ever want it to, so don't be too hard on simplicity. Good edit software will make utilization easy for you while backing this up with all the features that you might require for your cut.

Give others a chance too. The players in the intermediate home-user market are Premiere and Final Cut Pro (the latest versions uncannily designed by the same person). The lesser-knowns are not necessarily lesser-known

CUTTING EDGE
Final Cut Pro is the Mac's shining light of edit software. Now in its fourth incarnation, it's loved by business professionals and home users alike, demonstrating the versatility of its capabilities and the ease of its interface.

because they are inferior. Discreet, Incite, Matrox and Pinnacle are just a few of the others that should be contending for your cash.

Interestingly, the home-user market is now beginning to be infiltrated by programs originally geared to the high-end professional. Avid's Express has automatically made them an instant rival to Adobe and Apple because of their name. Their move could be merely a resigning sigh, a sign of the times that the home-user market can now be as professional—or as commercial—as the professional market. Why spend $25,000 when you could spend $1000 for a high-end product?

Of course, there are benefits to rent or dry rent, which are mainly client-based if you have them. A client will usually have a budget that allows them the privilege of an environment that isn't your home office or the box-room you rented. And just how good a runner are you anyway? This may be trite, but for corporations, they expect the best—and these are the little things that are expected to create an image of professionalism. If it is a corporation, it's more than likely that the budget won't be coming out of your client's pocket anyway—time permitting, it's a day (or so) out, and they'll expect everything to be laid on for them, just as you expect your directly paid suite to be faultless.

If you are renting, you should have established what kind of edit (i.e., linear/non-linear, online/offline, Avid/Lightworks, etc.) you're working with. You should expect your editor to be reasonably quick and maintain some kind of rapport with them (if not mind-reading as to what you want) and technically, the suite should be working perfectly. If any of these things aren't what you expect, you should expect it to give you some kind of payment leverage with the postproduction house. Everything is negotiable…

To sum up, the edit software should not just be compatible for your computer; it should be compatible for your product and compatible for you.

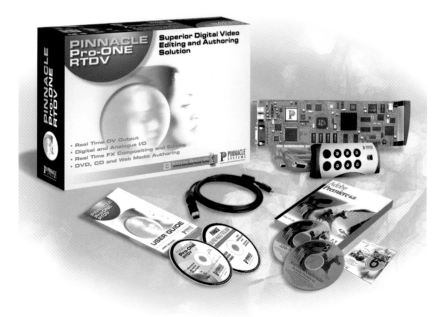

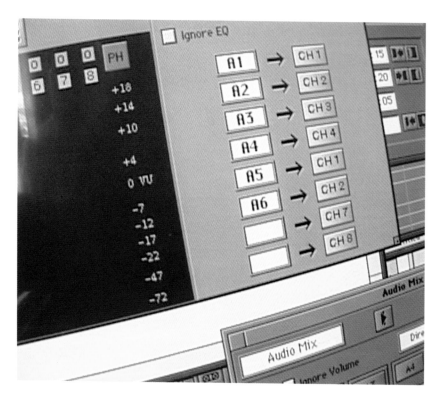

Top: Pinnacle's Pro-ONE RTDV edit application.
Above: AVID audio interface detail

BASIC SOFTWARE If you buy a Mac or PC specifically designed as a relatively cheap multimedia platform, you will have a capture card already installed. It is becoming more and more common that such systems will have appendage edit software to some extent.

On any Mac, it is quite simply a question of iMovie. On a low-end multimedia-enhanced PC, it's not so simple: there are so many capture cards out there that the software is equally multifarious and dependent on the preference of the manufacturer.

A low-end PC—and this is by no means a derogatory term; budget always requires limitations no matter where you are in the spectrum of software purchase—will be part of a standards "wave." This terminology refers to the particular rival standard at the time: the type of CPU, the amount of hard disk space and RAM, and the spec for the codecs and the CD-ROM/DVD. What is quite clear is that as time marches on, prices are lower and the standard spec is higher. With specific regard to the CD drive, a cheap multimedia PC will offer playback of CD and DVD, but with only the function of writing to CD-ROM.

The difference with cheaper models is that you're more likely only to have either analog input and output or a USB1 connection, which is not particularly handy for capturing digital video. A lot of the cheap software will be very much geared toward taking VHS as a source via a breakout box and allow a simple conversion and edit before exporting back to VHS. Dazzle, Pinnacle, and Pyro all produce very cheap edit software and capture cards for a compatibly cheap price.

IMOVIE, YOU EDITOR
Mac's iMovie is their standard edit application. The program makes it easy to recognize your clips, and just as easy to drag them into a sequence on your timeline. It's great for quick vacation movies or rough-cuts without too much of a fuss—or too many frills.

The thing to watch out for when buying a multimedia PC is that the edit software isn't just a "lite" version of the real deal. This can be a pain: the software is only acting as an advertisement to go out and buy the upgrade. We're back to the wonderful world of the Limited Edition…

Boxed-up full versions require you to install them yourself. They're usually a capture card with bundled edit software, which at least is indicative that your videocard will be compatible with the software—one of the biggest problems with digital video editing. Pinnacle have the widest range of different products that offer slightly different things. If you're buying really cheap, you don't get everything—i.e., either analog or digital. Spend a little more money within the realm of low-end and you get luckier.

The low-end edit software that Pinnacle bundles with their card is their Studio range, which functions as a simple drag-and-drop edit. Smart Capture is their low sample-rate capture facility, which allocates only 360Mb to a one-hour DV tape—something that at workable high-res should take about 12Gb. This is to preserve the smaller hard disk on a cheaper PC, and lets you work offline before recapturing your final edit. In fact, most cheap software will endeavor to save your hard disk at any cost to your picture in order that their product runs smoothly.

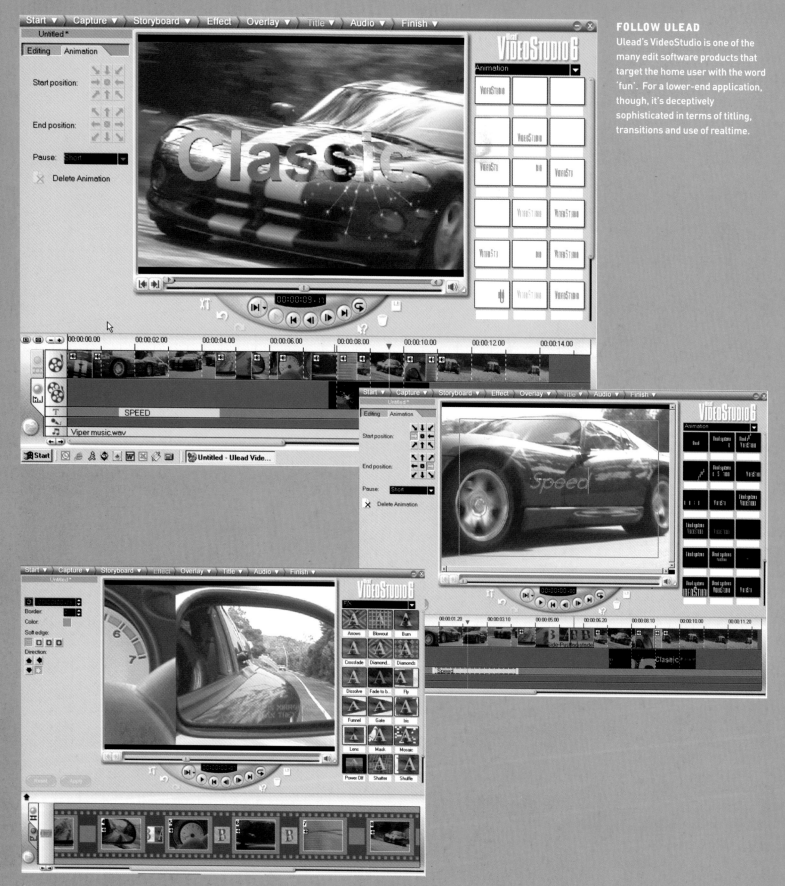

FOLLOW ULEAD

Ulead's VideoStudio is one of the many edit software products that target the home user with the word 'fun'. For a lower-end application, though, it's deceptively sophisticated in terms of titling, transitions and use of realtime.

Cheaper edit software will also have a limited number of transitions—but that's not to say that more expensive software is limitless. Some of the more elaborate transitions—probably the ones that you want—can be watermarked (branded) with the manufacturer's logo. The only way of getting rid of these in your edit is usually to go online and disable the function—for a bit more money. There's no such thing as a free transition… With PCs, the one factor in the operation of the edit software is a faster processor and a larger RAM and hard disk. Go to the brink of the budget that you can afford to get this and then work out the edit software with the budget that remains. And then at least you'll get edit software that works without worry.

Macs are easy in comparison. Their cheapest system offers iMovie as standard. The dichotomy is, of course, whether the cheapest Mac actually fits into the low-end spectrum. For the price, you could probably find yourself a middle-range multimedia PC with associated edit software.

iMovie's abilities are pretty supreme if it is going to fall under the low-end umbrella. Not only is it FireWire-enabled and operates a sophisticated drag, drop, transition, and audio effect (Skywalker, don't you know?), but your productions can be easily burnt to DVD complete with chapter stops. They make it easy for you because they're dedicated.

For the low-end user, design is one of the fundamentals for edit software: something that can intelligently guess what you're trying to do one step in advance. With this kind of feature, there is no learning curve and no giving up once confronted with head-busting jargon. The price you pay is that you won't learn and you can't do anything different from what the software is capable of and what it wants to do itself.

But if you want anything more than this, you'll probably be aiming for mid-range edit software.

CAPTURE TO CAPTIVATE

To get your clips from your camera to Sony VAIO's MovieShaker requires their installed DVgate capture application. Laptops don't tend to have an immense amount of disk space, so the program lets you monitor free space and plan ahead to some extent.

INTERMEDIATE AND ADVANCED Once your budget and editing horizons have broadened, the quest for your dream edit software can become a bit more directed. Mid-range products, however various, also become a bit more scrutinized due to home-users wanting near-professional quality at domestic prices. This results in a few of them offering a standard that makes them popular purchases.

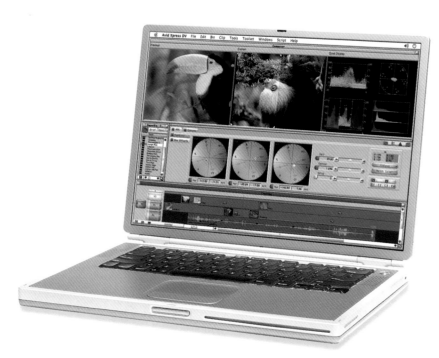

The spec for your PC or Mac is now vital to ensure that the software can run. Any manufacturer's websites will give the minimum spec for any product that they offer. It will be your job to guarantee that you have the right system, and not theirs that their software can run on it.

The Mac, again, offers a clear-cut choice: Final Cut Pro or Final Cut Express. The difference between the two is cost and features, Express being the slightly lesser version when it comes to color correction, allowing 24fps, and filters. Express also hides your source timecode and lacks EDL support. All these factors add up to one big question mark as to why the difference in price is so minimal. The answer is to do a bar job for a

LAPTOP DOG

Final Cut Pro on an Apple G4 Powerbook is a one-stop shop to portable capture and edit on location. As an instant solution to storyboarding or assembling a rough cut to see what shots you're missing, it can be indispensable.

couple of nights and buy FCP instead. Once you move into mid-range edit software, you begin to face realtime. This is something that will be discussed more in depth later, but Apple have identified the issues involved and let a user use the realtime either of the software or of an associated PCI card like Matrox's RTMac. This kind of PCI permits a Mac to be versatile rather than a rigid Apple-only platform.

Mid-range edit software is constantly updated to bigger and better versions. If you are buying, try to find out whether or not the newer version is right around the corner. Once you've bought one incarnation, you're going to have to pay a considerable fraction more to update—usually via a website.

Final Cut Pro's nearest rival is not as clear as the good old days when Adobe's Premiere was the PC preference. Premiere set such a good standard that other manufacturers have become keen to jump in. Even some of the snobbish high-end stalwarts have lowered their own standards to play the game—Avid specifically with DVExpress. The spectrum, though, of middle-range edit software is broad, and it's going to be a budget concern as to whether an extra $500 or so is going to buy you a better time in the edit.

Premiere, as the cheaper option, is bundled with some great (and sometimes expensive) realtime videocards. Cheaper, in mid-range, does not mean that your quality of edit will be lesser, as the functions are generally the same. If the spec of your PC is high enough, you'll be able to get maximum benefit out of your card and out of your edit software—in fact, the edit software almost becomes meaningless in the equation. Videocards tend to support specific edit applications, so if you're buying from scratch, it's best to look for the perfect card before it dictates the edit software that it is compatible with. You'll probably get it bundled too. This is equally applicable to a resident videocard if you're on the hunt for the right software. Check out the manufacturer's site of the card you've got and see if it recommends particular desktop editing software.

If your card offers such options, this gives you the chance to compare and contrast between NLE software, and this is the time that you will be staring long and hard at your budget. Try to see edit software in action. Despite their traditional drag-and-drop layouts, some are more user-friendly than others, so turn it into a question of preference. Most manufacturers also have free demo downloads on their websites, which are worth a go if you can't have a tinker with the real thing in-store.

Find out where the line is drawn between the software's handling of realtime and where the videocard becomes responsible. Demonstrations for videocards working with their associated edit software can be awe-inspiring, but often deceptive. Sometimes the two in tandem can deliver the realtime effect you want only if it's what they want…

CUT-PRICE PRO
Ulead's MediaStudio Pro is competitively priced against Premiere and Final Cut Pro, and still offers realtime capture, preview, and output. The latest version is particularly geared toward creating realtime MPEG capture and quick DVD authoring and production.

The question will always be what you want your production to be. Mid-range software tout broadcast-quality, which it is to the extent that better quality codecs permit. Edit software takes responsibility for making this happen with little fuss and to your requirements. Do you want good color correction? Do you want to run at 24fps? Would you rather it was more tailored for animation or effects? Indeed, the more specialized your requirements are, the more likely you'll be to use edit software that isn't FCP, Premiere, Avid ExpressDV, Vegas, or a mid-range Pinnacle product.

If you're going to buck the trend, make sure you can expect support for your choice from the manufacturer, the videocard, and codecs. Shelling out can be painful, but not as much as finding you haven't invested in a reasonable longevity.

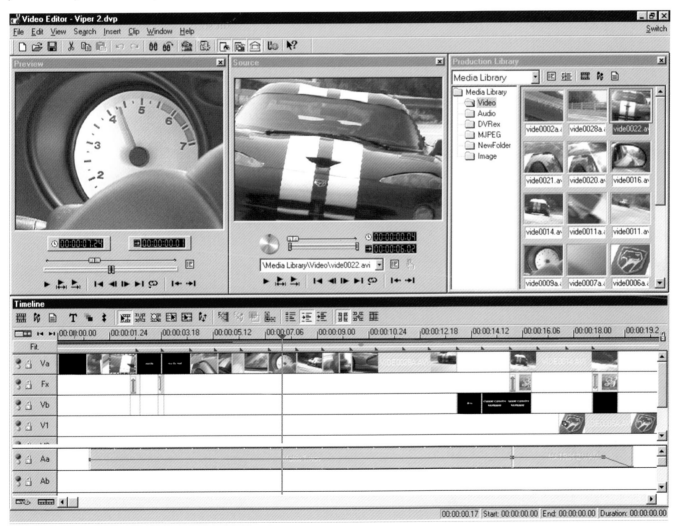

HIGH-END ALTERNATIVES

HIGH-END ALTERNATIVES When you get to high-end NLE alternatives, you're in the realm of renting with an editor, dry-rent, borrowing, begging, stealing—or else you've got far too much money. This is where you have to look at your job in hand and see what it is going to need.

Fundamentally, the difference between a mid-range and pro system is not the layout, nor the choice of transitions and effects, but the fact that it's where technology really begins. Because of the costs involved, it's where the investment starts. All high-end NLE systems are at the cutting edge of editing technology and anything that is available or anything that the media has caught wind of as The Next Big Thing is going to happen there first. Uncompressed editing, realtime, HDTV: it all begins there and gradually feeds down the chain in lesser, lower, cheaper versions.

All of the high-end editing systems are industry-standard—that is, the commercial industry relies on them to provide equipment to give them broadcast-quality results. A desktop editing system also vaunts broadcast quality, so what exactly is a pro NLE system giving you?

Today's reality is that "broadcast quality" is mere semantics—everything and anything is broadcast. News won't not broadcast the first close-up of Bigfoot because it's shot on Hi-8, just as they don't not broadcast warzone reportage with webphones or dropout-laden VHS-shot home funnies. However, industry-standard broadcast quality is largely to do with being shot on DVCAM, DVCPRO, or DigiBeta superior lenses and ADCs, HDTV CCDs, a larger bandwidth, and so on giving better quality images.

These images are being taken into professional NLE systems on robust, fine-tuned decks before going anywhere near any software, which almost makes it the weakest link. The reality is that editing is, as a client once said, just cut and paste.

Speaking of clients, a professional suite is usually what they would expect for their day out from the office. Runners with cups of tea on tap, a comfortable sofa at the back of the room, an editor quickly responding to their "could you just try?" requests, and a director being paid to quietly seethe at having creative genius overridden. They would expect nothing less for their company's money. The edit software is almost taking the back seat with them to the experience of being amid such intimidating industrial equipment.

Avid cornered the market with their edit software, which ranges from the horrifically expensive to the astronomical. Each variation either provides a technological step up from the last (Media Composer) or undertakes a specific task (Symphony for color correction and finishing tools). Because of the array of Avid products, a postproduction facility can easily feed between them from edit suite to edit suite, speeding transfer and conform. Storage and archive of files becomes easier in this respect too, with Storage-Area Networks (SANs) letting files be shared simultaneously among editors, graphic artists, etc.

Such high-powered equipment shares the production's burden with high-end edit software, and the software tends to be a lot more stable as a result. The investment in cost at a postproduction house tends to reflect this with high-spec computers that will run speeds which get the best out of the software's realtime features. Combine this with a quick editor and a professional edit takes away a lot of the frustrations of a low or mid-range desktop edit.

In effect, you get what you pay for in a professional edit, but whatever software your production is running with, you can expect it to work for your money.

AVID EDITOR
While conventionally found in busy, techno-busting edit suites (left) AVID's name can now adorn your tidy desktop as AVID Xpress DV and Pro (above). Without a doubt, its price still makes it the highest end for home users, but its abilities as a professional suite remain faithful to its origins.

SOFTWARE ACCESSORIES For every type of edit software, there are a dozen handy applications to use with it. Most of these you can live without, but some of them—if you try them out—might make your day. With most of these, it is essential that they support the format or other software that you are using, so be prepared for a bit of research.

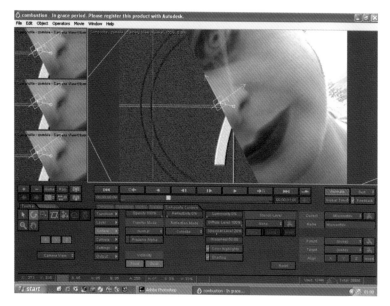

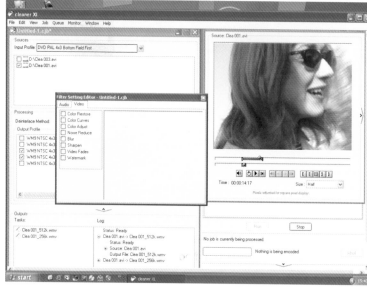

IMAGE MANIPULATORS

"It's never enough," as *Hellraiser's* Frank once said. Despite the image manipulation features in your edit and videocard software, users still want more. From crude, low-end shareware (home programming and the Internet can be a beautiful thing) to high-end whizz-bang-zoom, there's an application out there that can do wonders for your picture. Some transitions and effects work as virtual plug-ins and appear within your edit software menu. While this is a logical and immediate solution, sometimes the array of information can be cluttering and boggling.

A lot of the more professional programs work as stand-alone applications that require you to import your finished production into it and work from there. Pinnacle and Boris provide a whole array of sliding-scale products—the more recent and the more expensive, the more realtime capabilities they have. Discreet's Combustion is a prime example of such technology, with an intimidating interface and an imposing double-whammy of user guide and tutorials. Inside, though, are DVEs impressive enough to make your computer work hard for your money.

Work with your edit and videocard software—learn what it can do before you reach its limits and buy more in. And if you're frustrated by the aging edit and videocard software that you've got, think about updating those before you buy into image-doctoring applications.

Above left: **Available for Mac and PC, Discreet's Combustion allows for incredible manipulation of your images through unique paint and animation applications. When compositing, it also allows "space" to be introduced between layers, for believable 3D environments in which your moving pictures live.**

Above right: **Discreet's Cleaner XL contains a useful array of editable filters and encoders for video and audio. This ensures your production looks and sounds as good as it can.**

CLEANERS/TRANSCODERS

Video cleaners use compression algorithms to revise your video and audio settings optimistically without loss. Media Cleaner Pro, Discreet's Cleaner XL and EZ Cleaner are just a few of those available that allow for changes in image cropping, scaling, deinterlacing, field dominance, inverse telecine, noise reduction and filtering, gamma correction, audio gating, and audio enhancing. A lot of these cleaners have an aim toward transcoding your finished production into another format, whether streaming media or DVD—both requiring a specific set of settings for the best image.

Cleaners—especially the simpler ones—have standard media default profiles that will limit, clip, and adjust at the touch of a button. It is only certain transcoding, though, that can guarantee cleaning without recompression, such as a MOV to an AVI. Like codecs, the more complicated the algorithms, the more expensive the cleaners are, and the quality of compression is governed by the speed of your CPU. Cleaners are usually available for trial via websites.

TITLING

Your edit software, too, is likely to have some kind of basic titling software. It might even have a demo or full version of subsidiary titling software that enables you to create titles within a three-dimensional workspace.

Titling, like audio, is one of those things in edit software that can often seem to be a bit of an afterthought. Maybe you don't want to just scroll or crawl your titles, or open up a different video track for each word of your title in order to drag your various effects over. If you think that your creativity is somewhat stifled within your NLE parameters, there is plenty of titling software out there that will help. Boris' Graffiti offers a range of different animations for your titles, both in two and three dimensions. Costs vary depending on features, but it is worth pushing your budget to incorporate the use of cameras and lights onto your titles to let them complement your masterpiece and boost your production values.

ANIMATION

Animation applications tend to distance themselves in terms of stand-alone software from video-editing software. If you're an animator, you're likely to simply be working from a specialized application. However, animation applications can take your production from your edit software as a MOV or AVI and work with it as a primitive object for compositing, ink and painting, rotoscoping, and keyframe animating.

If you are going to work on your digital video images for animation, or you have created an animation using them in your edit software, a good animation application will reduce the time-consuming nature of working on your project frame by frame. An animator, though, tends to be an animator—and it may well be that if you decide that this is how you fundamentally want to use your digital video, a turnkey animation studio is probably better than using one bit of software in hand with another. If you are a casual animator, then you might want to think about an effects application like Combustion, which will let you animate your edit carryover.

Above: **Don't forget about your audio—your audience won't.** One of Discreet's Cleaner XL audio filters might brighten it up that extra bit. Below: **If you've got a production that you're proud of, let the world see it. Ulead's DVD MovieFactory lets you create and customise menus and burn a film directly from DV to DVD.**

DVD

The interaction that DVD offers with hot buttons, animated menus, and chapter stops has turned a simple user interface into an artform of its own. Because of this, various software is becoming available to allow the authoring and creation of such screens. It's really the frosting on the cake of your program if you're burning it to DVD and is one step toward making a truly professional product.

Sonic Solution's DVDit!, Ulead System's VideoStudio, and Dazzle's DVD Complete Deluxe are one-stop shops to getting your file onto DVD and upping your production values. They can be used in tandem with backgrounds or textures that you've created in image software to brand it entirely yours. This is very useful indeed.

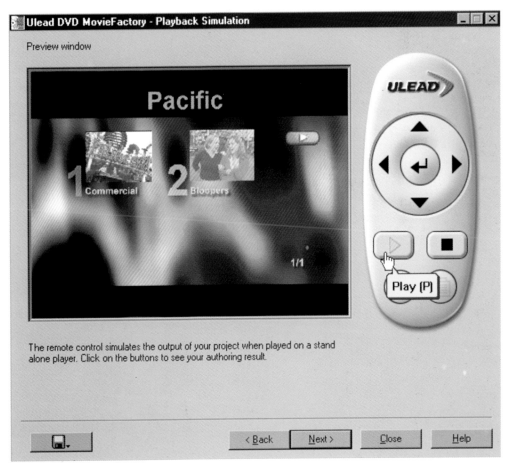

AUDIO SOFTWARE

AUDIO SOFTWARE A sequencer is essentially a timeline, just as edit software is a timeline. Just like edit software, the more features, the more expensive the sequencer. And also, just like edit software with a videocard, the better the soundcard, the better quality your sound.

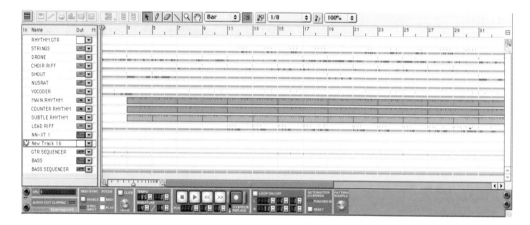

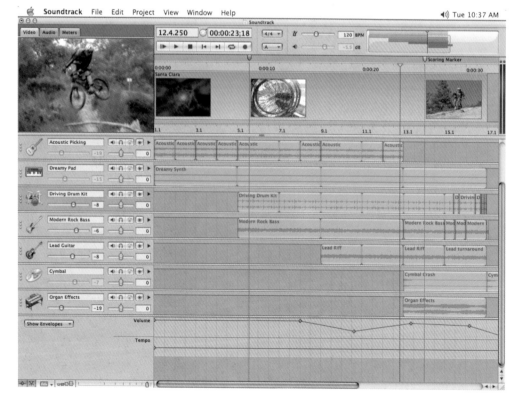

The parallels go on, but if you're thinking about good-quality video, you'll be let down if you don't think about good quality audio.

Edit software doesn't give as much consideration to audio as it should. While you might have hundreds of effects for your pictures, you will be pushed to find even tens of audio effects. And although you might have hundreds of video transitions, there is probably little more than a basic mixer on your desktop.

One of the reasons that audio gets such a poor deal is that it doesn't need rendering—and, more often than not, it doesn't need compressing. Therefore, while your computer works overtime with your images, your audio is quietly getting on with its own thing and waiting for the video to catch up.

The mixing of a soundtrack to your video is something that an audio mixer does. It's an audio mixer that would have a sequencer, just as it's an editor that has edit software. But seeing as you're already pushing the editor out of the hot seat, there's no reason why you shouldn't be mixing with a sequencer.

SOUNDS IN SEQUENCE

Top: Reason sequencer interface, with tracks on the left and the timeline running horizontally across the screen
Bottom: Final Cut Pro's soundtrack interface, with seven tracks of digital audio running through the timeline.

The dedication to either one thing or another still remains within the audio-visual world. The twain does meet occasionally with software such as VEGAS (now owned by Sony), which can operate like a sequencer that you can work captured images to. Acid is the audio-only version of Vegas—a sequencer with a video window that is frame-sensitive.

If you are thinking about separate audio software in order to compose your own soundtrack to your masterpiece, you'll probably find within the application a way of importing your finished work. If you are working like this, make sure that the frame rate in audio is the same as in your video. This is particularly relevant if you're separating your WAV from your finished production and taking it into the audio application to work on before dumping it back as your mastered audio track.

Don't dismiss an application like Logic or ProTools just because you're not going to become John Williams; audio software can also be used effectively for dialog and effects.

A system is only as good as its weakest part—different speakers respond to sound in a different way, for example. Good speakers with a good amp give out a very flat sound. Even though this implies that it reduces "colorization" of sound, what it is doing is giving you a very true sound. The only difference to this will be the acoustics of the room that you're working in, or whether you're working off open (bassy) or enclosed (flat, true). When you're working with audio, make it like video and shoot clean—or work flat in this case. Again, think about your distribution, where the production is going to be played and work from flat from there.

MIDI is a language developed for different audio sources and targets to talk between themselves. It works by telling the target to play, where to start and stop each note, pitch information, controller information (how the controller being used is affecting the sound), filter information, and so on. MIDI can also represent your audio source on screen as a digital replica—like a keyboard—letting you utilize the computer as you would the keyboard itself. MIDI is dependent on the right output from your source and the right translation software on your computer.

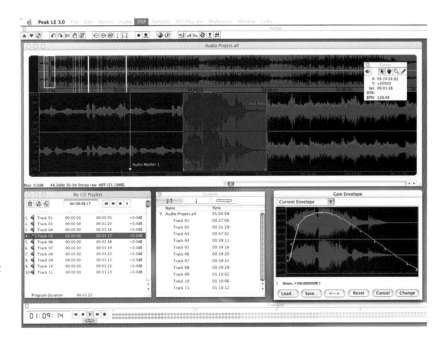

CLIMB EVERY MOUNTAIN
Bias' Peak 3.0 LE at work. A solid digital audio editor shouldn't just be regarded as a musician's application. With a range of effects and comprehensive editing capabilities, it's every bit as vital to the world of digital video.

Sound software is split into two camps: sequencers and wave editors. While sequencers control sound or MIDI over time, wave editors let you edit waves—visual interpretations of sound—manipulating the optical to affect the digital. Most sequencers have a small wave editor attached and most edit software is wave-led rather than MIDI-compatible, although obviously a devoted wave application will be a lot more versatile with the massage of your soundwaves.

Processing tools or dynamics processors let your video be compressed, expanded, companded, gated, or ducked. All these expressions refer to keeping your audio within upper and lower level thresholds. Digital audio peaking over 0Db is awful. It sounds horrific—if it isn't just instantly chopped and dismissed from your soundtrack by your camera during the shoot, or your videocard during the edit. Audio cleaners not only tidy up your sound, smoothing hiss and hum, but they are there to keep your audio safe within its dynamic range.

Production tools are there to manipulate your sound in the same way that video effects work. While effects such as reverb and distortion may well be available in your edit software, dynamics will give you choruses, flanges, phases, and wah-wah. Another mantra: audio is 50% of the deal.

FX/TITLING SOFTWARE No matter the level at which your edit software functions, it will always have options other than to just hard cut your pictures. Anything more than a hard cut is a transition. Your videocard too will have installation software that will usually contain video effects which you can apply to your images, as well as transitions. If these appear as options within your edit software, they're plug-ins.

Plug-in or edit software effects will, at a basic level, consist of some form of color correction and image manipulation—probably to the extent that your digital video camera offers. They will also have a way of creating titles that may require you opening a sister application, creating the title, and importing it into your project.

It is increasingly popular to see edit software that is a one-stop shop to all your wildest dreams, or is bundled with a whole load of plug-in toys. If you're using something like this, it may well be only a matter of time before you see something else and want to work with it in tandem.

Whatever options you ultimately end up with in your edit software may not be enough for your requirements or entertainment. Even if you are working with a reasonably high-end edit with a realtime videocard, there may be specific effects, titling and transitions that you want which you don't have access to.

For this reason, effects, titling, and transition software is available to purchase separately. Their compatibility with your videocard and your software defines whether they can be used as a plug-in or not. If they can't, you'll need to make sure that you can save your images in a suitable format—usually AVI—which you can then import into your NLE. And humans—especially editors—are fickle creatures. They get bored very easily with what's available to them and start sniffing around on other editors' territories and begin to covet the newest

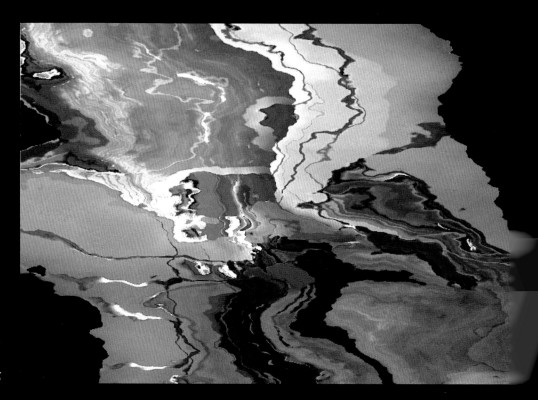

RED-HOT EFFECTS
The deftness with which Combustion lets your image be controlled without sacrificing resolution or color is impressive. Accurate keyframing can let you corrupt your image as much as you like when you like, as this crumpled image shows.

latest way of wringing pixels to death on a perfectly good shot. Effects, transition, and titling software is as self-explanatory as it gets. If you're not happy with what you've got, your search should be based on in-store and Internet demonstrations. If it's realtime that you're after, make sure you have a go yourself and find out the limits (there will be plenty) of what is possible in realtime with the videocard you have.

Some software, though, isn't a job-lot of jiggery-pokery. The more serious types available can concentrate on just one specialist algorithm to be applied to your image and then tailored to fit. Morphing is one of these. It's a complicated enough process to warrant its own software package, although it can be a budget-friendly one. The algorithms that applications such as morphing apply make

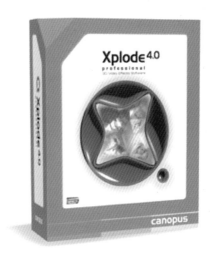

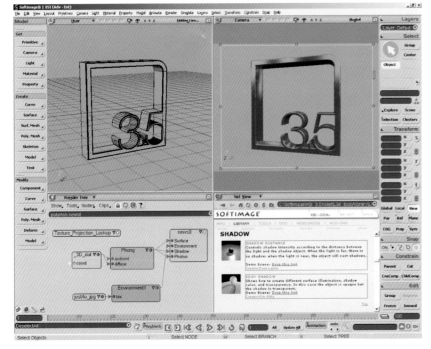

Top right: **Canopus' Xplode** is geared toward high powered effects and fast results. Its 3D abilities are excellent.

Top: iMovie, like most entry-level edit packages, contains a menu of standard preset effects.

Bottom: If you want a career in effects and you have a few thousand bucks in your pocket, AVID's Softimage will let you create the next 3D commercial.

your effects vector-based. A vector-based effect, transition, or title relies on the manipulation of image information rather than the image pixels itself. The information used is to do with an image's location, color, length, height, and so on, and the use of applied mathematics can then alter the image with precise scaling.

Non-vector-based software is bitmap-based or raster. A raster effect is likely to be a filter dragged over your pixels to change them and is therefore less precise and less customizable. It does, however, preserve your digital video image a little truer because it is relying on the existing layout of the pixels and not on processed data information.

2D vector-based software lets your picture be expanded, stretched, or compressed along the x and y axis of your screen. 3D effects, adding processor-heavy dimension, also add cost to a software package and turn your image into digital putty. Good algorithms cost money. And good algorithms can let you manipulate your image in the most subtle ways imaginable, not so much adding effects as effect. Used wisely, they can isolate images for transformation or composition to extraordinary effect.

This kind of software tends to be stand-alone and cross-platform—if not dedicated to Mac. They're pretty easy to spot: look for anything pyrotechnical on the shelves. After Discreet stamped their name on the market with Flame, Inferno, and Combustion, Canopus have followed up with Xplode and the rest use box imagery to infer the same. Whether or not this has anything to do with your CPU working overtime and blowing up your computer has not been clarified.

CODECS, ENCODERS, CONVERSION, AND COMPRESSION SOFTWARE Codecs, confusingly, stand for two things that do two things. The first abbreviation translates as **Co**der/**Dec**oder and is a chip used to convert analog to digital (ADC) and digital to analog (DAC). It's the kind of chip found in your phone or your modem.

The second abbreviation is the one that's more important to you—the **Co**mpressor/**Dec**ompressor. The latter is the vital hardware or software that you will need to process your video images and audio.

This kind of codec is basically an algorithm that deals with your binary data, compressing it in your digital video camera during capture and then decompressing it at your monitor. Your computer is also most likely to have basic codecs already installed if you have a FireWire port—and if you have installed your own capture card, the software will contain the codecs you need for it. The reason you need a codec in your computer is that it is required to decompress the clips during editing.

Like Coder/Decoders, Compressor/Decompressors can come as a chip. A hardware codec such as this is less in favor due to its cost. While they can make fewer demands on your processor and purport to increase quality, size, and color of image, they are sometimes slower as they have to send information from one part of the computer to another and back again. Software codecs are, alternatively, easily updateable via the Internet and are getting better at image size and quality. These days, the difference is slight, if unnoticeable. If you want to find out what codec you are running, you will find them alongside your compatible devices in your control panel menu.

Your codecs are essential for the quality of your output. Hardware codecs usually encode at a **constant bit rate** (CBR). This means that the video that you are importing will be capturing at the same time as the tape runs—**realtime**, in fact. The more expensive type are versatile enough to cope with a **variable bit rate** (VBR). And software codecs can usually do both.

The difference between CBR and VBR is straightforward enough. Running your video at CBR means that each image, no matter how complicated or simple the code, will be captured at the same number of bits per second. What this means is that your entire capture is likely to be compromised, the main outcome being that the more complicated codes are simplified, leading to your images being subject to pixelization— the dreaded **quantization** effect.

On the other hand, VBR, instead of giving your bits per second a meantime, gives them two parameters to work between. Reading ahead, the codec understands that some code is more complex than others and finds a suitably high bits-per-second rate to capture them at a more sophisticated quality.

This same principle comes into play for burning off your project, and for streaming video to the Internet, where a higher resolution is required for small details while keeping the speed of the stream tolerably fast. Similarly, the codec will read the simpler codes and find a bit rate that suits to keep the stream flowing at a constant viewing rate.

You recall that your codec is fundamentally an algorithm? Well, some mathematicians are better than others. Therefore some codecs deserve gold stars and others a big "see me after school." Good sums in realtime give outstanding results, but can be a burden on your processor if you're using a software codec—and as hardware, they can simply be outpricing. If you're using a quality software codec, although it might take time, it has the benefit of being able to encode with multiple passes. This means that it can always refer back to the original source tape and make tiny adjustments each time for better quality encoding.

Once you have edited your masterpiece, it is always best to avoid **transcoding**. This is the process of converting your file or clip into another format. With video, this might be a compressed .avi to MPEG and with audio, a compressed .wav to MP3. Try to avoid this. Likewise with **re-encoding**— the process of taking a compressed clip and converting it to, say, a higher sample rate in the same format—because all it's doing is compressing your compressed binary values yet again and taking further information from it. If you think you are making your images or audio better, think again…

CRACKING CODECS
Aside from cleaning up pictures and sound, Cleaner XL is extremely versatile when encoding. Broadband and DVD are the two factors that have changed the emphasis of encoders to concentrate more on streaming formats and MPEG settings.

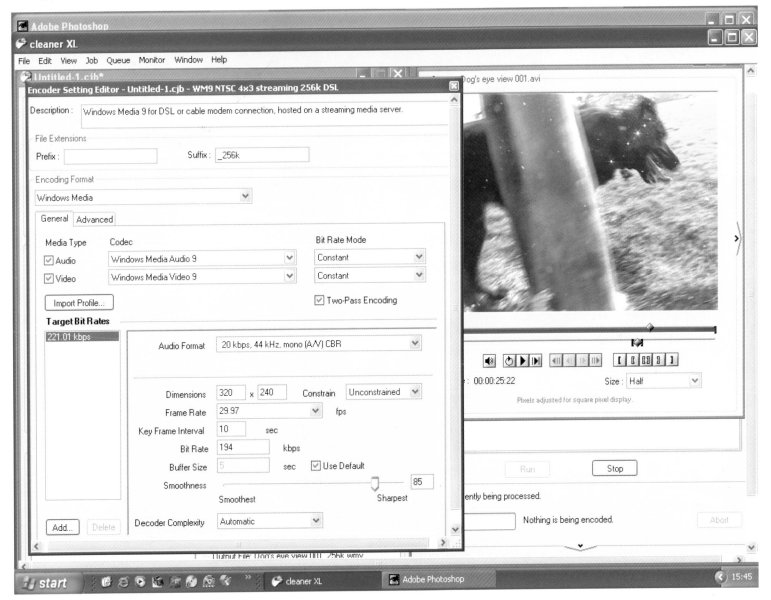

BURNING YEARNINGS
Sonic's DVDit! (above), Mac's DVD Studio Pro (below), and Ulead's DVD Workshop (right) are just three of the many products on the market specific to the authoring and burning of DVD. Applications such as these tend to have extremely user-friendly interfaces to make the creation of menus and the importing of images, textures, and buttons a very logical process with very professional results.

BURNER SOFTWARE You don't have to anticipate far into the future to know that if you're going to have large video files, you will probably need to be able to archive them. Further than that, you may see your project distributed on CD-ROM or DVD for convenience.

Traditionally, computers have used CD-ROM for archiving and video playout. VCD (Video Compact Disc) or SVCD (Super VCD) can hold, respectively, 74 minutes or 34 minutes of video on a 650Mb disc—their difference being in resolution. VCDs are encoded with MPEG-1 and their quality is slightly better than VHS. Curiously, they are still popular as a movie format in the Far East.

DVD, on the other hand, can hold nearly two hours of video on a single side of a disk at a much higher resolution using MPEG-2. This is preferable and it is the better alternative.

The difference between simply transferring files to archive and DVD playout is the process of encoding to MPEG-2, authoring the DVD, and burning it off.

In order to write to DVD, you have to make sure you have at least a DVD writeable or rewriteable drive. From there, you need to be able to compress using the MPEG-2 codec. If you have good-quality edit software, it should facilitate the burning off onto DVD. If you haven't got access to compress with MPEG-2, then you will need to find some burner software incorporating the MPEG-2 codec that will help you do it.

Burner software has spent a long time being dedicated to burning audio to CD—something that has been revitalized with the advent of MP3 compression for audio. Video has lagged behind, somewhat, because of the complications of computers handling large files—a CD can only hold, typically, 650Mb of video information, resulting in heavy compression and low frame-rate and resolution. DVD's arrival heralded new possibilities for desktop NLEs, just as it had revolutionized the movie rental and the sell-through market. This has led to burner software becoming a sophisticated application that incorporates all your compression, authoring, and burning requirements to emulate that professional-level movie market.

ULead, Canopus, GEAR, Dazzle, and Sonic Solutions have all released solid software that becomes a one-stop shop to create a reasonably high-end looking product. The Mac has Studio Pro and iDVD. The idea is the same in all of them: by exporting your finished program as MPEG-2 and importing into the software, you can create basic menus with hot-spot buttons that trigger text or the playout of your masterpiece. When you are happy enough, this can then be burnt to any writeable or rewriteable CD or DVD and used in most DVD players.

The most versatile feature with such software is the ability to be able to import menu background JPEGs that you might have created out of stills from your production in a graphics application. This gives your product the individuality that is just one more notch in your production value. Print off a designed jewel case inlay and you've got something with quality.

There are lots of format issues in burning off DVDs, which will be discussed later, but you should be aware when buying software that there are still some of the dreaded compatibility complications. These are not just with your platform and Windows versions (although manufacturers are tweaking them to make them cross-platform), but with the make and type of your DVD driver itself. There are thousands of drivers on the market, so you might want to check out a few Internet video forums for compliance first.

THE SHOOT

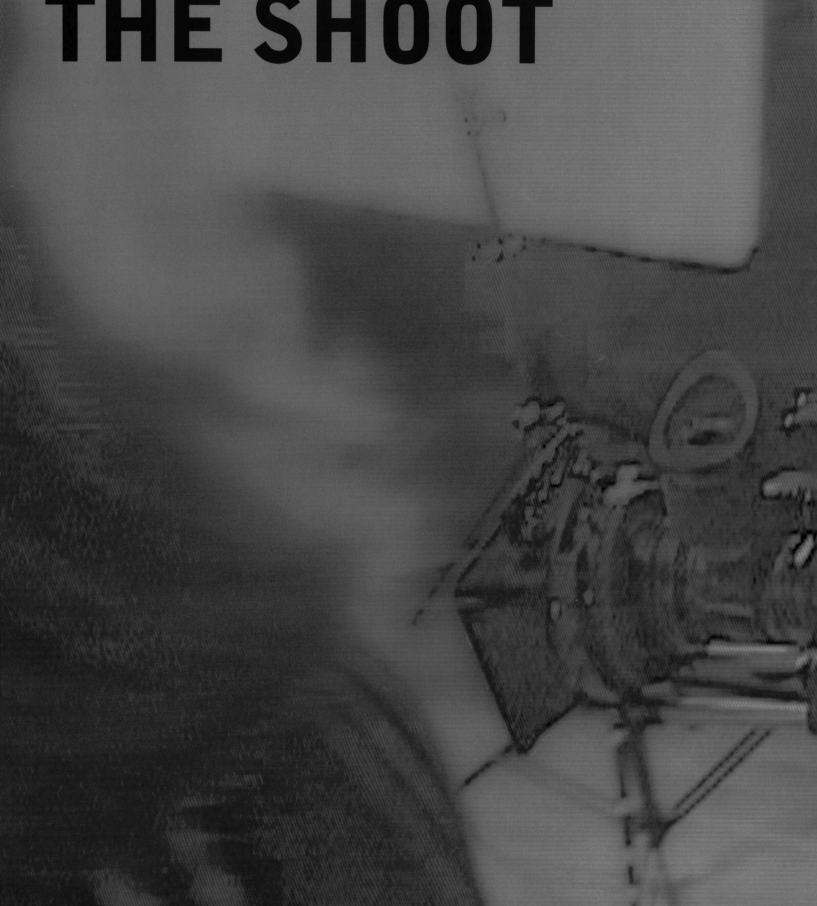

03.01

Preproduction is not so much an art as it is a temperament. It is organized and chaotic; bolshy and seductive; demanding and giving. It's the personification of any good producer. And if you haven't got the temperament, give the job to someone else.

If you can't make cold-calls, be on call 24-7, if you're not organized, or can't sell your product in twenty words or talk about it for twenty minutes, then stay well away.

Preproduction is where the fun starts for a producer—or you, as an auteur, in your role of producer. Even if you're only shooting and cutting your fortnight in Botswana, some of the job isn't directing or aiming a camera or editing—it's producing. Who's going to book the hotel? Get the camera back if it's confiscated at the airport? Ask for permission to shoot in the local mud hut town hall? Find out which night the weekly frightwig parade falls on? Arrange for more DV tape to be sent out?

Of course, the more professional the production, the more likely it is that a production assistant will do these jobs—but even PAs are puppeteered by producers who are far too busy wrestling with the budget they've been given. The less professional the outfit, the more likely the producer is going to be yourself as auteur. If you think you can handle it and spare the time for it, then do it. Otherwise, find someone who can.

PART 03. THE SHOOT

CHAPTER ONE

PREPRODUCTION

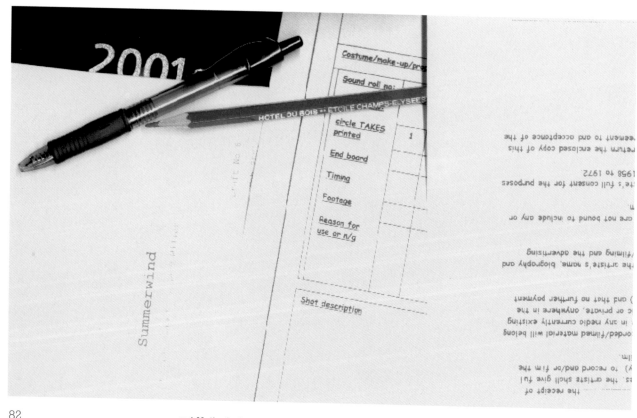

When embarking on a production, the key is always to think ahead, and to think laterally. Some examples—with answers depending on the kind of shoot—are:

- What is going to be shot?
- When is it going to be shot?
- Are there any interviews?
- Will there be dialog?
- Does anyone need to be informed?
- What is the time of the event?
- How long will it last?
- Who is our point-of-contact?
- What's their job and mobile number?
- Who is your best speaking, best presented engineer?
- What time and where should the crew meet?
- Do you need a map?
- What crew members do we need?
- What cast members do we need?
- Will it be dark?
- What will the weather be like?
- What kit will we need?

Again, depending on the kind of shoot, your questions might have to be more obscure:

- Are there computer screens in the background?
- Do the interviewees need to be told not to wear blue/green?
- Is there a lift?
- Where's the nearest coffee shop?
- Does the caretaker speak English?
- What time do the workers stop for lunch?

ACTING THE PART

Time is money, money is time—but if you have it, then try to spend time with your actors prior to production. Discuss their part as a whole, their character, their dress sense—and yes, their motivation. Actors do like to be reassured of what they're doing and have an input. It will help you determine shots, emphasis, and pace.

Preproduction is the time to spend looking ahead to every need and every eventuality. It is almost like crisis management, too: if you can possibly anticipate your worst-case scenario for the shoot, then you will be leagues ahead if the tiniest of problems arises. Shoots can be difficult enough without being unprepared for the tardiness of your crew or the breakage of an essential prop.

If you can be as organized, it will save you time and money—guaranteed. It will also help you get the best out of your crew, cast, or just the tribe leader. Your confidence and assertiveness as auteur will not only rub off, but open doors to better shots, better performances, better interviews, and

MEETINGS Part of the preproduction process is that of meetings and discussions. You may still just be shooting Auntie Marge's birthday, but at the very least you'll want to know what time you need to come. Of course, this is not particularly helpful to anyone shooting on the fly and editing later, but for any auteur with production values greater than this, it is imperative.

Gaining all the facts is going to help you cover all eventualities and know exactly what you are going to shoot. A storyboard is fine to an extent, but if you can't get access to a location, you're going to have to think fast. In order that you don't have to think about it at all, it's worth nailing everything in preproduction.

Despite the readiness of production with the ease of access to digital kit, the word "filming" is still generally an exciting prospect to a lot of people. There are the more jaded: any PR who has worked for a national transport system or, Bloomingdales, for instance, will not be remotely excited about your project, no matter how much you are.

They might even know more about production than you do. If you are thinking about approaching a press office about shooting in a particular location, remember that they have an agenda too. They'll be thinking whether it is worth their time supervising you on site; whether they get a **location fee**; if it is helpful to them; if it hinders work hours. Most of all, they'll be thinking of their branding: are you going to endorse them in a way that they would like? If you're not, you might as well forget it. The adage that "all advertising is good advertising" simply won't wash in such circumstances.

Back to those "generally" more excited. There's a psychology in anyone who is allowed to be involved in "filming" that they get more useful to the auteur. This doesn't mean to say that you hand over complete editorial control, but that you consult your contact to inform and discuss your shoot with an appropriate regularity. Like your actors, interviewees, and crew, this inspires both confidence and

PROACTIVE PROFESSIONAL PRODUCTION

Right and below: Your production break-down should be succinct, prioritized and logical to the point of obvious. For each day's shoot, make sure that all cast and crew—even those back in the office—have the latest schedule and contacts list. Your mobile is going to be switched off during shooting, so all of these people—especially those in the office—need to be informed of any changes or slips.

FILMING SCHEDULE

DATE OF FILMING:
LOCATION:

PROG CHARGECODE:
DIRECTOR:
AP:
PRODUCTION CONTACTS:
Work:
Home:
Exec Producer:
Series Producer:
Producer 1:
Producer 2:
Production Assistant:
Production Secretary:
Assistant Producer:
Researcher:

CONTRIBUTOR CONTACTS:
PSC CREW:
Camera:
Sound:
Equipment:
TAPE STOCK:
ASPECT RATIO:
RELEASE FORMS:

```
Hire car to be delivered to work for 6pm Thursday
in the name of AP. Hire car is currently hired
out for 24 hours.
0800    AP to pick researcher up from home
        Address:
0900    Production and crew RV
        The TV company
        Contact:
        Directions:      See map
        Parking available for 2 vehicles

1000    Actor required in make-up
1045    Actor due on set
1200    Lunch (This should be flexible depending
        on when TV company break for lunch)
1300    Continue filming on film set
1800    Wrap and travel back to base
```

worth—even though the only payment they're receiving is the promise of a copy of the final product.

Your contact might be a PR or it might be someone at a local authority, in charge of a store, a magistrate you met in a bar, the chairperson of the Harry Belafonte fanclub—anyone. They might be critical for gaining you access to a location, access to a prop, a legal consultant for your crime drama, a supplier of background music… The important thing is to make sure that you keep them briefed and on-side.

With your contact, you'll want to make sure that they can get in touch with you if there are any changes to what they can offer, and that they know exactly what their responsibilities are. If you need them to find an interviewee for you, don't just ask for that, ask for someone who'll suit you: specify a gender, ask for a talker, someone presentable, or someone who doesn't look as though they do the job they do. Once you've got them on-side, you might be able to push it. Is there a cherry picker on site that you can use for a crane? Can you get access to the members' enclosure? Can you mount a CCD to the cockpit?

Producers need to be seductive and they need to be bolshy. If you smooth the shoot in preproduction, it will help your production values disguise the budget.

STORYBOARDS AND SCRIPTS

Pre-production is governed by organization. No matter whether there is only yourself involved (which, as discussed, is unlikely—even if you don't have a crew), or you're adopting guerrilla tactics, organization and preparation for the worst is the key to a successful shoot, edit, and product.

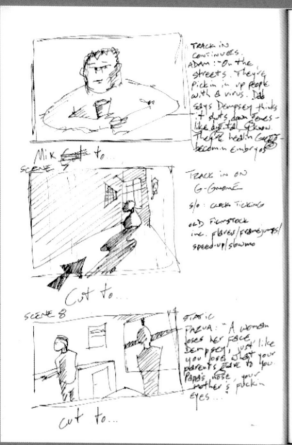

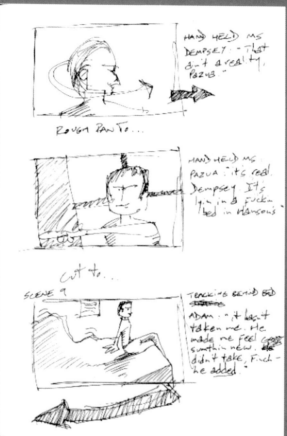

Whether you are shooting narrative, documentary, travelog, diary, events—whatever—there is always some administration that you can tailor for the job. The psychological glitch is that it sounds laborious. The reality is that not only can it be the most necessary part of the production, but that imagining how you would like things to look and sound can also be the most fun. Keeping an original concept in mind while letting yourself work on it (or compromise) will keep you focused and inspire your enthusiasm in the most trying of production times. Preparation can be broken down into the following:

STORYBOARDS

Anyone who is familiar with Hollywood or DVD extras will probably be familiar with the storyboard. Aside from being a baseline for directors when they're shooting, it can act as reassurance to producers and creditors that the director knows what they're doing. It's also reassuring to anyone thinking about a storyboard that directors sketch so badly (unless they're James Cameron or Clive Barker).

To you, the storyboard is more likely to be a personal reference to plan your shots, and a useful tool for your camera op. Once you've got a script or an idea of what you will or want to shoot, it's the next step to your production. The good thing about a storyboard is that you can scribble out what you don't want; you can see pacing; you can block actors and plan elaborate shots. The only limitations to a storyboard are your creativity, but bear in mind the practical limits of the shoot itself. There is no point in planning for 360-degree shots around your subject unless you've got all four walls available as a set…

Storyboarding software is available that may help—or hinder you. They contain interesting quirks such as adding a recorded background once you've scouted for your location, but whether or not you could have shot and edited your movie by the time you'd finished finding the best library character likeness to your actor, nicest font for your dialog boxes, and most appropriate library prop is another thing. The best way of pushing their use is to find a program that enables animatics, particularly if you're shooting very complex sequences. An animatic is your fantastically drawn still as an animated computer graphic and is more used for effects scenes before lengthy—and expensive—processes of rotoscoping, texture mapping, or rendering.

SHOOTING SCRIPTS

You've written your script and you've maybe even sketched out a storyboard—and if you have, you've done the hard work for a shooting script. This is a script for the director and producer that breaks every scene down and numbers them in order that they can be reordered to shoot practically (i.e., location by location or actor by actor) and financially astutely.

A shooting script may also contain references to camera angles and moves and production notes made along the way, again for the benefit of production, rather than for the actors and lesser crew.

CALL SHEETS

Nearing production, certainly in broadcast or feature production, a call sheet is distributed to both crew and cast. They tend to contain concise details of a day's shoot and are very useful for yourself, as an individual, should you need to marshal your troops.

The information that you will need to incorporate at a bare minimum will be a list of those involved, call times, and RV points. If you anticipate your day's shoot to be more intricate than that, then incorporate all the information they are going to need. It is certainly a good way of getting a better night's sleep before the shoot…

SHOTLISTS

If none of these preparations seem appropriate for your production, then you may well be shooting something a little more out of your control (or you're not organized). In this case, a shotlist might be more conducive.

A shotlist can be a way of logging your shots during your shoot, but it can also refer to a calculated guess as to what you might need on the day. If you have only a rough idea of how the event will occur, then make a list of the shots you'll need to create the edit you want. If you are at an air display, then make a shotlist before you go to act as a checklist. A wide of the entrance; a tight of the banner; a top-shot of the crowd; a close-up of a wind-cone—all these things will be as invaluable in the edit as the fly-bys, and a shotlist will make sure that you don't forget them.

ACTING DIRECTOR
On set, the advantages of solid preproduction come into play. Show the actors your storyboards and let them understand how they'll be shot—and their significance in the scope of the production.

REHEARSALS/DRY-RUNS To expect the unexpected, prepare those involved and thereby preserve your budget is a video-maker's version of crisis management. Even if you're simply having preproduction meetings, it can allay any fears and give those involved a chance to air concerns. As an auteur, it will also give you a chance to keep everyone else informed within a group dynamic—which never fails to inspire debate, and is often the perfect chance for someone to ask why they are actually present.

It is not just your crew who should be involved. If you are relying on external parties such as PRs, event organizers, tour guides, or even the caretaker, invite them along too. If everyone is confident and singing from the same song sheet, your results will show on the day.

Try to imagine worst-case scenarios and come up with Plan Bs to avoid panic. If you can't get the top-shot that you want, is there another roof that you can get access to? If the weather forces everyone inside, do you have the appropriate lighting? If the guest-of-honor turns up late, will it be too dark to get your exteriors?

Work out your day's shoot to make the most of everyone's time and cause the minimum fuss or disruption. If you can store kit overnight at the location, set up, or simply mark your territory before anyone else arrives, you will be saving some valuable time.

If you are lucky enough to have access to your location prior to the shoot, go for the fullest rehearsal you can. If it is an event, your camera op will need to know which people are important and what they look like, where they are arriving, sitting, if they are going to speak… If it's a wedding, get your crew along to the dress rehearsal; if it's an air display, contact the organizers and try to get invited to one of their pre-show meetings. There is always a way to advance your knowledge— even of things that are out of your control.

If you are making a narrative video, you will be working to a storyboard and script. If you can't get the location before the shoot day, recreate it in your living room or garden. A full rehearsal is the perfect time for you to find out if your work will come to life, for your actors to find their characters, and your crew to find their positions. Block everyone, establish beats, conflicts, and backstories, be encouraging and enthusiastic, and listen to feedback. Again, remember the edit: if you at least rehearse the scenes in their correct order, you will be able to determine the right tone for each scene when it comes to putting them in place.

DISCUSS AND MAKE-UP
Actors like to be encouraged, motivated and, above all, to understand what you want them to do. They also like to be pampered. A good time to discuss and clarify everything with them on set is when they are a captive audience: in the make-up chair.

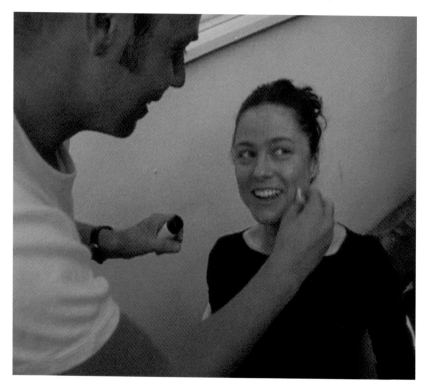

part 03. the shoot

BUDGETING There is no such thing as a no-budget video. Even if you were given a free digital video camera with a tape to shoot a free-entry freedom march and given free rein of a desktop editing system, there will be some outlay at some point—even if it comes to buying a sandwich for lunch. And no, there's no such thing as a free lunch in video-making.

There is such a thing as low-budget video, though. And if it is a home project, then you probably don't want to structure it so you know where each cent is being spent. If that's the case, then you should simply take into account that you should always be prepared and cater for the unexpected. Make sure you've got enough cash in your pocket to bung a $20 bill to a 10th-floor apartment resident for the top-shot you want, or buy a potential interviewee a drink, or to get a cup of coffee for yourself when the weather turns cold and dark and you're still waiting for your star to turn up at their premiere.

When it comes to video-making that obviously requires some money to be spent, stick to your own rules. Along with your budget, invent a cash-flow sheet during preproduction. If you are renting equipment, call around for the best offers and then play them off against each other—and make a note of their costs on the phone so that they stick to their prices. If you are renting for a 24-hour period, find out what the leeway is so that you don't end up paying for another day if you are five minutes late.

Your budget will always be tight, so fix it hard to your cash-flow sheet. The secret is always to think about what's up on the screen: if money spent isn't going to change the production values of your program, then leave it alone. What will change your production values tends to be the more lateral things on your shoot day: feed your crew and talent well and you'll get the best out of everybody; divide your time and make everybody concerned feel that they are needed, if not special.

Above all, be professional. Don't reimburse unless there's a receipt—and take the receipt. Be strict with your budget—and honest. And again, make your money work for you and your production.

Having investors or clients are a different thing. An investor will want their money back; a client will want a product back. Either way, they have an interest in the production which you have to control as tightly as the budget that you have prepared for them. You don't have to be honest with these people: they are the people that you are trying to make money out of. Be reasonable, though—you are answerable to them, after all, and you should always be prepared to negotiate.

There are two ways to budget for clients. The first is the standard business practice of breaking down true daily and hourly rates for crew, talent, music, editors, graphics, etc. and then adding a 20% production fee—which is yours. The second way is to factor in a rough 20% (or whatever you are cheeky enough to ask for) to each facet of production (pre, shoots, and post) and come up with a project total without necessarily giving much of a breakdown of costs. Although you might be able to earn more this way, the gamble is that your client won't ask for re-edits or changes that will see your profit margin diminish at every request. Once again, be reasonable and incorporate changes, but if you feel that it is one edit too many from your original budget, tell them that you've now reached re-edit stage, which will have to be charged for.

PRODUCTION Whatever project you have decided to work on, make sure that it works for you. The only way to see a project through from storyboard to distribution is to plan everything from the start. Your enthusiasm at the beginning should be revitalized with every part of production—and if it isn't, you're doing the wrong job. The everyone-is-a-director theory could apply to you…

Sure, you'll get days where nothing goes right, where nobody is playing ball, and it seems like you're making negative progress. A good auteur who is focused and believes in what they are doing will see these through. The everyone-is-a-director director will have a whole load of unmade video ideas under their bed and a whole load of disparate clips captured to their hard drive—and nothing much else.

If the project's not you or there's somebody in your crew who is unsure what they are doing there, get out—or get them out—at the start.

Note that the only exception to this is the corporate director who will sell their soul to the devil to make anything… They are paid to believe in their project.

We'll start at the top. Hollywood is a commercial business—a business like any other in the way that it's there to make money. Entertaining you is the way Hollywood works to make you part

KIDDING ABOUT

If you have to shoot kids, get them involved and interact. With a recent statistic that over 80% want to work in the media, they're likely to become disobedient, tired or temperamental if you don't. And there won't be any eager runners in five years' time.

with your money. In that respect, there is nothing different about any other genre of commercial film or video-making. A television commercial—if it is doing its job—will sap money off clients and public. The only aberration is the guerrilla or amateur video-maker. Their projects may be for vanity, for education, family pleasure—for something other than financial glory. And even if it's not for cash gain, it is always good to ask yourself at the beginning: why am I doing this? You absolutely will do when everything goes horribly wrong on a day halfway through production…

Your mantra (think about the edit) is not the only thing to have in mind always from the start. You need to know exactly what you're intending to do with your production. If you're thinking big with theatrical distribution, you've got to think about everything from formats to production stills to release forms. Anything put in the public domain, even on the Internet, requires a few simple copyrights put in place. Seal your storyboards and scripts and send them to yourself by registered post—even if you're just sending jotted ideas and random doodles. Think about publicity and marketing, of tricks to gain backing and distribution. Don't expect an instant success story: even the ones reported are simply marketed as overnight successes—it's not something that even seldom happens…

There is also still a lot of snobbery in the business regarding video, despite the success stories (*The Blair Witch Project*), the genre adoption (dogme) and the odd arthouse experimental (*Timecode*). It is still a medium far more suited commercially for the Internet, television, and corporate distribution because its resolution as digital isn't currently ideally suited for large screen presentation.

Ironically enough, it is still bound by some of the same rules. While digital video has become a reality-inferred medium, you still have to work hard to excise continuity mistakes, jump-cuts, and visible booms. And it won't tolerate bad acting, bad scripts, and bad editing at all…

Aside from the language of the moving image, which we'll come to, there's another unspoken dialect.

EYE SPY

Sunglasses can be essential for a talent's character. They can describe a hard night, a shady side, a physical condition. And they can also show the camera op...on the other hand, sunglasses should never be allowed to be worn by an interviewee (unless they have a physical condition)—for the aforementioned reasons.

THE LANGUAGE OF THE MOVING IMAGE Video and film-making create a world of their own. Just as it has a language, it also has rules. And just as MCs or txt-perts develop dialects, so video-makers break, bend, twist, and turn around these rules. The constant mantra, though, is that this is fundamentally impossible unless the rules are learned.

SHOOT TO THRILL
From award-winning English shorts such as *Summer Wind*, (left) to award-winning American features like *The Blair Witch Project* (below), the language of the moving image is the same. Deploy all cast and crew, shoot on site, and engage the audience.

Mass media, the everyone's-a-director theory, and the availability of equipment have positively encouraged the population to dive headfirst into a deceptively familiar world. The fact is that critics don't make movies.

We'll start with genres. How do we know that a movie is a movie? Because it's feature length? Because it's got a story? Because it plays in a movie theater? Surely all these things can describe a contemporary documentary too? And what about *The Last Broadcast* or *The Blair Witch Project*? There were plenty of American preview audiences who thought that they were watching a documentary.

The truth is that there is a language to each genre of video and film-making—and the two instances mentioned are of interest for taking one language over to another genre. In order for this to work, of course, they're relying on an audience to subconsciously understand the difference in the languages that dictate what they think they are watching.

It works the other way around too. With broadcast channels becoming more and more competitive, winning audiences is essential to their success. Commercial channels rely on sponsorship, which will always be withdrawn if the ratings aren't coming in.Even government-regulated channels demand a broad spread of programs accommodating all. This isn't an argument about so-called "dumbing down," it's more a comment that even with the globally less popular documentaries, ways are being found to make them more appealing, more sensationalist, or more narrative. Reality shows, which are basically documentaries, became popular because they were cut into something resembling a soap-opera, staple diet for a home-from-work audience.

And round and round we go: the popularity of the reality gameshow inspired Marc Evans' *My Little Eye*, very much a movie—but shot through the eyes of multiple DVs and cut to a broadcast format.

INTERVIEW
Maxim Jago, Corporate Producer/Director

"

I mainly shoot both documentary and fiction on DV—corporates, music videos, exhibition stands—whatever they'll pay me for. I take whatever I've shot into Avid ExpressDV and Storm, cut it, and then spit it out back onto DV or as MPEG-1 multimedia CD. If clients want streaming media, I tend to use Windows Media Player and make it available to download off a client's website.

I'm a lazy consumer and I prefer Media Player because it doesn't ask me if I want to Go Pro all the time like Quicktime. And RealMedia is always cluttering up your desktop and asking you to sign up for sales promotions and registering this, that, and the other that I just try to avoid—although I do understand that Real is better for audio. I like the frame rate and interpolation with Media Player and the smoothness you get as a result—and frankly, I use Media Player because it bothers me less. The open architecture of Windows doesn't worry me so much any more now that XP Professional is about.

I do believe that a client-base is very much word-of-mouth. You can advertise yourself until the cows come home, but unless somebody actually starts the ball rolling and gives you a job, you're not going to get any work. I think for small-scale

freelancers like myself, it's almost all to do with who you know and repeat business. There's the other echelon of corporate video-making where you're spending quite a bit on advertising and you've got an account manager, but it usually stems from when you have one really large client who keeps you ticking over and gives you enough money to advertise and pick up more blue-chip clients. The money's not in broadcast any more, it's in high-end corporate production.

I think that the Internet is the key to advertising. If you can get on Google or suchlike, there are a lot of people out there who want a video made but don't necessarily know where to go. I even know of one company with a couple of Avids that just make home videos for customers. Clients don't have to come into your office as long as you make yourself available. All you need is a good idea, nice letterheaded paper and so on. The workplace that is an office is only another level of production. I've met a lot of people who are using their spare room at home as a suite and producing high-end productions—it's just that some clients do want to come and sit with you and it's simply not possible when you're working from home.

One-man band-ism is an immensely significant problem. When you've got edit, effects, everything in one box, you can really only have one person controlling it. It all comes down to multi-tasking. The problem is that people become alienated as media professionals, and unless you're working for a production company, you don't tend to get to know people who make programs. This is why webforums like Shooting People can be so important—when your project gets too big for your one-man band, you can find someone to hold the boom or get a whole crew. If you are a one-man band, you have to rely on a client's ignorance to get sensible money out of them. It's hard telling them that you are a multi-tasker and get to be taken seriously financially. If a client pays you for your production, they're paying you for your skills—all of them—and that's something that is hard to get them to understand.

"

One of the dialects of the moving image language is made up of your shots themselves. Hand in hand with editing, they form a complex, variform vernacular of their own. It is up to you to make this accessible…or not. However you decide to approach your shoot, be deliberate and focused as to whether or not you wish to follow rule-of-thumb or be avant-garde. Again, in order to break the rules, you first have to know what they are.

If you look in any book of technique or attend any course, you'll be told that there are a certain number of shots available to you. This is true to an extent, but the combination and effect of them can change everything from forced edit decisions to the meaning, emphasis, or spin of your program.

There may be many miscalculated shots in professional video and film-making, but few are uncalculated. That's not to say that everything is storyboarded and rehearsed to perfection. The rules just make things a little easier to know what you want even in the most unpredictable of situations.

As noted in this chapter with terrier-like fervor, you should remember this: however intense, fun, or traumatic the shoot is, the one thing that should always be on your mind is the edit. You can shoot all you like to your heart's content—or for sheer coverage—but your program becomes a different beast entirely when you're confronted with it for days in the edit. If you haven't got the shots you need, you'll be making desperate compromises that you'll quietly curse but always justify in company. That is the way of the video world.

PART 03. THE SHOOT

CHAPTER TWO

TYPES OF SHOT

PIER PRESSURE

Perspective = depth = enrichment. Imagine this shot without the carousel: dull-ish, possibly. Look for objects or subjects within your location to clip the frame and convey the depth of your shot. Passers-by can be really quite obliging when it comes to walking into frame and stopping near the camera to survey the view.

THE ESTABLISHER

There is no getting away from the establisher. Aside from the cutaway and the pay-off—to be discussed later—it is possibly the most important shot of the shoot.

The establisher is an opening **wide** that gives a viewer all the information that they need to begin watching the edit. Of course, you may wish to hide things in order that a narrative might progress—or simply to dupe the audience. The point is that the establisher is designed to give them all the information that you wish them to have.

An example of the polarities of establisher would be that found within a **Broadcast Library Tape** (or **VNR** [Video News Release]) against that found in Maya Deren's *Meshes of the Afternoon*. The former relies on a news editor to understand the story that a PR is trying to sell them. If the story isn't obvious, it's not worth the editor's time to try and make it make sense. For this reason, a library tape establisher would be as wide and as omniscient as necessary to set a scene. Fundamentally, it's saying that this is the place we are in and this is what is happening.

Alternatively, the establisher for *Meshes of the Afternoon* is a **close-up**, contradicting almost everything just said. In fact, this is a near-perfect example of understanding the rules to break the rules. The convention is the wide, which is exactly why we're being given a **tight**: the rules are understood but being broken, which makes us slightly uneasy and gives the film an aura of mystery from the start. The close-up establisher in *Meshes* is followed by another, and yet another. A whole series of shots such as this is termed **fragmentation**—individually nonsensical, but together an establisher.

SETTING THE SCENE

An audience wants to know five things: When, Where, What, Why and Who. An omniscient eye can easily fulfil the first two and give perspective to your magnified scene that describes the rest.

THE LONG SHOT

Typically the most abused shot in amateur video, the long shot is pretty much an establisher during the course of the program. It puts an entire person in place; it captures an environment; it can talk of hope and loss, scope and loneliness; it conveys perspective; it adds significance and insignificance. These are some of the good things about it when it works and there are many textbook examples to be found in cinema: *Badlands; 2001: A Space Odyssey; My Own Private Idaho*. Indeed, the growing enthusiasm for **anamorphic** lenses has truly had an effect on the use of the long shot.

Where the long shot is less likely to work are those occasions where an auteur is trying to capture an entire scenario without making any choice as to specifics. Worse still, the auteur is doing it without a tripod. On a boat. Okay, so maybe that's going slightly overboard, but it is the one shot that will ensure that a camera's instability is noticed, and never to deliberate effect.

Long shots should be used sparingly. They are never as interesting as action or a subject unless **mise-en-scène** or the **golden sector** are applied, or unless careful consideration has been gone into how thematically they'll be used. Think of them as establishers for different locations and not as a way of shooting everything without trying.

THE MEDIUM SHOT (MS)

We're getting closer now. The medium shot tends to warm more to one's subject than to a location. If there is a subject involved, the medium shot frames from the waist or chest up to include a portion of the background over the subject's head. Most interviews and dialogue scenes are conducted as an MS because the subject can be seen in a recognizable environment without losing facial animation and, practically, a microphone can be held unobtrusively.

Within the MS, it's also possible to maintain a **two-shot** (two subjects, usually engaged in conversation) or a **three-shot** (likewise, but with three subjects and adding the complication of working the triangle).

TAKE YOUR BEST SHOT
Introducing the foreground into a long shot adds a realism to a scene that can implicate the audience as voyeur (top). And while your actors may require to be a bit more emphatic with their physical performance, a medium shot will let their faces do all the work at the expense of location (bottom).

THE CLOSE-UP (CU)

Yes, Mr DeMille, we're all bored of waiting for ours, so we've gone and shot our own instead. And, boy, are they gruesome.

The close-up is a dangerous thing: it can divide families, scare small children, and send sales of paper bags through the roof. It can also absolutely make an edit work and for that reason it has a power not to be underestimated.

The CU frames an entire face—any closer and it becomes an **extreme close-up**—and is often used with dialog. In order to avoid an **eye-line** that might possibly be perceived as a **point-of-view**, the CU in dialog may be shot **over-the-shoulder**, introducing the other character as a shoulder/side of head edging into frame.

But a CU doesn't have to be a facial reaction or line delivered—it can simply be an object or an action (a phone replaced, a ring on a finger). The power that it has is that it can help pace your edit with a rhythm and is invaluable as a **cutaway** (soon to be discussed). CUs can cover continuity and audio and let scenes or shots be reached easily without any additional coverage.

THE FRAME GAME

If only life was that simple. Nestling between the above are (clockwise from top left) the XCU (extreme close-up), Wide Close-Up, Medium Close-Up, and Medium Wide. They don't vary wildly from the framing described, but all have their effect—or practicality. Use your imagination: if your subject is wearing a kilt, opt for either a wide or a MS as a walking shot—a hem riding in and out of frame is merely distracting.

THE CUTAWAY (AKA INSERT)

As said, cutaways are an essential part of a video-maker's edit. Aside from pacing—i.e., adding to the variety of shots to add to the rhythm of an edit—they provide the perfect patch for any cut whether narrative or not.

A cutaway is a shot that will allow transition from the shot on either side that would usually juxtapose, such as a jump-cut. A press pack with cameras, an audience, people watching the event being shot—their breaking up of the action will always create the illusion that the action itself is seamless despite the editor having pared away at the master shot.

Reverting to our example of the Broadcast Library Tape, a news editor would be lost without cutaways. When faced with a tape of possibly chronological, but probably meaningless shots, using a cutaway pastes over any inconsistency in the edit—and better still, makes it easy to cut for timing, especially later in the day when other stories begin to eat into its running time.

CUTAWAY FROM IT ALL

This sequence is made up from the master medium shot, the close-up dialog shot (character, left) and the pay-off close-up reaction shot (character, right). The coffee-cup shot is inserted as a cutaway to let the dialog shot continue using a second take, without reverting to another master or the pay-off reaction.

THE MASTER SHOT

If this were a book dedicated to the modern narrative Hollywood movie, the master shot would probably have topped the list of important shots. If you are shooting a narrative or have the privilege of repeat actions within a documentary, then this shot will be your priority.

A master shot is your entire scene from beginning to end at a wide enough angle to take in all the action. The reason for the master shot, unsurprisingly, is that when it comes to edit, there is always a shot to refer to—and to use, helping the scene back into perspective. It can also act as a quality **blocking** and line rehearsal if you are pushed for time.

As we are not dealing specifically with that genre of video-making, it is hesitant advice to suggest that the master shot is used to cover a one-off event. It may well be tempting to shoot a wedding, an air display, or a birthday, as one long master shot, but in reality all these events occur over a duration of time. You will have a chance to get all the other shots needed for an edit.

SHOT/REVERSE SHOT

Use a reverse shot to create a mini-suspense. The convention of an Over-the-Shoulder shot has been replaced with more of an 'Over-the-Elbow' shot, and knocked out of focus whatever our subject is recoiling in horror at. It is only the reverse shot that we are permitted to see through her eyes, and the full picture.

The suggestion here is that rather than playing safe and eventually creating the most tedious video with zero edits, the auteur plans their production: if the action is brief—a Red Arrows fly-by, for example—shoot it as a master shot, but make sure you've shot your **cutaways** of the audience looking to the skies. Anticipate that their expressions may change before and after the fly-by. What will you need for the edit in order that you simply don't just have the master shot and no edit at all?

For that indeed is the key. The master shot is your main reference to be cut into to build rhythm, pacing, and perspective.

THE POINT-OF-VIEW (POV)

The POV is simply I, Camera. It is the camera becoming part of the action. In documentaries and non-narratives, the camera operator is a—usually—silent witness to events. In narrative film and video, the POV has now firmly become part of the language to identify an individual within the structure of the plot. The POV is often used meaninglessly—a binocular shot, a rapid glance around a room—and is usually conducted as a **hand-held** operation to insinuate a human/(inhuman) perspective.

Within **non-genre** (i.e., not horror/sci-fi movies) cinema or television, the POV is not generally used. The reason for this is that it has the curious effect of drawing an audience back into being an audience and making them aware of the superficiality of the scenario before them. This is not only because it is heightening the awareness that there is a camera operator, but also due to the fact that if it is used and the character is engaged in dialog, the language forces the **reverse shot** of the other character speaking directly into the camera—i.e., straight at the audience.

Perhaps the most important use of POV that changed commercial cinema's convention was the opener to John Carpenter's *Halloween*. The camera stalks around a house and then into it. The mask is put on over the camera restricting our view through eye-holes. The hand emerges side of frame, the knife is picked up, the stabbing ensues until "we" run from the house toward our returning parents. We then cut out of POV to an omniscient shot (possibly parents' POV) to find the small boy, knife in hand. The reason it works to perfection is that aside from hiding the assumed age of the killer (he's just a boy), we are incriminated in his action.

The slew of horror and sci-fi movies that took Carpenter's lead on such a use turned cinema's language around and the camera (and therefore the audience) became the killer. Should you choose to utilize POV within your production, you might be best remembering this…

CAMERA MOVES

CAMERA MOVES Over halfway through the chapter and it's only now that the camera operator is being credited: finally the camera is beginning to move. That's not to say that it hasn't already. It's only when the camera is locked-off/down that it is really static.

The camera op—if it's not you—should take instruction from the director as to the mood, the style, and what is supposed to be framed, while the director should pay attention to what the camera op says—especially if they are experienced.

Be warned, without a **monitor**, the director's power is even more diminished.

Camera movement has accelerated in the past few years. There is an eagerness for kineticism and the forced reality that, certainly, **hand-held** camera allows. With digital cameras especially, a freedom like no other has been experienced within the field. A constantly moving/roaming camera has been attributed to an attention-deficient MTV generation, but this stigma is merely the use of the effect to thrill an audience with an experience that often disguises the fact that they have watched something of no substance at all. For every Michael Bay movie, there's an *ER* or a *This Life*, a *Natural Born Killers*, a *Blair Witch Project*, or any Brian DePalma production.

That's not to say that your camera has to keep moving. If you are shooting for news broadcast, only **statics**, **cutaways** and **sedate pans**, **zooms** and **pulls** are currently acceptable for primetime bulletins. Consider your edit again: are there themes of movement or unsettlement? Are you making a road movie and want to work against freneticism? Or is it a dialog-driven, character-emphasized production? Are you cutting your travelog to music?

And bear in mind that Andy Warhol's *Sleep* held the same camera position for eight hours without a noticeable edit…

There are many ways a shot can move, and many more effects to be had if that movement is combined with the shots discussed earlier. There are three ways of creating movement: either the camera operator physically moves the camera; the camera makes a digital/optical move; or both. Get excited, too—it was only in 1977 that the combination of a **zoom** and an exact pull-back on a **dolly** let us feel Chief Brody's dizzy shock on witnessing the shark attack in *Jaws*.

HAND-HELD

Exactly as it says, and a healthy alternative to using a **tripod**. The camera operator holds the camera freestyle with no option but to move the shot. Even if it's a supposed static, it'll be an edgy static. Due to its on-the-hoof use by documentary makers, it brings a "reality" to narrative film and video-making.

TRACKING

The term comes from film production, where the camera moved on tracks to follow a subject. Video-production has bastardized the term and it is generally used for any shot that tracks a subject, keeping them—or it— within roughly the same portion of frame.

DOLLY

The camera is mounted on a dolly—a tripod on wheels—and guided along a track, usually by the camera operator. The term is often used to describe shots where the camera moves smoothly into or out of the shot. Dollys are commonly used for walking **two-shots** or **three-shots** or circling a conversation.

HANDY CAM
A hand-held tracking shot can create tension and unease simply because it doesn't provide an easy explanation to an audience. This shot would usually be a POV of a character approaching, but the subject's non-reciprocative gaze back into the lens takes away the comfort of comprehension.

ANGLE OF MERCY

Be kind to your subject with a flattering camera angle—or don't. Your sister won't thank you for placing the camera at her feet shooting upward when she's at the altar. Conversely, a bad guy can be made more intimidating this way by creating height. Or try a **dutch** (also known as "on the piss" to one of my cameramen)— shoot slightly crooked for a sense of oddness or madness, a device particularly used to convey a character's disturbed psychological state.

TILT

The camera tilts on a vertical axis. This can be hand-held or with the camera on a mount and is most often used to locate a flat in a high-rise or to mix off to another scene from the sky.

PAN

This is the most bastardized term in video-making and, aside from the **zoom**, perhaps the most used and abused shot. The camera moves along a horizontal plane with either the operator (hand-held) or tripod (mounted) as the pivot. A pan can place a subject relative to another, but it can also disqualify a cut instead in the edit which may have been more interesting. A **whip pan** describes a movement fast enough for the area between the start and end of the shot to be little more than a blur.

CRANE/JIB

Instead of a dolly or a tripod, the camera is mounted on a crane or jib, allowing freedom of movement—essentially upward. The use of a crane tends to indicate perspective, relativity, and a larger budget.

STEADICAM

This is an invention that became an institution. The camera is mounted on a counterbalance rigged onto the operator. The operator moves with the camera and the counterbalance counteracts any of the "wobble-cam" effects of a hand-held shot. Just as the rig physically dehumanizes the operator, so the shot dehumanizes a tracking shot's "reality." The ironing out of the camera op's humanity (although they sometimes still get paid) quickly led to DV incorporating a digital motion stabilizing device, which is pretty much a standard option for all DV Cams in circulation.

ZOOM

The zoom lens on the camera is used to get closer to the subject (**zoom in**) or farther away (more often termed **pull out**). A **crash zoom** is a less gentle—and therefore sometimes much more effective—approach to the subject. This can be achieved through the manual use of the zoom and "crashing" into the subject. Ensure that you find your end shot and pull out from it first before zooming in—and vice versa. Nothing shows up an amateur more than a shot that doesn't know where it's going.

IN-CAMERA TRANSITIONS If you're thinking through your edit in preproduction, or during your shoot, you should be thinking about transitions as well. You have probably done it subconsciously in your storyboard—a scene ends when somebody walks out of the frame.

Moving from one scene to another, though, can be a bit more fun or a bit more significant than that. If the idea is that one scene to the next is with progressive time, you might want to find an in-camera transition that effects this on-screen. The same goes with two scenes abutted together that are to be recognized as simultaneous actions.

Film as an analog medium involving physical, forward-running, back-cranking stock at variable speeds, mediated light exposition to sensitive surfaces, chemical processing, and viewable, scratchable frames offers infinite ways of trickery and transitions. Digital video-making, on the other hand, is far more suited to transitions in postproduction than it is in production itself. That doesn't mean, however, that you can't try to achieve the same effect while shooting.

Two things: think about your edit—and you don't just have to cut.

A **blur-out** is a technique that involves the camera op knocking the entire frame manually out of focus. If this action is performed with a telephoto lens, an excess of light and minimal depth of field, you will be able to take the focus beyond recognition at the end of the scene. If this is duplicated in reverse at the start of the next scene, your edit should reveal a smooth metamorphosis between the two scenes.

A **burn-out** is exactly the same thing, but here you utilize light rather than focus. Go through your f-stops to create the burning out of the frame to white-hot exposure at the end of a scene and then down again to the next scene, if your soundtrack or dialogue supports this.

While a pan can take you from one scene to another with steady control of movement in both shots and a slow mix in the edit, a **whip pan** can do the same with more of a dramatic or cartoonish effect. Best effected on a tripod with a jib, spin the camera away from your scene at its climax. The hardest part of working the same with the next scene is getting your camera from a whip to its focus without a jolt. What you may find easier to do is to enact a brief medium shot of your subject in the second scene before whipping off and then mixing this in reverse in your edit (see sequence shown left). The second scene can carry on after a cut from your reversed shot.

In short, once you have found a rhythm for your edit, these kinds of transitions can help to break up the beat and up the ante.

NEWS PAPER

Left: Broadcast news often use a setup. This is a version of the establisher that lets an interviewee be introduced as audio overlay. The setup may just involve the interviewee sitting down at their computer or simply walking down a street. News are looking for only one or two twenty-second soundbites, which negate most of the interview. Cutaways and visual overlays may be used to paper over the audio cuts, but more frequently wide two-shots of the interviewer and interviewee are being used. Make sure you get these prior to the interview when both parties are candidly engaged nailing the questions and answers.

DIM IN DIMMER

Below: Always observe your environment for something that might give you a more interesting shot. This might have been a slightly tedious sequence shooting some home DIY, but a full-frame reflection in a chrome dimmer switch saves it and provides an appealing cutaway. Reflections tend to drain color and contrast, so fix this in your edit.

THE REVEAL

Above: Instead of shooting to cut within the same location, you might want to try revealing whatever you were going to cut to in the same shot. This either involves moving the camera, the actors, or both during the shot. Reveals offer the element of surprise while keeping it in perspective to your subjects. In effect, it can be rather less of a cheat than a cheap cut.

If you are going to reveal, make sure that it's not accompanied with a pregnant pause. Keep the action going and you won't draw attention to your choreography.

COMPOSITION The composition of your picture will separate the auteurs from the amateurs. Composition, if used in tandem with an understanding of the language of moving images, enriches the depth of your program. Without this understanding, you might as well be a bad Bruegel.

If you imagine that your audience is made up of wannabe-directors, composition can be a good head-start by informing them that they're not just watching some arbitrary knock-up-job. The more thought that goes into your work—and this is essentially a preproduction gambit—the more control you will have over your audience.

Composing your picture can be a good technical challenge—if you have the time. Using different lenses, focus, and camera movement, you can tell the audience what they should be looking at. It's been bread and butter to the horror movie for years to guide the viewer's eyes to one part of the screen and then surprise them in another—and even this simple device can indicate a good director (focus pull; crash zoom) or incriminate a bad one (a cut with an amp-busting sound effect). Experiment with lenses before your shoot, rehearse your camera moves, and discover esthetics and techniques that work with the overall theme of your program.

Training a viewer's eye on something within the frame is known as favoring. Human psychology—probably more to do with survival than anything else—is that we'll tend to look at either the biggest thing, the fastest thing, or the nearest thing. If you go down this route when composing your picture, you will determine exactly what your audience will be watching and when.

Your location and your subject/s will threaten to dictate how you shoot them. Controlling them is either a job for the storyboarding auteur or the professional DP. Sometimes absolutely letting them run riot is completely the right thing to do (reality narratives, documentaries, etc.), and sometimes you might want to give them some strict rules. We're back to Bruegel.

The Golden Section is a line segment divided into two parts where the ratio of the short half to the long half is equal to the ratio of the long half to the whole. Got it? This rule was invented by the Greeks as "the mean and extreme ratio" and later adopted by artists as the most beautiful and simple mathematical construction for esthetics. To the modern-day auteur, it now means the **rule of thirds**. This transposition of ratio esthetics divides the screen into thirds both vertically and horizontally. These imaginary lines form a grid in which you can compose your images. For example, close-ups thread the eyes onto the upper horizontal; a landscape runs along the lower horizontal; an interviewer, eyes left, supports the right vertical; the corner of a room with a two-shot is placed on the left vertical (creation of depth).

This is a rule that you'll begin to notice in every aspect of visual media. It is now a rule that is more of a language of its own—and if you can understand its use, again, it's a rule to be manipulated or even broken.

FRAMING HELL
If you're shooting a narrative, don't be afraid to knock your speaking part out of focus. This shot goes another step by fragmenting the other actor, preserving a suspicious anonymity. Add a dutch shot and you can craft a sense of discomfort.

DUTCH COURAGE

Sometimes your fixed aspect ratio will force you to shoot dutch (above). It's never a bad thing, and can allow you to keep both the perspective of the backdrop and include your presenter.

ME'S ON SCREEN

Composition—otherwise known as *mise-en-scène* (right)—can describe characters, create metaphorical divisions and unities, almost become a character of its own. And if you fancy studying a bit of math, some people even apply the Golden Section for technical estheticism.

Your lighting will be an essential part of your shoot—and it tends to be the one thing that low-budget productions consider as an afterthought. Consider, instead, that if it is the amount of light hitting the CCD that is the crucial element to the existence of your images, then a basic lighting setup is the least you can do for your pictures.

The more thought you give to your lighting, the more flexibility you give to your camera and the higher your production values—and remember, it's thought and not cash that you should throw at lighting. Creativity through resourcefulness is always half the battle.

Understanding light itself is the best place to start. All objects emit and reflect electromagnetic radiation, some of which takes the form of visible waves. The human eye and brain perceive this as light. The intensity of this light is interpreted as brightness and the length of it as color. If we see red, the signal that we are receiving is reflecting the red wavelengths in the spectrum while absorbing the others.

Color temperature is measured in Kelvin (°K)—for example, the sun at noon is 5600°K. This is the perceived natural color of light encompassing the complete spectrum that is visible to us (red, orange, yellow, green, blue, violet) as well as the huge proportion of the spectrum that isn't (ultraviolet, infrared). The intensity and color temperature of light change throughout the day and make lighting a challenging task for a professional shooting one scene in one day. For the amateur, this can be a nightmare.

What you are doing when lighting a subject is compensating for the intensity and color of that light as it changes. Within the professional world, interior sets and studios assist time and budget by containing light sources that can be controlled as a constant.

PART 03. THE SHOOT

CHAPTER THREE

LIGHTING

CANDLE IN THE BIN
When reviewing your footage, don't expect your lighting (left) to be well represented. A party—crystal clear on your LCD and in reality—can become a shot of crushed blacks and flaring. Add autofocus and you may as well trash it.

NO HAIR, JUST A REDHEAD...
Above:...as the old gag runs. Redheads are very useful and adaptable lamps to have at the ready. A blackened deflector reduces the glare, and another working as an overhead carries a blue gel to cool the scene down.

CONTROLLING LIGHT

Light can change subtly during the day or dramatically from location to location. This is why white balances are so important to preserving true color. Understanding the warmth and coolness in degrees Kelvin of different light sources will help you not only to correct light, but to control it for exactly the right mood.

By eliminating the complexities of changing daylight, interiors can contain other forms of light source. Incandescent light is a by-product of heat and is a yellowish-white light that brightens warm colors and mutes cool ones. Candles, matches and—for your money—tungsten emit incandescent light. Tungsten offers initially cheaper lighting but uses a lot of power. The bulbs also get hot quickly and the shadows it produces tend to be hard—which is not necessarily a bad thing.

Halogens are a longer-lasting form of tungsten. A trace of iodine or bromine in the bulb itself returns a small amount of tungsten to the filament when burnt, adding to its lifetime. Halogens, using dichromatic filters, give out a high intensity and uniform light close to that of daylight.

HMIs (Halogen Metal Iodide) lamps are used far more frequently in the business of lighting. At 5600K, they have the same color frequency as daylight. They are more expensive than tungsten but the power they use gives better value for money than tungsten—and they give off about half the amount of head. Most HMIs perform better between 500 and 800 hours of burn time. After this, the color temperature or quality of light may become erratic and replacement bulbs tend to be expensive. Like tungsten, the shadows they produce are harsh and you may find that diffusing the light or using a softbox helps if you don't want so much contrast.

Fluorescent light is emitted from electrically charged glowing phosphors (like those in a TV screen). Because they use electrodes rather than burning gas, fluorescent lamps tend to last ten to twenty times longer than tungsten and don't waste energy in heat (i.e., they don't get as hot so quickly). However, they do generate narrow wavelengths of light rather than a continuous spectrum, and this can result in untrue reflections of light (like you might find in a clothing store).

Understanding the light source, reflection, absorption, diffusion, and shadow—and then how to control it—is a profession of its own. As a starter, it might be useful to simply understand the terms and techniques under which light can be controlled for your production.

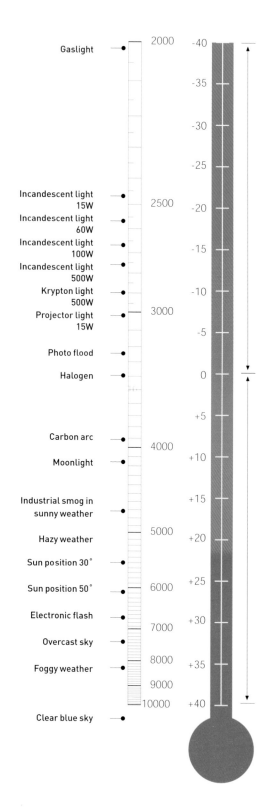

THREE-POINT LIGHTING Within most locations, you will have ambient light—the light available from pre-existing sources (daylight, a window, a computer screen, a mirror reflection), and practical light—light available from your location (a streetlamp, car headlights, a candle, a television). These are the lights that you have to balance to create exactly the right scene.

If you are shooting a documentary or reality, everything is excusable as long as your image is close to being correctly exposed. If you are working with narrative, interviews, or anything professional or compositional, there are no excuses. If your ambient light is glaring, shoot away from it, diffuse it, reflect it, or get rid of it altogether. If your practical light is harsh or too soft, use all you can to emulate it or add to it within the logical grounds of your location.

Any light source can have its intensity, beam, spread, direction, and color corrected to exactly what you're looking for. This can be done with **barn doors, diffusers, dimmers, reflectors,** or colored gels. What you need to find is the right light source suitable for the task.

Basic three-point lighting will work every time to give you a stock issue, well-lit shot. It works for interiors and exteriors—although it is a harder task in broad daylight. Three-point lighting consists of the following:

KEY LIGHT
The key light for any subject is one positioned to light them directly. Without any other lighting, this will give you a dramatic effect with well-defined highlights and shadows. If they're close to a background, a shadow will be cast onto it—and if your subject is distanced from the background, it will be lost altogether. If you find a comfortable distance that lights both subject and background without a shadow, you'll notice a lack of separation between the two. If there is any light that you can get away with using on its own, this is it.

FILL
The fill light softens any of the shadows created by your key light. Because you don't want it to overpower the effect of your carefully placed key light, you will probably want to change the quantity of light without changing the spread of it. This can be done by angling the fill away from the subject and reflecting the light back onto the area of shadow.

BACKLIGHT
If your key light is lighting both subject and background and the separation between the two is being lost, use a backlight to highlight the background. This is particularly good at preventing dark costumes or dark hair merging into your background.

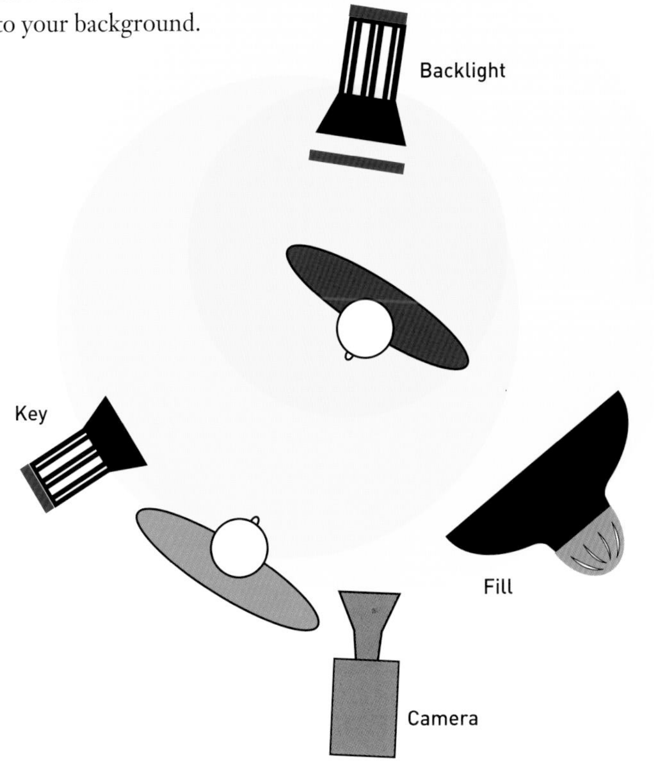

Backlight

Key

Fill

Camera

SPOT HIGHLIGHTS, KICKERS, EYELIGHTS Your three-point lighting is the basic setup. If they're rigged right and you're exposing correctly, your only problems will be everything else. Working with these lights will give you a well-lit and very standard look, but nothing special. The following lights can add a little extra production value that can take your image beyond the norm.

OUTSIDE IN

The difficulty of shooting night exteriors can be overcome on an interior set with amber gels as window flood and blue gels to highlight the darkness. Grazing brick walls with light from above adds texture and relief.

BACKGROUND LIGHTS

These lights work with your background or scenery to give them an extra lift. Whether you are shining a light through a frosted window, grazing brickwork to create stark contours, or creating an abstract slash of light, background lights should add, not distract.

KICKERS

A kicker is usually a low-angled light, set on the fill side, somewhere near the feet of the subject (hence the name). A kicker will add a glare to the side of the face, hair, and shoulder, picking them out dramatically from the background with a crisp line of light.

SPOT HIGHLIGHTS

A spot highlight is usually created with a tight beam and is used on your background or part of your set. In a realistic scene, they work to imply light spill from somewhere off-set or to suggest either a reflection from something out of frame, or accentuate one that exists on-set. If you're working with practical lights— everyday lighting that is already on location— spot highlights can be used to replicate their effects on your scenery or subject.

EYELIGHTS

Eyelights are used to add a little personality to "dead" eyes. Sometimes the key light will add the sparkle you need, but otherwise find a place where these can work with your subject. If you're shooting as a close-up, try reflecting or diffusing the light to conceal the source— and not distract or blind your subject.

PRACTICAL MAGIC
Practical lights (top) might look the part, but if they're not efficient enough as a light source you might want to boost it with gels and diffusers.

MAKING LIGHT OF IT
If your light's going and you haven't got an HMI (bottom), a blue gel on a tungsten added to natural daylight won't look too far off the real thing.

NIGHT LIGHT
Don't be afraid to add spurious lighting to night shots if they're near residential areas (top). An audience will always assume spill from windows and you'll be able to light your subject dramatically.

LIGHT THE WAY
Don't be afraid to be bold with lights (bottom). If you think you can make a strong shot out of a single on-set practical and your own lens reflection, do it.

TECHNIQUE AND TIPS Lighting doesn't have to be rocket science, despite what a pro-lighter might tell you. It has the potential to be if you are using reflective surfaces or ornate camera moves, but even if there isn't an artistic bone in your body, you can achieve effective results simply by using artistic logic.

If you want to increase a subject's fearsomeness, light them from below. If you want to "angelicize" them, light them from above. Think about the mood of the scene and—if you're using talent—the characters. Work against them or with them, but above all, be bold. Here are some more tips:

■ Always white balance before you add gels or filters.

■ Don't under-light for darkness. Digital video is well-known for artifacts within crushed black areas and you won't be able to recreate any of the detail that you've lost.

■ Don't over-light. Even the brightest of sets needs some relief.

■ Only light what the camera sees. If your light's not doing anything, either use it where it will do something or not at all.

■ If your subject has dark or black skin, use a warm amber gel or a green background to bring out texture.

■ Distant lights mute shadows and reduce contrast. Either use this to the advantage of your shot or move the lights in with the camera.

■ Watch for reflections, especially from people wearing glasses. Key your subject slightly more from the side and higher than usual to ensure that you see eyes and not reflections.

■ Use foil (preferably blackened) and white foam or card as reflectors.

■ If you have no option but to use the fluorescent lighting on location, put the warmth back into your shot with compensating red and blue filters.

■ To simulate fire out of frame, aim a redhead with a red gel away from your talent and shake a reflector to bounce the light back onto your subject. For television, do exactly the same but with blue. For water, smash a mirror into water and use this as a reflector. And don't forget your audio effects...

■ If you're conveying a reality, make it real. Light through windows, through doorway, from practicals. Don't fake lights if there's no reason for them being there—your set will look as artificial as it is.

■ You can't control the sun, so don't even try (unless you have a large diffuser). If you are shooting exteriors, you will have been checking the weather report—but make sure you know where the sun is going to be at the time of your shoot. Don't compensate for a lack of sun during your wides with two keys or you'll fall victim to the *Dukes of Hazzard* double-shadow syndrome.

■ And talking of 1970s television, a blue gel may be a convention to convey nighttime, and shooting day-for-night (blue filter; low exposure) might once have been acceptable, but your alternative of using practicals or calculating for your requirements in your software effects package might be the better solution.

INTERVIEW
Graham Berry, Camera Operator

"There's not a lot of difference between shooting on a digital camera or a Beta SP analog camera because the set-up is basically the same. If you want to shoot onto a hard-drive system, you either have to have a digital camera or an ADC to get to it.

I prefer to use digibeta cameras because they are more robust and act like Beta SP, but are more controllable. I don't think DV gives that much better a picture than Beta SP. If you're going to use digital, use digibeta, although it all comes down to price in the end. High-level top-of-the-range documentaries tend to use digibeta above anything else. The better broadcast stuff is done on digibeta. News is done on DV—the cheaper, lower-grade digital version.

They've altered the chips in digibeta cameras to make them more light-sensitive, so you don't need as much light—but if you're going to light something, you light it with balance. If you're going to light something professionally, you really need a lighting operator rather than someone like me who does both. Again, it's down to expense. I'm often told to use just the two lights, the one light, or the camera light, which isn't going to give you the best effect. I would always prefer to just sort the pictures out and have a lighting op—or even a sound man who doubles as a lighting op—so where you used to have a three-man crew, you have a two-man crew.

I carry a mini-DV to get into places that you couldn't get into with a broadcast camera. I use it a lot for clamping to vehicles, strapping under vehicles— limited-access stuff.

I work a lot with Pulnix cameras—pencil camera, tiny little things—that give out an analog image. I've just started putting Pulnix into timelapse, which can now be done as digital instead of the old SVHS system as film. The analog camera goes into the ADC and then into the digital hard drive recorder, and then you set the intervalometer to dictate the delay for your captured image. You can get this down to one frame every 24 hours. I use this on construction jobs, plant-growing—things that usually take a lot of digital editing time. It saves money.

I always thought newer technology would make cameras get lighter, but it doesn't seem to have worked. I'm still carrying batteries, tripod, and camera around with me because the way to shoot things is still the same. A good director takes a lot of weight off me literally—and figuratively when they know what they want. A good director can get a program out in about five tapes, whereas a bad one takes ten and then spends time looking through them all in the edit.

Chromakey is a nightmare for a lighting-cameraman. It's great in a studio because you can key it as you do it so you can see all of your problems. When you're on location, your lighting has to be equal across the whole of the Chromakey, nice and bright. You have to backlight your subject and you only need a small shadow and that gives you your one big problem when it comes to key it. When you're on location too, you're in danger of not having a lot of light, which is exactly what you need for Chromakey. The only 100% way of doing it is in a studio."

03.04

Your time and your budget will be the prime consideration for shooting coverage. Setting up for your scene or shots will almost always take longer than you anticipate, and you may have scheduled to be at the next location within an hour. Indeed, you may have paid for a location and either have to vacate before you have finished shooting or make sure that you're there in order to make the most of it.

For all of these reasons—and more—you have to make sure that you have coverage of whatever it is that you're shooting. Put simply, you can't cut to the same shot in the edit. If you've made a shotlist of all the shots that you require, you should shoot at least two versions of each. This will be your shot, and your safety shot—another take just in case there is a picture or audio issue on the original.

If you haven't made a shotlist—maybe you're shooting on the fly, or have abandoned it with time pressing—there are a few things that you need to make sure that you've got the shots in the can. The first is that you've got enough cutaways. If you don't have them, you can only consider yourself lucky that you get as far as an edit. If you're working with a single subject or talent, make sure that you've got close-ups of their hands, eyes, feet—anything that will let you cut away from the one shot (and the safety) that you have spent your whole time getting in the can. There's nothing remotely involved here: just get the shots while your subject is getting their mike fixed, working on their lines, or primping their hair.

SHOOTING COVERAGE

THE EYES HAVE IT
Cutaways of eyes are popular, especially in profile. Eyes draw a viewer in and provide clues to the subject or talent. They're also difficult to cut into your program as the position and expression has to complement whatever your cut has them saying. The tighter you go, the less you'll have to deal with the additional expressions of laughter lines.

HANDY CAM

Hands are the easiest cutaway in the book. Everyone fiddles with them while they talk—and most people gesture. Tilt the camera down during a pre-interview chat and they'll probably do it more naturally than they would during the interview itself.

MIGHTY TIGHT ON

Shooting tight onto a subject from a distance for a setup shot lets them operate a bit more naturally. Because of the zoom's use in fly-on-the-wall documentary, it also lends reality to a very set up setup shot.

NO BUTTS?

Just as any good cowboy walks off into the sunset, shoot your subject or talent leaving you behind. When it comes to cutting, you might just need it for your pay-off line. Just don't leave their script sticking out of their back pocket...

The other tip is to point the camera in completely the opposite direction from your subject. This will give you either a fresh perspective of your location or the point-of-view of your subject. Make this shot count. Shoot it wide for ten seconds, zoom into an interesting tight for ten seconds, and then pull out. This will give you four useful shots that can save an edit.

Always get an establisher—preferably one while your subject is in shot, and one without. If you are using a subject or talent, shoot them walking onto your set (into your frame) and off (exiting the frame). Again, this can be done in the most candid of moments and provide quick wallpaper for an intro or pay-off with either music or voiceover.

MONITORING Monitoring shots—particularly framing—is an integral part of film-making. Where production is expensive, the last thing a producer needs is to have to reassemble cast and crew to shoot the whole thing over again. Not only did digital video take this consideration on board, but it went one step further. Because analog to digital isn't as cut and dried as shooting analog to analog, monitoring can become important to control levels within broadcast and playout source limits.

FIELD MONITORS

If you are shooting anything intricately framed, extremely light or dark, anything requiring absolute focus, or anything live with a multi-camera setup and a mixer, you will need a monitor. And some directors simply insist on them anyway.

Typically, a field monitor on set or location will let you see images only prior to the analog signal reaching the ADC and therefore what you are not seeing is your true digital signal recorded to tape. However, a monitor will show you the analog image as your digital video camera is seeing it, and this is enough for your compositional and technical requirements.

A field monitor uses a CRT, but, unlike a television set, doesn't make any automatic corrections to the image—exactly what you need. The controls that it does have will let you view your image with only a blue hue or in monochrome (like a high-end digital camera's viewfinder) in order that true focus and exposure can be seen.

Your monitor should also let you use an underscan control. When you are shooting, you will be overscanning. This means that your captured image is slightly larger than necessary. When you eventually play your finished program on your standard definition television in front of your proud friends, family, and dog, the television will always cut off a proportion of the edge of the picture to ensure that your picture fills the screen. This is underscanning. By using the underscan control on your monitor, you can see exactly what the dog will be watching—in black-and-white too.

OSCILLOSCOPES

If you want to ensure that you always have correct exposure, whether out on location, set, or in an edit, you will want to use a waveform monitor. The image is displayed as an analog visualization of your picture's luminance. The brighter parts edge toward the top of the screen and the darker parts toward the bottom. Along the horizontal wave, the left, middle, and right sections correlate to those sections of your image. Any

REFLECTING BADLY
Try to keep your monitor shielded from on-set lights—and if you're shooting exteriors, always attach the hood. Reflections have a knack of hiding the one thing that you don't want to be in shot.

peaking of the waveform in either direction above or below set PAL and NTSC guidelines will tell you that your camera needs stopping up or down to compensate.

A vectorscope is another form of oscilloscope that measures the chrominance of your image. Displayed like a wheel, the closer to the rim, the more saturated the color within the image. Vectorscopes are essential with analog cameras and in an analog edit. They are far less essential with controlled CCDs, as the problems of bleeding and streaking are absent in digital video. However, the point of all oscilloscopes is to tackle any image problems before they become part of your image.

GOOD PRACTICE, GOOD HOUSEKEEPING Whether or not you are shooting professionally, there is no reason not to act professionally. If you start with good practice, you'll carry on in the same vein through different kit and different productions. If this sounds like a chore, it's not. It's a couple of minutes of time and consideration before shooting—and a whole load of time saved in your edit.

Digital videotape is just that: tape. It is physical and it's prone to the elements, to digital flaws and misbehaving camera mechanics. At the beginning of every tape—mini-DV or DVCAM—record at least twenty seconds of bars, and preferably a minute. The bars (and audio tone) that the camera records will not only give you your color reference for the tape, but will allow the first part of the tape to play through. If you don't have bars on your camera, shoot the same length of black with the lens cap on. The reason this is important is that this is the most likely to be damaged. With digital videotape, it's the probable area of any dropout, mechanical creasing (clogged heads), or inconsistent coating that could cause corruption of the data stored.

DESIGN A LABEL
Back in the edit, your simple scrawls are going to save you from time-wasting rummaging and spooling.

Want to save some time, some money, some...hair? Here's a few tips that might keep them in your favor, your pocket, and on your head—and you on your toes.

■ Do your white balance—and your black balance if you've got one—and do it manually if your camera will let you.

■ Focus your viewfinder eyepiece if you've got one—and turn everything that's automatic to off if you want some kind of control over what you're shooting.

■ Switch your zebras on and check your exposure on your shot. Add any gain that you might need or relight to compensate.

■ Use a monitor if you can; check your screen-safety for your chosen ratio on the complete camera move.

■ If possible, set your timecode specifically for each tape that you shoot.

■ Label your tapes while you shoot (there, that'll give you something to do...): Date, roll number, and production are the least you can provide; interviewees, scene numbers, and takes can be very useful, but you may want to leave these for your shotlist.

■ Watch your tape remaining; try to stop a minute or so before the end of the tape, which is as vulnerable as the top of the tape.

■ Always rewind your tapes before boxing up; if you fall victim to clogged heads either in-camera or at the edit, you'll want it to be over your stripes and not over your last shot.

LOGGING SHOTS; TIMECODE Logging shots is like a washing machine: it's not a luxury, it's a necessity. Having said that, you can make it difficult for yourself and go to the laundromat. Whether you're using a pen, a Personal Assistant, or a ScriptBoy, the time, effort, and frustration you will save in the edit will make you thankful that you went that extra mile on the shoot.

01.00.00.04

That's the summary; the practical side of things is always on the shoot itself. As has hopefully been driven home by now, there are so many things to think about on a shoot as an auteur that running around with a pen and paper in your hand will probably be either the last thing on your mind or forgotten entirely. Try to remind yourself that even carrying a scrap of paper and a pencil around is as much a tool as the camera itself.

What you are looking to do, at the very least, is to note both the timecode of what you're shooting alongside a brief description of what you're shooting. This is basic good housekeeping. Where this becomes difficult is if your capacity on the shoot runs to being camera op as well—especially if you're under pressure of time to get the shots. This is where you should seriously think about a PA, a runner or just a pal—somebody to write the code down as you shout it out.

Similarly, if you are conducting an interview, you won't have the time or concentration (if you want to ask serious questions) to take down the key responses and the raspberries. And this is where logging comes into its own. Your best take—the one that you are most satisfied with—will tend to be the last, but in the edit, you may find that the response doesn't make sense without cutting it with a sentence from one of the other takes. This is exactly the same for narrative dialog.

If you're paying for your edit, you'll appreciate that time is a lot of money. And if you have a client, then you will want to look as professional as possible by knowing exactly which timecode to spool to.

If you're taking sync from a DAT, you will have your work doubly cut out for you. Make sure that your audio log is talking the same language as your shot log. If your audio op is notating (it is easier to monitor sound and log simultaneously), then make sure that they are running with roughly the same description as you or your PA are with the visuals. In this case, your audio op will be looking for airplanes in the background just as your camera op will be looking for a microphone entering the frame—anything that will ruin the take.

TCR 10:05:01:

INTERVIEW

Mark Baynes, *Big Brother* UK Website
Executive Producer

"

The fundamental thing is not to get overexcited about streaming media, and recognize the limits of the technology. Always remember what the end-user will see. Even though things have moved on in leaps and bounds, the problem is still the middle stuff: the encoder and the server.

You have to make a choice whether or not you'll encode in Real or in Windows, and those choices are based on commercial issues—the various costs involved—and whether or not your users can be bothered to download software if they haven't got it. What you're looking for is the lowest common denominator in pre-installed software—and not everyone has got DSL.

You've got to have a server that can stream to the user on demand. You buy a certain number of maximum streams and there's a cost issue there. Most people overestimate the number of users who will be wanting a stream.

In *Big Brother* we hooked in directly to the broadcast track, which allowed a mixer to make the decisions on which pictures were going to be sent to the encoder. The house was basically a TV studio with high-end cameras, so it was all designed for broadcast—and there's not that much difference between broadcast and webcasting, the ideal being a newsreader sitting down with a plain background behind them. And if you're shooting, encoding, and streaming that, you'll get an extremely good image. In the *Big Brother* house, a lot of the time they're just sitting on the sofa which, again, made it ideal.

The extreme for a webcast is someone playing football. That is obviously bad news in terms of streaming, with lots of people running around a lot and especially green grass, which comes out looking like green soup. You've got to think not what the best shot is in terms of action, but what the best shot is in terms of encoding.

The big issue with *Big Brother* was the load on the server and getting enough video streams for the people who wanted them. There's a tolerable load for the UK Internet and a lot of the service providers wanted an idea of users for *Big Brother 2* because on the first one we nearly brought down the whole of the UK Internet because the load was so high. You've got to have a server in the middle with the capability to send out 50,000 streams. For *Big Brother*, we had about 50,000 concurrent users, which is very high. On a normal gig with a reasonable band playing, if you get 2,000 users you're doing very, very well. The big one after BB was the Madonna gig, which had a maximum number of 9 million streams.

There's also a very big difference between encoding and streaming live and encoding and streaming almost live because it's easier to control after the event. If it goes out live and you've got half the country watching it, it can bring down the server.

Streaming codecs will get better, but the problem is the delivery to people over the Internet. If you've got the money, you can have a delivery system especially for the delivery of video. It's called EDGE and there are video servers located in all the main ISPs. The central server that you're using delivers copies of the video streams to the EDGE servers, and then the user is automatically directed to their nearest stream, so it distributes the load throughout the Internet.

The secret to all webstreaming, to be honest, is to underpromise and overdeliver.

"

SHOOTING FOR THE INTERNET Too many contrasts, too much movement, too much detail. These are just some of the issues facing those who try to put their movies on the Internet. Because the Internet relies on data streams, it is important that your movie doesn't have too much information to transmit or download. All your data needs to be compressed and decompressed, so the quality of the codec that you use will be vital.

CONTRAST
If you want mean and moody, go tighter and lighter.

Your main consideration is your audience and what capabilities they might have with which to view your masterpiece. Expect the worst from their machines, their software, servers, and codecs and work up from there.

TOO MANY CONTRASTS

When you're shooting, try to keep your light even throughout your production. This doesn't just mean within one scene, but requires you to imagine your program cut together. If you haven't managed to do this during your shoot, there's always post-production that will help. As ever, this is something best tackled in the early stages rather than fiddling around in the latter.

Most codecs work much better with medium tones of lighting and contrast. Anything that you shoot dark is always more problematic to compress and reproduce without the inherent digital graininess. The best tip while shooting for the Internet is to keep your zebras on at all time to make sure that you've got a good and correct exposure for your shots. If you're losing detail in your picture, you can be sure that this won't magically reappear using a codec…

TOO MUCH MOVEMENT

When you're viewing an Internet movie file, your frame rate (movie download) or bitrate (streaming media) is dictated by the way that the file was originally put onto the Internet. This is the number of times that the image will refresh itself every second to give the illusion of a moving image. Of course, the higher the rate, the better the illusion.

A high rate balances the amount of data that you're giving the codec. If there's a lot of information, then your rate will be a lot lower—and vice versa. A crucial method of reducing the amount of information in your moving images is to mitigate the number of times that the picture changes. A codec reads between the lines (technologically, the deltas between the frames)—and if an image doesn't change, then it doesn't have to work on that part of the image again when refreshing it. Any slight movement requires your reshuffled pixels to be read again. Your job while shooting, therefore, is going to be the mitigation of any unnecessary movement. This you can do with a tripod. Use sandbags, shield yourself from the wind, tighten everything rock-steady. Any movement from the camera that moves your pixels is going to work against you. This includes camera moves themselves, of course. Zooms, pans, and pull-outs are notoriously good at destroying the illusion of the moving image. By the time the image has refreshed, the frame has moved on so far into your shot that you might as well have simply cut to a wide, close-up or a different shot altogether.

DETAIL

The combination of a long shot and relative darkness makes the detail in a small low-res download almost impossible to decipher.

MOVEMENT

Left: If the frame rate or bitrate at which a movie was put onto the Internet is too low for the amount of movement within it, the image can show signs of ghosting or jumping.

PERFECTION

Right: Bear all these things in mind, and don't raise your expectations, and your Internet movie image can sometimes be a thing of relative beauty.

TOO MUCH DETAIL

Similarly, detail in your picture will simply become a whole load of unnecessary data to the codec. The kind of thing that you really don't want to slow your process down with are cars, trees, dogs, birds, or people moving in the background of your shot. These are the more uncontrollable aspects of a shoot once you're on location. If you are on location, try a narrower depth of field to knock the background out of focus, or point the camera toward a less complicated horizon. Within a controlled set, you can concentrate on your subject without being victim to the wind or your natural environment. Your codec will handle close-ups very well. And if your subjects are wearing clothes, then try to stay away from patterns, stripes, and checks.

All of these can be applied to the audio that you're using. Although audio doesn't need compressing, different hard and software owned by your global audience will treat the audio in different ways. Keep it as uncomplicated and as clean as possible, just like your pictures.

The best way of dealing with the production implications of shooting for the Internet is to try it first. Don't think that whatever you shoot and whatever you cut will automatically be appropriate for web distribution. What you may find is that another cut from your rushes is far more suitable.

CHROMAKEY

CHROMAKEY Chromakey for digital video is always a poor-man's Hollywood, a special effect that is so transparent that it's a wonder it's still in use. However, it can be used effectively in some circumstances and can save you a lot of money in others.

The rudiments of Chromakey are that in the edit, the computer can be told to recognize a certain color (usually blue or green) and be told to introduce another image wherever that color exists in your frame, creating a composite image.

The reason that Chromakey is usually keyed with blue or green is that these are two of the three primary outputs for a video camera. Traditionally, Chromakey has used bluescreen as it's both the complementary color to flesh tones and because it's easy to incorporate the screen itself into a blue sky. Red is rarely used as it is found in all human skin. Greenscreens are becoming increasingly used because green paint or fabric reflects light more readily than blue—it has a higher luminance—making it easier for a clean key. The problem with keying on green is that any bleeding of the color in the edit tends to be far more noticeable than blue bleeding. This, however, has become less of a problem with modern software and green is now the recommended choice.

Keying in the edit is based on luminance. Your luminance control will decide how much of the keyed image is allowed through into the composite image. For this reason, light is the key to a successful Chromakey.

In the edit, the key will remove the single primary color that you choose—i.e., your screen color. In the bad old days, this used to be a harsh and rough outline.

KEY TO SUCCESS
Chromakeying using Matrox's RT.X100 Xtreme gives you additional adjustments for spill, noise reduction, and transparency, making for perfect Chromakey around the usually difficult areas of hair, smoke, and shadow.

Nowadays, software tools can allow not only this mat to be smoothed off and thereby disguised, but a secondary color to be used if your image is rife with primaries.

For a designed Chromakey shoot (rather than artistic fiddling in an edit), you will need either your blue- or greenscreen and a lighting setup. Lighting your screen is crucial. If you're looking to key a different background in on a subject and are looking for a very real key, your lighting for both background and subject will have to be synchronized. You won't be fooling anyone by lighting your star with a key from the left when your background sun is blazing from the right.

To get the correct lighting for an authentic Chromakey, you need to light the subject and the background separately. It's easier if you've got a physical distance between the two, and it helps to eliminate shadow from your screen. Any darkness on screen will be read at a different luminance and hue—and the same goes with areas of excessive brightness. Try to create as even a light as you can across the entirety of the screen.

When you are lighting your subject, an amber gel can help stop wash out some of the spill you may get reflected from your greenscreen. This tends to be most noticeable around the areas of the hair, the side of the face, and shoulders.

Because the lighting is so crucial to a successful Chromakey, a test run is always advisable before you start. Use a friend or crew member to stand in for the talent and practice a few setups. If you can get your hands on a waveform monitor, it will show you exactly how even your light is. A vectorscope can also be worth its weight in gold, informing you of the RGB composite within your subject's clothes.

Monitor your frame too. Keep an eye out for any part of your background that isn't within screen safety or your illusion will be destroyed. The only way of redeeming this common adversity in the edit is by losing resolution with a digital video effect zoom.

Indeed, issues of framing aren't the only camera op involvement here. Motion conflicts between your subject and your background give the game away entirely and may well force you to shoot both your subject and background with a tripod.

Most times, the most invisible Chromakey is one lit by the sun. Chromakey exteriors are where the effect can become as natural as the light itself. Add a slight blur effect to the background in the edit, and you might even convince yourself that you took your talent off to the Mohave Desert for the shoot.

If you can pull off a convincing Chromakey, you can then start pulling the convention apart. Green paint exists solely to do the job, and instead of painting a wall, try painting other parts of your set or shooting your subject or background in motion to destroy any kind of reality. Be brave…and not a little artistic…

MAT EASE

Compositing images with mats requires a bit of experimentation, but can be used to paint your screen with busy visual artistry.

MATS

Chromakey is just one way to create a composite image. Most of the others are to be found hidden in your edit software, but it's important that you know the capabilities while you shoot. Serendipity in the edit is one thing, but it is truly rewarding when you've managed to shoot a composite image by design.

The outline of a key is called the mat line and with digital video it can sometimes make itself intrusively obvious and unsightly. There's a fine line between having a horrible pixelated halo around your subject and your subject missing the ends of their hair, their cheeks, or their ears. While you've accomplished all you can on the shoot to get clean pictures, you have to make sure that the edit doesn't let you down.

The aim of the game is to apply a low-pass filter to interpolate your images before applying the key to composite them. Some videocard codecs can do this very efficiently by

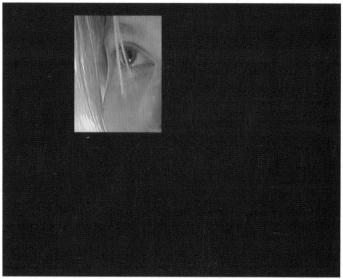

changing their settings. Because the color in your images is being sampled once (NTSC) or twice (PAL) for every four times the luminance is being sampled, it means that through your RGB setting, you'll have only one color sample for every fourth or second pixel and get an aliased color image.

This is fine as far as digital video is concerned. The human eye is far more sensitive to luminance than it is to chrominance. But what a Chromakey is doing is taking just your lower-resolution color image and finding differences in it in order to make the mat. Those important differences in your color are to be found in the luminance and saturation of the color.

If your success with color mats is based on color difference, a composite RGB setting is not ideal. Try looking for a component YUV setting instead. YUV was originally introduced with the gradual changeover from black-and-white to color televisions. Y separated from the other channels gives a monochrome image, while together they form your full-color picture. YUV transmits your video signal as three channels: Luminance and sync (Y), red minus Y, and blue minus Y. The green signal can be deduced from this information.

Alternatively, when you're capturing your two scenes for Chromakey, try using your analog S-VHS (Y/C) input. Your chrominance and luminance signals here are traveling down two separate lines with a greater bandwidth (read resolution) and your connection will have pre-filters that smooth both signals.

DV, relying on light hitting the CCDs, has a great capacity for storing all the information that you need for a good Chromakey or mat. The point to all this fiddling is to draw this information from your tape comprehensively.

If, after all this, you're still getting aliasing problems with your mat line, apply one of your edge blur or feathering tools in your edit to make it less of an issue. If your software doesn't have any, there are Internet downloads available that you can use to filter, soften, or blur your images to your heart's content.

MAT BLACK
Controlling mats to mask parts of the screen offers a very classy look to title sequences. Letting the images run while mixing on and off provide a smooth background to any text you might want to add to the masked area.

MIX AND MAT

Mixing through your various composite mat layers is a great way of smooth editing without having to use cutaways. In this instance, the singer is slightly out of sync with her (backward sung) lines, and a slight mix through loses her mouth in the mat for the brief duration before bringing her back.

Right: A simple composited iMovie animation can work as a stand-alone movie or as a background to a title sequence.

Below: Having shot and edited the video and exported it as a Filmstrip, an animator can take each individual frame and work on it. It's as painstaking as it sounds, but the finished work comes alive in a way that the original video never could.

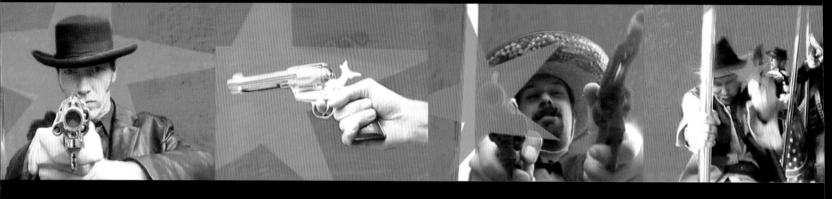

ANIMATION Animation is very particular with edit software, just as the people who use it are. Like Chromakey, animation is just one of those things that you either do or don't. Your NLE knows this full well and knows that dedicated computer animation software can do the job a lot better. This is why there are plenty of specialized animation software applications out there that can understand what you're trying to do.

A lot of them can even read between your keyframes and fill in the gaps of your animation, saving a lot of time and effort. Needless to say, this method is hardly for martyrs or purists. What your NLE can do is facilitate animation should you require it. It does this by letting keyframes or still frames to be used to build an animation sequence.

If you've got the patience—and if you're an animator, you have—then you can animate to digital quality using your digital video camera. The best thing about a setup incorporating a camera FireWired to your edit software is that you can animate next to your desktop, straight into your machine and build as you go. This is perfect for stop-motion animation, especially if your video camera has a simple one-touch still button.

LABOR DEFENSIVE
Because the process of animation is so time-consuming, animation software is getting better and better at making it less laborious. Reading between the frames, applications can make judgments by default, eliminating tedious "filling in." Purist animators, though, tend to turn these defaults off and remain the most patient, almost too laid-back professionals in the business.

Sequential stills or graphics can be imported onto your timeline as well. This will give your Plastercine or your Amazing Moving Cigarette Packets a leg-up on the production value scale. If you introduce mats or Chromakey into your stop motion, you can key stills for the background this way. If you've really got the patience, use keyframes from AVIs to pan or zoom with your stop motion. If you are using stills from graphics applications, make sure that you make your adjustments to the square pixels before importing them. What you're looking to do is to have the same frame size as your edit project settings without the stills being subject to interpolation, something that will cause distortion of your background.

Combining graphics applications and edit software can work the other way too. Any AVI in your edit software—if your software allows it—can be exported as a filmstrip. The resultant exported file is your video clip as a sequence of stills that you can work on in a graphics application. It may be painstaking, but you can get some great, almost physical, effects simply by using paint and draw all over your sequence of stills. After you've done this, your NLE will let you import the file again, drag the sequence back onto the timeline, edit it, and then export it again as a movie.

Using the same technique, you can shoot your original AVI to be designed for your animation by using Chromakey or mats. In doing this, you'll be able to make your live action integrate with an animated background, or vice versa.

Your exporting options might also permit you to create a .gif (Graphics Interchange Format) file. You can perform any of the above mentioned animations, import them into your NLE, and export them as a GIF. The drawback, however, is that these files tend to have a small frame size, with a limit of 256 colors, making them more applicable to graphics than to the moving image. GIFs won't incorporate audio as a file, and are most used to animate on the Internet as they are simply a quick sequence of bitmap files that can be easily sent from server to user without the need for a plug-in of any description.

In short, you won't be creating Shrek in your NLE, but there's certainly something to be said for animation that can be far more experimental in a less-tailored and less easy environment.

NATURAL TRANSITIONS If video is a time-based medium and one of its capabilities is to deceive the viewer about time, then you'll be working with transitions a lot. Transitions between scenes are mainly undertaken in the edit, something that will be discussed…in time.

For the moment, though, during the shoot, you have options as to how you might want to convey these transitions of time. What your digital camera can do is capture the ideas you have in the physical real world and let you use its natural resources instead of digital after-thought after-effects. On-camera transitions in this case are well worth considering because a little thought in your storyboard process (and you almost certainly won't be shooting in scene order) goes a long way toward your production values.

We've discussed how your lens can work to link scenes (white-outs, blur-outs) and how the tripod can pan from one scene to another. Another method is to use a movement within the frame—the most accessible being your actors.

A **body wipe** offers a number of solutions for moving from one scene to another. A typical example is for a character or **walk-off part** to lead the camera away from the tail end of your focal conversation as they walk past, breaking the space between the lens and the action. This is an extremely valuable device as it adds breathing space from one scene to another. It's used to death in any bar scene of your favorite soap opera. Incidentally, a **walk-on part** can introduce your (bar) conversation in exactly the same way.

Body wipes can also work within your scene. Without breaking the 180-degree rule or jump-cutting, a recognizable close-up of a walk-on or walk-off can wipe directly in front of your lens at the end of your first shot and the beginning of your second. This lets you cut flawlessly between them and bring you close to your subject. This same technique is also the tricksier version of a transition between one scene and the next and a keen-eyed viewer will find you very clever if you pull it off…

Which brings us to the subject of pulling it off versus just showing off. There are many directors around that draw attention to their techniques—and many that prefer not to in order that a viewing experience is not compromised by the viewer being made aware of their audience status. There are arguments both ways.

There are ways of really showing off— and if you're going to work with an edit or effects package that allows morphing, you'll need to get it right on-set. If it's a location morph, you'll be looking to simplify your sets and maybe match props. If it's a prop, portrait or eye morph, exact framing will be your ally. Either way, color temperature and lighting matches between scenes (unless you're cheating day to night or vice versa) will assist your success for a fluid morph.

PASS WIPE
If your accidental walk-on isn't walking, moving the camera around them will give you a body wipe and a reveal.

AUDIO 1 When you get into the edit, you'll find that you can make or break your production with audio. A driving soundtrack can always move things along nicely, or you might be importing a voiceover or doing additional dialog recording. Fine—you can do that in the edit in a controlled environment.

For the rest of it, though, you're going to be relying on the sound that you shoot on the day—and getting this right is crucial. Your worst-case scenarios in the edit will be such that you either have to leave that annoying hiss, hum, or pop in, compress and clean it beyond audible recognition—or leave a shot (and probably a scene) out entirely. Getting it right on the day is the only way to avoid these nightmares.

For this reason, there is no need to skimp on the budget by giving yourself a PA, rather than having a dedicated sound op. There are plenty of camera and sound and lighting ops out there, but the more you can divide these crucial jobs, the better. If you do have a multi-talented camera op like this, it's probably more important that they're responsible for the lighting rather than the sound—even if they are monitoring through an earpiece while they shoot.

A dedicated sound op needs to work in tandem with your camera because both the visuals and the sound have usually got to be faultless simultaneously. While your camera op should notice if your interviewee has a tree sticking out of their head, or a helicopter hovering above your Elizabethan drama, your sound op will be able to tell you whether you've got an intrusive nearby highway or grasshopper.

The crucial thing about sound is that while in everyday life we're used to general background noise—and don't even notice it—once you've isolated an image and put it in a viewing context (your program), sound becomes a character all of its own. Airconditioning systems are a usual suspect—and airplanes can be a walk-on part all of their own. Airplanes are a great example of how human psychology works. If you're

SONIC BOOM BOY
Enclosed headphones don't let any air in. For this reason, they're great out on location because they block natural audio diversions. On set, though, open headphones both let your sound op hear what you're saying and let them monitor bass easier—something more prone to roofed environments.

undertaking an interview in a "real" location, the viewer will completely forgive the intrusion as long as it introduces itself during the course of an interview. If there is a forgivable background sound but it's there at the top of your interview, or it's there at the point of you cutting hard into your interview, it becomes unforgivable, purely because it's sudden. It sounds like a mistake.

Pity the poor narrative video-maker, who becomes a victim of the genre's creativity. Because everything is designed within the framework as narrative video, anything out of control becomes instantly noticeable.

Audio is 50% of your deal. Deal with it at the time and you're halfway to a sound production.

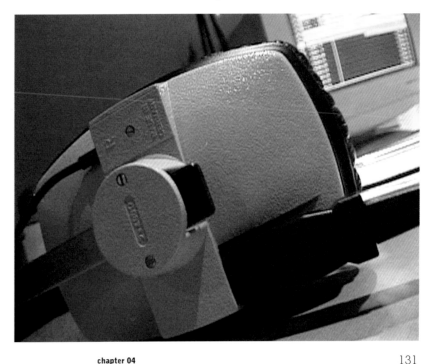

INTERVIEW
Tull, Audio Mixer and Composer

"

The way I start off with digital audio is by using hardware-based equipment and slowly moving toward a computer and computer-based software to do most of the recording, sequencing, and mastering. I've worked on projects for promotional videos, commercial videos, a few bits of audio for short films, and multimedia projects—all of which usually require the full scoring of a piece of music.

If I'm working with video, I prefer to have a basic timecoded cut provided so that I can preview it in Logic Audio and sync it up with my audio on a frame-by-frame basis. Along a timeline, I can work crisply and precisely to the images, and any problems I have tend to be frame-rate related, so I try to lock the audio in with the video as much as I can.

It's a good idea to keep all the bits and pieces you're working with in a recognizable and separate folder. If you're sampling and importing, you need to keep a track on what you're loading into the sequencer and make sure that you've got everything you need. If you're doing any mix-downs, make sure that they're in the same folder to save any confusion about which version you're working on.

Keeping separate audio tracks alive in your sequencer lets you mix between different instruments. More tracks mean that if you're going to add an effect, you can add it to the whole track rather than have little audio clips all over the place with different effects all over them. It's worth naming every track you use to let you know at a glance whether it's a vocal track or a bass track. Sequencers help you to some extent by telling you the kind of track you're working with, but it's always more helpful to know whether it's a MIDI sample, the original video dialog, an external instrument, or a computer-generated sound.

I've got a fair amount of experience with live instruments, but you don't have to be a composer to work with a sequencer. Gigging with a band is quite a useful experience to know how sound works and interacts in a given space or a physical environment, and working with an analog mixing desk—that kind of thing. All of these things are relevant because they're all incorporated into audio software as a digital representation of them. As for being a classically trained musician, there are plenty of people who work with audio software and even compose without any previous experience of music at all.

Some of the software gets quite complicated—high-end professional sequencers like ProTools. Certainly something like Logic has all the utilities on it that you would expect to find in a fully fledged studio. On the other hand, you've got programs like Acid and Cool Edit where somebody who's not used to composing music can simply arrange different chunks of audio, including full pieces of pre-sampled music. This kind of software then lets the user lay loads of other bits of sound like your strings and your snare over the top wherever you want it, which makes it extremely easy to create a completely new track.

If you've sampled something from CD and you're using it in a commercial project, you've got to be very careful and apply for rights and pay for the privilege. Home- or art-based projects have a lot more leeway; your viewing audience is obviously a lot smaller, and you can get away with using stuff. The best way to look at it—and it's certainly how the rights holders look at it—is whether or not you're intending to make money out of your project.

"

AUDIO 2 There are three main types of audio that you'll work with over the course of your production: dialog, music, and Voice of God (VOG). This is not to say that you'll be working with all three in your production—or even if you are, during the process of production—but you should at least be aware of their differences while you shoot in order to plan your audio edit.

EASY ON THE EAR

If your sound op's going to be wearing headphones all day, make sure that they're comfortable, lightweight—and not too hot. These Sennheiser HD200 cans are closed and bassy, and their reduction of ambient noise reduces chances of getting feedback.

DIALOG

Dialog is not limited to narrative video. Dialog is anything that anyone says on screen (or off) that is intended to be audible and part of your production's discourse.

If you are working with dialog, then that is the most important part of the audio that you will shoot. Capturing it precisely will require as much effort as getting the shots that you want. The technical issues that you'll need to shoulder are various—and probably the most crucial will be that if you're recording to DAT or a non-linear source, you need to make sure that your frame-rate matches the speed of your camera. Even if you are certain that both are running at 25 fps, it might be worth testing prior to the shoot that your sync matches. If it's even slightly out in the edit, you'll find yourself cutting breathing spaces into or chunks out of your audio in order to sync it—an extremely painful process. If in doubt—and for best results—try to find the best possible means of recording directly to your videotape with an external mike and monitor it.

If you're confident enough to be recording to DAT and you can afford the luxury, there's no harm in leaving your audio running as unbroken. Audio can be the best wallpaper in the world and any candid line recorded or accidental sound can be very useful in an edit as an audio supplement or transition. Alternative versions of dialog—even outtakes—can be handy to cut with if the intonation is better than your take. Just make sure that your audio is properly timecoded.

MUSIC

Generally music is added in post-production. Sometimes it's not—and sometimes it's not even meant to be on your audio. If you're shooting music live into one or both (or all four) of your audio channels, you may be doing it the wrong way. Music—by very nature of being complex in its different offering of sound and layered in depth—is best monitored and controlled through a mixer. Even without quality XLRs on mini-DV, it is possible to get the mixer directly in through your audio input mini-jack and straight to tape.

Because camera mikes are extremely sensitive, listen out for music that shouldn't be there. Even if you decide to go along with it as ambience in the edit, there might still be copyright issues that you probably don't want to get into when you're over a barrel.

VOICE OF GOD

Again, Voice of God is best achieved in a controlled environment or studio in post-production. Logistical problems, though, such as the unavailability of crew or talent, might force you to record on the day of the shoot.

Voice of God is the term given to an unseen voice-over. It might be a character in your narrative as monologue, or it might be simply a voice-over for your documentary. If you are cornered into shooting on the day, try to find a room that will give you the dull, flat audio carcass for your shoot. Furniture can help absorb unwanted high frequencies and give your voice the qualities that it needs to be softer and edit-tweakable.

USING MICROPHONES As mentioned, there are three types of microphone that you can possibly use: omni-, bi-, and unidirectional. While shooting, there aren't many instances where a bidirectional will be useful as its two areas of pick-up are at 180° polarities and you won't be shooting in two opposing directions at once unless you've an elaborate live event camera setup.

Omnidirectional mikes, on the other hand, are particularly bad at live events as they can generate feedback from any surrounding speaker. Their use is limited to general ambience or "real" sound, such as capturing a singer in a room and the hushed atmosphere of an audience.

Unidirectional mikes come with three varieties of pick-up pattern. The most used is the cardioid pattern, so-called because of its heart-shape. While the tip of the mike isolates your focal sound, it allows a small amount of general atmosphere frequencies in from around the rest of the mike. The problem with it is that you have to be reasonably close to your focal sound in order to get the best out of it, which won't help with your wides or long-shots.

The other two versions are the supercardioid and the hypercardioid, which respectively get narrower in field—and more difficult to aim while keeping the same audio level. If your subject isn't a frantically moving target, though, a supercardioid such as a shotgun or rifle mike will keep them audible. These are available with different distance ranges (short or long) and with different preferred frequency ranges.

On set, it is wisest to stick to a cabled mike. You are working within a controlled specific space, so there is no reason why you can't work with cables. In this case, use your cardioid on a boom and mike from overhead. This will generally produce the most natural of sounds—certainly for dialog. If your framing doesn't allow for booming overhead, your next best bet is to mike from underneath. This often provides more bassy dialog as you're picking up words or sounds more from the subject's chest cavity. The other reason why this is slightly less preferred on-set is that your floor-bound **fishpole** is going to add that one extra obstacle for your crew. Your other option in this scenario is to plant boom mikes within the set if your speaking parts are reasonably static. Use **c-clamps** and stands to keep them in place—but always keep an eye on them. With all of these, work your mikes with your widest frames shot. The point is that the mikes follow your talent, not your camera moves.

CALL OF THE WILD
Getting the sound right when you're on location means that you won't have to face one of these in the edit.

If you're undertaking an interview on set and your focus is on one static subject, consider using a cabled lapel mike that will take their sound straight to one channel with a discreetly hidden mike. These small mikes come as cabled or wireless and are globally termed lavalier mikes. Interviewees are flattered by these (despite or because of your sound op's wrestling to get the cable up their shirt) as the attention tends to make them feel important. Use your camera mike for your second channel to let yourself not only pick up any atmosphere that you might require, but to keep the interviewer's questions audible as a reference. If you want their questions, take any mike to them (as they'll be out of shot for the moment) and to your second channel.

Exteriors are similarly treated: boom mikes are the *mic du jour*. However, exteriors

tend to offer a versatility of distance and depth that can get any auteur carried away. For this reason, wireless lavaliers begin to come into their own. From "walkie-talky" shots to long shots, you'll be picking up the dialog or monologue from your talent loud and clear. This, of course, is entirely unrealistic and will usually look ludicrous in an edit, but like your pictures, shoot clean and you can adapt in postproduction.

The sound precision—and the harshness that prevails—from a lavalier can be eased by relocating the mike on your talent's body. Lower down on the body will not only allow a little more ambience in, but pick up a bit more bass from the chest cavity. Work this out around their clothing too. A long shot may disguise the mike, but if you're using distance with a telephoto, you'll have to disguise the mike itself with the clothing. Colored tape works well for camouflage—and remember the psychology of the viewer—they'll be used to seeing lapel mikes used in the media, so find somewhere where they won't be looking. The brim of a hat will certainly take the mike away from any sound-disruptive jewelry…

This is one of the other issues with lavaliers. As sensitive as they are, they'll pick up the rustle of clothing or a gust of wind, or they'll lose your vocal audio if your talent

WIRELESS FOR SOUND
You may find that your crew members need wireless communication as well as your actors on a large location (above). If you're operating with multiple wireless systems using several channels, the Sennheiser 500 series includes a receiver with 16 frequency pre-sets to save some time.
Sennheiser's EK3052-U (above right) is a miniature stereo receiver designed for receiving signals from their own SR3054-U and SR3056-U transmitters. Using everyday alkaline batteries, it'll give you eight hours worth of use.

speaks while looking over their shoulder or leans over a prop.

The conclusion, then, is to use wireless as little as possible (and steer away from radio mikes entirely: they'll pick up all sorts of local frequencies that you really don't want on your soundtrack). If your long shot cuts to a close-up, re- mike with a cabled cardioid, which you should always carry as a back-up anyway.

The other essential is to monitor, monitor, monitor. Your sound op will need a good set of enclosed headphones, which will become as wise an investment as your choice of good mikes. Be a friend to your sound op, too: they can tell you all sorts of things they have heard when your talents have forgotten that they're still wearing their mikes…

RECORDING Your sound op—or yourself in audio mode—has a job on their hands to supply something that's going to be useful in the edit. If you're doing this properly, you will already have decided on open or enclosed headphones depending on your environment.

WIND-CHEATER

Invest in a muffler for your mike. Wind in your audio is intrusive and distracting. It will also keep your mike warm and cosy...even when you're not.

If you're recording to an external source rather than the camera, such as DAT or mini-disk, make sure that the recorder is set to the same frame rate as the camera. Even recording at the same frame rate can cause slight sync problems in the edit, so the more that can be done to eliminate problems from the start will only help later on. There is a huge digital audio debate, here—almost as big as digital audio versus analog audio. The recommendation is, though, always feed to the camera. The other setting that you need to sort out from the start for your recorder or in the menu of your digital video camera is that you're shooting at least 16-bit 48kHz of sound.

Digital video audio operates differently from analog in that your monitored mixer levels will peak at 0db. Anything over this will simply be distorted too much to be usable. Your peak should be set at –20db for reference: low levels of sound aren't a problem with digital audio if you can use a normalization process in your edit. This will boost your low levels as near to 0db as possible without your audio breaking up, and anything over 0db will be automatically clipped. Don't be concerned about recording at low levels as this is digital. Analog tape has an associated hiss and the reason it is less noticeable with a high signal is merely because it's being hidden by a high signal: it's still there. With digital, you're looking out for any hum more than anything else—and any feedback.

Because the 0db limit is such an issue with digital audio, it can be very difficult if you're operating the sound yourself to monitor your VU controls as well as your picture. Set your AGC and your audio will limit itself in-camera.

But other than the sound that you want, what other sound do you need?

When you're shooting your bars at the top of the tape, make sure you're getting your tone through too. It will provide good reference for the edit later.

Like images, some of the most useful tools in your edit will be some of the things that you didn't mean to shoot. That doesn't mean to say that you should keep recording no matter what, just to be safe. Your shooting ratio will only make capturing tedious. But there are things that you can deliberately shoot and make sense of them in the edit.

Take time out and record two minutes of atmosphere. If you're going feature-length with your program or most of your production is set within that location, record more: there's nothing worse than hearing the same owl in the background time and time again. Recording at 16-bit is only going to give you two tracks, but your edit will allow you countless layers, so find yourself a tape that you can dedicate to strengthening your audio. Record video at the same time, and even introduce the sound with yourself in shot. When you're spooling through tapes in the edit, visual references can really help you locate the right bit of audio. Keep your crew and cast quiet or just send them away. Atmosphere is ambience, not ambience with schoolgirl giggling.

If there are any particular visual references in the background to your shoot—rivers, cars, sheep—make a point of obtaining their isolated sound close-up. They can be very useful for adding to your sound mix when your master audio didn't pick them up. Sometimes hard-to-hear audio becomes annoying and a stronger signal is more appropriate—audiences can make their own audio-visual assumptions from your program even if you're boosting a sound that would naturally only be distant.

Remember that you will have audio tools in the edit and distortions of sounds can provide fantastic effects and ideal companions to transitions. Try to tune your ears to the sounds around you and think about how that sound could transform your images.

RAISED VOICES
Whether in an audio suite (right) or on set (below), raised mikes are not only practical for staying out of the way of a script or out of frame, but they also reduce bass from the chest and are ergonomic for your talent.

THE EDIT

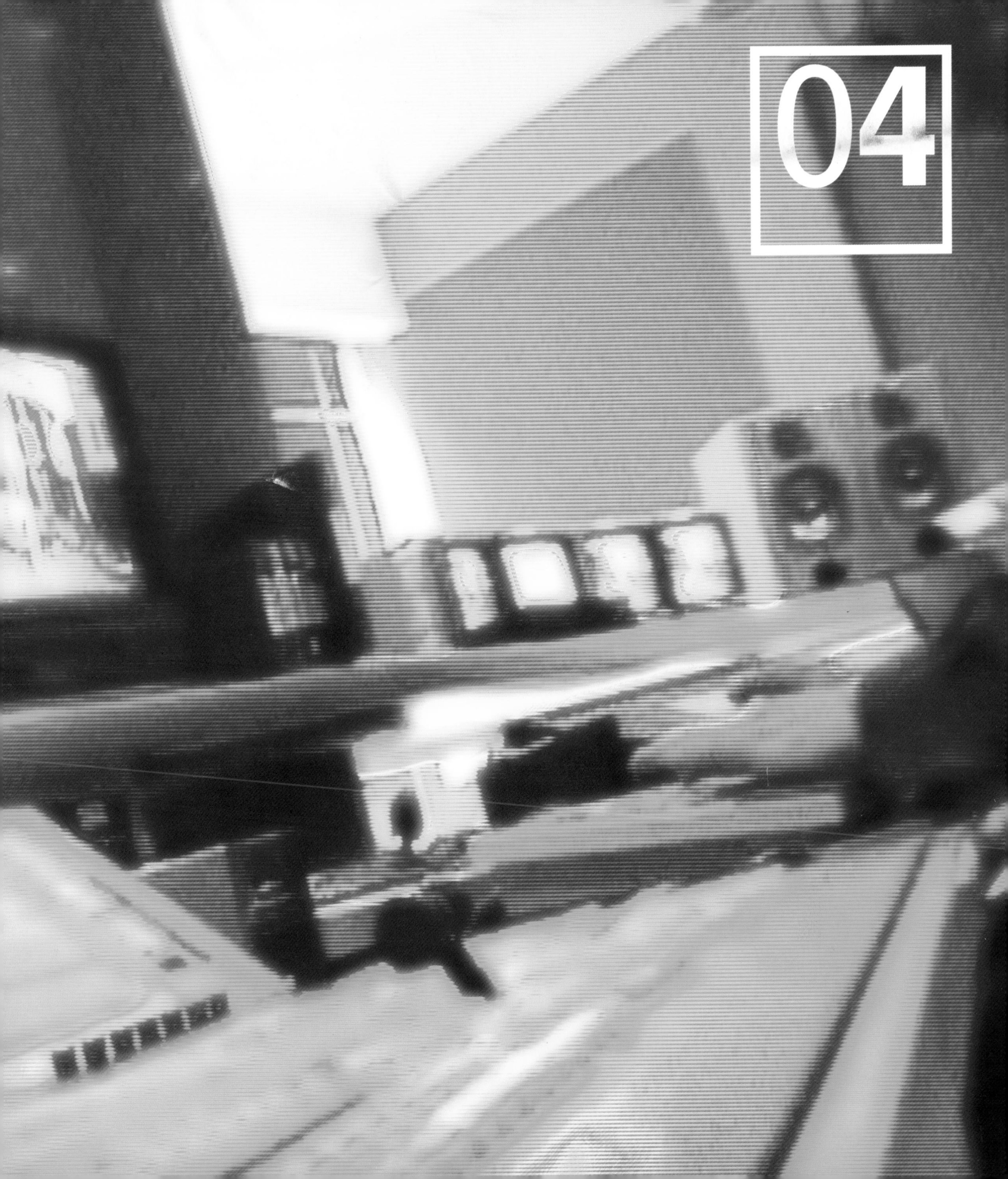
04

You've labored through preproduction, burnt off 40 pounds with your shoots, and now you're faced with the sweaty claustrophobia of your edit. Just like beginning to write a book, you're staring at a blank screen, wondering how you're going to fill it…

…Except you're not. Hopefully by this stage, you'll be excited about what you've shot and the possibilities of what you're going to do with it. The edit is the point at which understanding the language and the craft that you've learnt, both by textbook and through sheer experience, is about to pay off.

Video editing is a craft—and uses an entirely different language from that which you've learnt. It's artistic, it's technical, it's logical, and it requires a clear idea of what an audience understands from the moving image.

Just like the temperament required to act as producer, an editor works far better when they're patient, methodical, and organized. Even if this sounds like you, the auteur—and remember, you know the footage and you know how it should play—yes, even if it sounds like you, one of the most suitable attributes for an editor is that they are objective. More often than not, an experienced editor can do things for you that you never dreamed of—and guess what, they will work better than whatever it was that you had in mind…

Having said that, if you are starting out as the director and editor of your production, it's the perfect hard way to learn how you can direct and shoot better. What's more, your knowledge of the more technical aspects will enhance your future productions: indeed, knowledge is power.

PART 04. THE EDIT

CHAPTER ONE

THE ART OF VIDEO EDITING

A CLASSIC EDIT SETUP

... circa 1997... Edit suites can be as elaborate or as minimal as you wish—or as you pay for. This is a linear suite controlling Digital Betacam tapes and decks. For an effects-heavy broadcast-standard program, this may be the kind of environment you will still find yourself in.

There are a few fundamental facts to editing. The first is that it is a time-consuming process that requires full knowledge of what the final product is to be. If it is a glossy marketing tool, it will probably need to look esthetically pleasing or brand a product correctly; if it's a pop promo, it might need to be monochrome or degenerated; if it's a wedding video, do the clients want a cut of the whole shebang, the highlights, or a music-driven two-minuter?

The second thing that you will need to know is that no matter how you are structuring your time in the edit, the more you do and the more pressure that you're under, the worse the product is likely to be. If it gets to three in the morning and everything is taking an age to edit—let alone to render—go to bed. Cuts can look very different in the cold light of a new day, whether cruel or kind.

The third applies to auteurs and editors with clients. If you're being paid to have a moral obligation for a job, you have to either find a happy medium for decision-making, or a

Above: **A fast, mind-reading editor is going to be your best friend.**
Below: **Saving time—and money— in an edit suite even comes down to peripherals such as talkback systems with the VT department.**

healthy distance from your work. You're likely to find neither. The fact is that the clients may be paying or pressuring for your time and expertise, but they're also paying or pressuring for the product that they want. And television and cinema are a terrible thing: they have made pretty much everyone into a director.

Remember two more things here: if you are precious about the way that you have shot and cut a sequence which your client doesn't like, you must have a reason why you have shot and edited it like that. Be prepared to justify what you've done—it's good self-discipline even if there isn't someone in the edit who objects to your use of solarization or the font you've chosen for the title sequence.

The other thing to bear in mind is that if the client objects, ask them for a reason. If it's not an unreasonable request, then sometimes working within the client's set parameters can be a healthy challenge for a creative auteur.

Finally, be prepared to re-edit. If you're in charge of your own production, it's highly likely that you will never be completely satisfied. If you have clients, the project will probably have to go to higher bodies that will ask for changes. And if you are going Hollywood with your production, a test audience can even send you straight back to the storyboard…

trilogy

Eduardo Sanchez, Co-director, *The Blair Witch Project*

THE STORYBOARD

It's the only film that I've done that I haven't storyboarded, but on *Blair Witch* it would have been ridiculous because we wanted that spontaneity and improvisation on set. You still have to work out what you're going to do, though—what you're going to shoot and how you're going to shoot it. We had to work out all these details before we shot anything. The storyboard lets you concentrate on the logistic and technical aspects of the script and identify the challenges. I actually think it's very foolish not to do a storyboard. On location you should be spending your time on lighting, working out your characters' performances, sound problems—a million different other things.

THE LOCATION

With independent film-making you have to keep locations to a minimum because every time you move it costs a lot of money and a lot of time—and that costs a lot of money. Our challenge was to find some woods that looked as though they were in the middle of nowhere yet not be in the middle of nowhere, so the actors didn't get lost and we could get camera batteries and supplies to them.

THE SHOOT

It must be one of the only films where the actors didn't read the script before the shoot or while we were out there shooting. We gave the actors three different sets of notes so they had no idea what to expect from each other—it created real, genuine moments. That was our thing about making this movie—we didn't want it to be like a hoax, but the experience that we had as kids where it was 100% real—like those old Bigfoot documentaries. The video was integral—the shaky camerawork that you're used to seeing on *The World's Funniest Video Show*. We used every trick in the book to make it absolutely real, including making them shoot the whole damn movie.

THE SOUND

We were confident about the images because we had three people in the woods just shooting it, but the big problem was the sound. It had to seem like they were really out there—sometimes the sound is too low, sometimes it's too high, sometimes they're too close to the mic. You've got to think about sound issues—when the sound is horrible, it makes an indie film look like an indie film. The sound for *Blair Witch* was simple: Mike Williams—who played the sound guy—took out a DAT recorder to record all the sync sound stuff from Heather, who had a 16mm camera. So we used that, but most of the sound came from the low-end Hi-8 RCA video camera mikes. Basically there was just the cutting of the dialog from that audio track and then the sound mixers added background tracks and sound effects of trees snapping that made the film a whole lot better than we'd edited it. The majority of the dialog is said off-screen—which is very rare—so it was easy to chop and splice audio. Renting a proper sound mixer on set for your indie film is essential—if you can somehow make your film sound great, you're way ahead of the game.

THE EDIT

There are a million different questions you have to answer before you shoot a frame of film. Will it be non-linear? What decks are you gonna use? What editing system? How much drive space will you need? And crucially, what format is this movie going to end up on? We edited *Blair Witch* first on an Avid and then on a Media 100. We'll use Final Cut Pro for the next film we're planning, but pretty much any desktop system will do the job for you now. What we did on *Blair* was transfer the Hi-8 to Beta SP; batch capture it to Media 100, and then edit out to DigiBeta before transferring to 35mm. We used Hi-8 because this was supposed to have been shot in 1994, but Hi-8 has no timecode, which meant that there was no way to automatically sync, so we had to manually replace everything back into the Beta SP.

THE UPSHOT

The great thing about this kind of non-studio independent film-making is that you can do anything you want. This is where the artistic jumps will take place—nobody in Hollywood would have made *Blair Witch*. This is the level where it's going to happen. It's not going to happen out of LA.

BASIC EDITING TECHNIQUES Offline editing is the practice of any non-linear edit undertaken with images at around 30% picture quality, making it quicker to manipulate and render pictures. Storage capacity on computers can force an offline too when just four minutes of DV at best quality consume 1Gb of hard disk space—and offline can become absolutely essential when the program (duration and quantity of captured clips) is long.

An offline is the process of making edit decisions and the tangible product of the edit is an EDL—an edit decision list. This list contains all the in and out timecode points in the right order, which is then taken into the online suite. Onlines can either be linear or non-linear and the information from the EDL results in the program being auto-conformed using the original source tapes, this time at 100% picture quality. It will also render any effects, transitions, and text to complete your finished production.

The processing speed and disk space of computers now, though, is beginning to change this tradition of edits, and it can often be cheaper and quicker to capture at 100% picture quality from the get-go. It certainly makes editing a more enjoyable and rewarding experience.

If you have the capabilities (or budget) of working at 100% picture quality, your entire process will be in online. You will still be making edit decisions, though, and the way to confront your blank timeline is as a rough cut. This rough cut is likely to have few effects, maybe a couple of experiments in colorization, little text or graphics, and a general bagginess to all shots included. It's the first real draft of your program (bar your capture selection process) and its fundamental purpose is to put all the shots that you want to use from all your tapes into roughly the right order.

This remains the best way to begin any edit. A rough cut will let you see exactly what you've got to play with—and exactly which shots it looks like you're missing. And as this is at such an early stage, it gives you a chance to go and shoot anything that it looks like you're going to need…

Your rough cut will be the broadstrokes and the base for your program to build on, which is why it's a good idea to leave your shots long on your timeline. You'll be cutting into it, chopping it around—and if you're going to be adding some transitions, you'll need excess frames at the top and bottom of each of your shots.

Once you've got everything in place, you'll get an idea of what length and type of program you're really dealing with. It's going to help your composer, your script, your imagination. With desktop non-linear editing, your rough cut will be everything you do up until your final tweaking of your program.

If you are going into online after your offline edit, your computer should indicate which tapes are required at which point from the information on the EDL. Any timecode complications that arise—i.e., if the computer doesn't understand the reference—are likely to be either from clips with matching timecode or from a timecode break in your original source tape. Sometimes these can be a real headscratcher—especially if you have a lot of tapes. Hopefully, though, you'll have watched the whole damn thing so many times that you'll know exactly which shot slots in where…

THE TROUBLE WITH OFFLINES

Offlines are good for clients, and clients are notoriously bad with offlines. If you're working at 30% resolution (far right), there's still another 70% of picture and effects for them to criticize later (right).

SOFTWARE INSTALLATION

SOFTWARE INSTALLATION If you're confident enough to have built a PC from scratch, you'll be confident enough to install your software tailored to your own requirements. If you didn't go along the separate component path, and either bought a Mac or PC from a store, you'll probably have a whole load of things bundled onto it that you don't need, and a stack of software with it that you don't want. If you bought a machine tailor-made for your requirements, you're likely to have everything loaded and ready to go.

If you are loading up your own software, it's a good idea to register with manufacturers you trust for software that you value. New versions, drivers, and better codecs are often available and they are likely to pass you by unless you're reminded online.

Once you are up and running and ready to dive into your empty timeline, start up the edit software and make sure that your device is being recognized—i.e., that your digital video camera is saying hello via your FireWire or breakout box. If you're not told otherwise, you should end up with your first settings screen where you can find out for sure.

If your edit software is compatible with your videocard, it should refer to it as a preset option for capture either for DV, analog, or both. This is the first option that you need to activate in order that you can benefit from your chosen videocard's hard and software. Okaying a box is usually the method to route through the card, which should open up a new project in your edit software.

And there you are, salivating to start capturing—but it's the project settings that you need to stop off at first. These will predetermine how your production will be edited.

Project settings for an edit are all reasonably logical, and your capture card is likely to choose a lot of its own default settings, which means that you might not have to think about it at all. If it doesn't do this automatically, find the card's recommended settings online or in accompanying literature. Here, though, are a few of the less obvious quirks among the details that might aid any decisions that you might have to make:

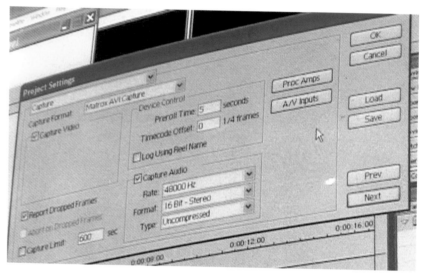

DROP-FRAME TIMECODE

If NTSC is the format to your edit, you should have a choice of 30fps drop-frame timecode or non drop-frame. Because the frame rate for NTSC is actually 29.97fps, drop-frame timecode allows for the first two frames of each second (i.e., :00 and :01) to be dropped from your timecode. For every hour, 3.6 seconds are thereby lost from your program to make it broadcast standard. What you have to remember is that this is merely for editing. You are not losing the first two frames of image—and the only reason for selecting it is if your program is destined for broadcast.

PIXEL ASPECT RATIO

Your pixels already exist on your digital videotape. Therefore, this setting should always be set referring back to the ratio you shot your footage—not as to how you would like your program to finally be seen.

SETTING STANDARDS

Always revisit your settings. Default options can kick in when you expect them—and want them—least.

PROCESSOR AMPLIFIER

Whether or not you feel like changing the settings on your processor amplifier depends on your perfectionism. Of course, you really shouldn't need to change any setting on your processor amplifier unless the lighting on your shoot or the settings you chose were way off, in which case your purism is somewhat questionable, if not sullied. Using the processor amp allows for changes in hue, saturation, contrast, and brightness during capture. The benefit of tweaking at this stage is that you are messing with the signal and not (in your edit effects) with the pixels.

These are all particulars for your project itself. Your edit preferences can be found in another menu and you'll need to tweak them to suit you and the computer you've chosen.

Most of the edit preferences are straightforward tickbox options. Certain preferences like auto-save require a little bit of contemplation: you want it pretty regularly (computers crash; projects are lost), but you don't want it to constantly interfere with your rendering. The most important setting is for your scratch disks. This is the area of your hard disk where you want the edit software to make space for capture and preview of files. Because video clips are large, you will need to make sure that the disk is capable of their temporary storage. For best performance, it is advisable that your audio and video previews are assigned to a different drive than that for your captured movies in the likelihood that you are editing with large files.

INTERLEAVE

This is the frequency at which you let your RAM process audio for every frame of video on your timeline. The lower the value of interleave, the longer the audio segments stored—and the more RAM you'll need. If you hear your audio breaking up, it tends to be because your setting is too low.

ENHANCE RATE CONVERSION

Set this to "off" while you're editing unless your project is strictly audio-based. This toggle refers to your audio sampling during playback. While working with the timeline, a better sampling rate will just slow you down, so don't change this to a better quality until the final render or export of your program.

LOGARITHMIC AUDIO FADES

The logarithms that this setting applies to your audio make increases or decreases of gain smoother to the human ear—again, at the cost of processing time.

FIELDS

Like your ratio, your method of scanning is dependent on how you shot your footage. It's likely to be interlaced on digital video, unless you specifically shot with a progressive scan setting. If your rushes are interlaced, you need a "lower fields first" setting in your edit to preserve smoothness of motion. If your rushes aren't interlaced, choose "no fields." "Upper field first" is a setting that tends to be used more for importing analog footage or for particular ratios dictated by your videocard. Again, check for certainty with the manufacturer's recommendation.

LISTEN WITH FERVOR
Don't forget that your audio is always there somewhere, waiting to be tended to. It has almost as much versatility on your timeline as your pictures and likes to be played with occasionally...

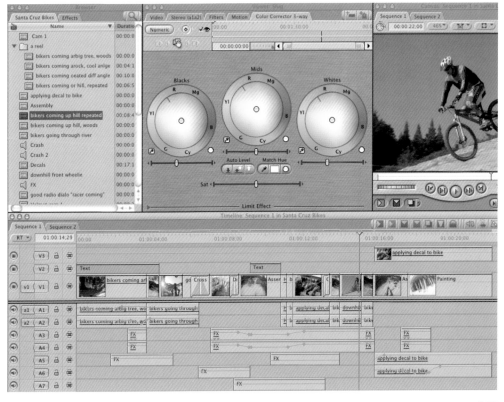

IMPORTING FOOTAGE Once you've got an empty timeline staring ominously back at you, you'll need some pictures to hang on it. Capturing from digital video is made extraordinarily easy, thanks to FireWire, timecode, your device controller, keyboard shortcuts, and a computer that thinks it knows what you're trying to do.

Your computer's memory, the length of your program or your client's tendency to demand changes at inappropriate moments will now in turn demand of you whether you are going to be working online or offline. Make your decision wisely: exporting off sections of your program is just as tedious as the process of conforming…

TIME TO START CAPTURING

Batch capture is for all you professional shotlisters out there who logged every shot or take that you wanted from your tapes. It lets you automatically capture everything you need and nothing you don't by simply typing in every in and out timecode reference. It sounds tedious, but a five-minute typing session will save you from spooling, rewinding, pausing, umming, and ahhing through an hour-long tape.

Movie capture, on the other hand, lets you do precisely that—with a little versatility. You can type in timecode if you really want to be frame-exact, but it's always better to leave shots baggy to enable transitions and have pre-captured cutaways at your fingertips in the edit. To do this, record and escape will take the chunks you want. The flexibility that higher-end users will have is the capacity to log in this screen for batch capture, and to make additional reference text comments on the clip.

Animation or stop-motion capture will collect a series of stills for you, either from your connected digital video camera or an associated image capturer such as a digital stills camera.

Audio capture is to be used to take any live audio into the edit with a microphone, such as a voice-over. Doing it this way is a bit hokey. Using separate audio software is more of a recommendation for all of its tweaking properties when recording live audio. It is a hard job to control the pops, atmosphere, and hum in an edit environment. It's an easy one using a dedicated tool such as Acid or Pro Tools with clippers and cleaners, saving it off and importing it into your edit.

Because of the different compression formats of video clips (i.e., MPEG, AVI, MOV), you'll have to tell your computer how you would like your clips captured. Your videocard will have its own way of dealing with this information through the capture options on the project settings menu. Your options here will involve certain allowances via the card, and certain allowances or prohibitions without it. If you are faced with a dialog box informing you of a device control recognition problem, check that your driver is present and correct in your device control menu. The best advice here is to stick with the options available through the card that you specifically bought for the job. If you're still having problems, there may be dreaded compatibility issues, which can be confirmed through many an online video forum or through your videocard's manufacturers. If they can be fixed, it's often by cheating the computer. If they can't, you can only blame your videocard research…

When capturing any clip, give it a name that you're going to recognize, and one that differentiates it from any other clip. If it's another version, or the clip is your safety shot, label it the same with a "002" or "/safety" extension. Your clips will usually first be laid out alphabetically by their text names, not chronologically, and it makes sense that you want two of the same shot next to each other to avoid tiresome scrolling and confusion. Be logical. Imagine another editor taking your place: how would they make sense of what you've captured?

Try to keep your clips in view as thumbnails as well as text—it helps no end. For each scene or each theme within your anticipated finished program, create a new bin to put the clips in—and rename it to suit. Any kind of methodical separation can only help once your eyes begin to glaze over fourteen hours into the edit. A bin works just like any storage file in a computer system, devoted to one particular item or items for easy retrieval.

As mentioned, FireWire tends to take precedence at another device's expense, so if you are capturing from multiple sources, disconnect it if you want, say, DAT to plug-and-play for preview and capture. This is particularly important for two FireWire inputs. For analog input, you will have to change the settings for your project, which will usually start right back in the load screen to your project.

During capture, a dialog box will tell you how many frames—if any—you've dropped. This is really an indication of the power of your system, the frames dropped being those that have missed being encoded. If you are experiencing a lot, try a different codec. Certain compressors are extremely good and use a lot of processing power (DivX); others use less complicated algorithms that don't have a high compression ratio and therefore don't put your processor to task as much (Indeo). If you're finding that it's only one source tape that's causing you problems, it may well be due to an unstable recording speed during your shoot. You might find a patch

iLOVE iLINK
Your iLINK or FireWire output will become your new best buddy when you come to capture clips.

online that will help you or simply keep your captured clips short.

This leads to another issue: the length of clips. Longer clips captured are likely to fragment your hard drive and slow your machine down. Shorter clips, although filling up your bins with textual brain-damaging information for yourself, won't bog down your processor so much. Editing also becomes a lot quicker once you can simply remove a used clip from your bin, rather than keep a longer one there because there's a part of it that you haven't used. It's actually more satisfying to eliminate clips from your enquiry as you progress through the edit.

If you already have clips on your drive or on CD or DVD that you want to use, which you've taken across from another machine or demo templates (yuk) that your software has taken liberties to install, then you will need to import the clips. Again, your computer will make this easy for you and copy whichever file you select to any bin that you option.

And when you have exhausted your source tapes, it really is about time you began to reap the rewards of all your effort. About time, that is, to edit.

WORKING WITH A TIMELINE AND SAVING
The timeline of any edit software is one thing that you will become awfully familiar with. By the end of an edit, you will probably know the layout of those organized blocks as well as you know the cut itself.

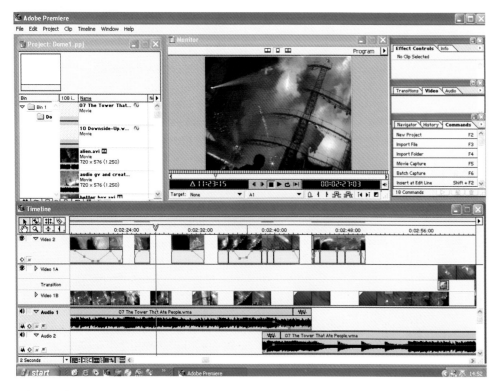

The timeline is easiest used down at the bottom of the screen with your on-screen monitor somewhere above. Timelines are usually found here as an emulation of any computer operating system, but click and drag all your clips, FX, and navigation boxes to where you feel most comfortable and practical—it is, after all, going to be a long ride…

Starting at the top of your timeline box, you'll find the work area slider, which will help you focus on areas that require rendering. Directly below it is the play indicator, which will tell you at precisely which point you are monitoring. As a shortcut, use your space bar to start and stop play (or capture).

WHAT A DRAG

It's not just clips and transitions that are dragged into the timeline. Any change you make to a clip that's been placed there needs to be dragged onto the clip itself. The amount of control you have over the pre-rendered effect (color balance, contrast, etc) will depend on the quality of your edit software. There should be no limit to the number of effects that you can layer onto your clip, but use your render preview and preview tracks to save time undoing and re-rendering.

The timeline itself may begin at 00:00:00:00, but this doesn't mean that you have to start there. Allow room for maneuver at the beginning of your edit. Remember that the rendering process can be slow and software packages will render every field to the progress of the timeline. Just moving your cut forward or back a second can invite the computer to re-render the whole show again. Anticipate what you might need at the beginning of an edit, bearing in mind that an audience will need at least three seconds for any text or any image. Are they going to fade up? How long will your fade or transition be? This may seem like an obvious point, but it's worth bearing in mind as most editors or directors tend to start cutting a scene or part of a program that they feel most comfortable with to get things going. And some sections may well have not yet been shot.

Timelines are broken up to make them look complicated but easier to work with. By understanding the reasoning behind each track, you will be able to get the best out of your software. You'll probably find that your timeline is topped with the track Video 2. This doesn't mean that the track is inferior to your Video 1 tracks—on the contrary, the higher placed the track on your timeline, the more control it has to override the others. Most semi and professional editing software will have many inactivated video and audio tracks available to it. To find them, simply right- or double-click on a track and add either another video or audio track. Try this with Adobe Premiere and you'll find an additional 96 tracks each for video and audio.

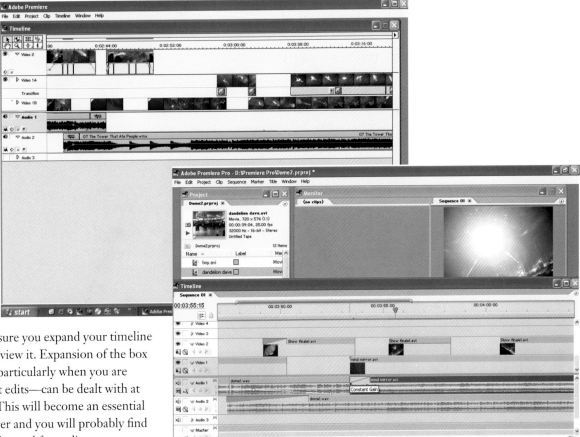

Once you've added a track, make sure you expand your timeline box in order that you can actually view it. Expansion of the box to magnify what you're cutting—particularly when you are dealing with transitions over short edits—can be dealt with at the bottom left of your timeline. This will become an essential tool for you once your edit is longer and you will probably find about 100 additional tracks for video and for audio.

The audio tracks function slightly differently. Instead of superseding each other, whatever is placed there on any audio track will be played.

A AND B ROLL

A and B roll is a term originally used for film. It refers to the fact that if you want to operate a transition which is anything other than a cut, you'll need two rolls of film. The reason for this is that you need to overlap the footage to let you operate a simple physical mix between the two rolls.

Video bastardized this term slightly, using it to distinguish two different tracks that could visually represent the "checkerboard" look. Fundamentally, the way A and B works is for track A to take the body of the edit until a transition is placed on the transition track to carry into an overlapped clip placed on track B. If there is then a transition from B, it can be dropped onto the transition track to move back to using the A track.

The rest of the video and audio tracks are used for overlay, mixing through effects, and for cutaways if you are not razoring away at your master clip on the A or B track.

What would you do without A and B roll? The answer is that you'd work simply with Video Tracks 1 to whatever, with no As or Bs—and no transition track. Instead, the

THE TIMELINES ARE A-CHANGIN

Now you've learnt your A and B...it's time to unlearn... Premiere 6.5 (top) works with A/B roll with a transition line in between. Premiere Pro (above) simply lets transitions be placed and stretched onto either clip for tweaking. Audio, too, in Pro lets transitions be applied between clips as well as the usual rubber band manipulation.

transition itself is dragged onto one of the clips just like any effect. Unlike an effect, though, the transition needs to be applied to the end of the first clip, or the beginning of the second. Adjusting its length or settings is a question of either dragging or right-clicking or using keyframes. And it is exactly the same with audio.

As digital video continues to stamp its mark, there will be fewer "film" hand-me-downs—certainly as the illustrated difference here between Premiere 6.5 and Premiere Pro shows. Digital video works with copies of files of 0s and 1s and, as such, the non-A and B roll method alludes to the fact that you can have as many as you want on as many different tracks in an instant—rather than splicing precious, expensive, physical film.

Remember the priorities of the tracks, be logical with your clip and transition placement and save, save, save…

A PRACTICAL GUIDE TO EDITING
In the world of linear editing, there's very little room to maneuver when editing. Any changes made to analog—or even onto digital—tape has to be undertaken as an assembly edit. This is the basic laying down of shots chronologically and eating into them with the next shot as a cut. A transition required A and B roll playing and the transition itself marked at the correct in and out points to be recorded onto the record deck.

The implications of editing like this ensured that any changes that had to be made to a program were either applied to the master edit as an assembly insert edit or else required the whole program to be laid off onto another tape to allow cutting between the two masters and any new source tapes.

This was always a problem with analog tape, not only losing another generation of quality, but disrupting the existing timecode.

Non-linear editing gave birth to a freedom that had never been experienced. The idea that clips lived virtually on a hard drive that could be played around with infinitum before finally playing out to a master was something that saved the day. Editing with NLE means that assembly edits are out with the dinosaurs and insert editing can be conducted in a number of ways.

Because editing virtual clips is so versatile, there are four different types of insert editing—the ripple, the roll, the slide, and the slip. All of these affect your clips on the timeline and effect the clips specifically on either side of your insert edit. Here's how:

ON THE BUSES
While an effects bus in a professional edit looks complex, it actually does little more than a solid semipro effects card and edit application on a desktop NLE. What this setup does allow for, though, is accurate pre-roll monitoring and true picture monitoring output. The Matrox Parhelia card can help you do this on your desktop with a separate broadcast monitor, giving full-screen output and monitoring—particularly useful for scrutinizing graphics and effects resolution.

■ Don't waste time using the monitor edit option: it is easier to drag than clip.

■ Dedicate one bin to used clips, and get into the habit of dragging them there once you've placed them on the timeline.

■ Right-click on your clips and transitions for quick options.

■ If you're working for broadcast, make sure the monitor window is showing correct safety margins.

■ Use your keyboard arrows to exact your edit marker.

■ Even if you're not using sync sound, lock your video and audio for reference and so that you don't get your timeline littered with odd bits of leftover sound.

■ If you are cutting to a soundtrack, expand the audio track and let the visual image guide your rhythm.

■ Expand your time zoom when dragging clips and tighten it down when editing.

■ Double-click on a clip to view it at full-screen resolution.

■ Lock tracks and clips that you're not working on or that you're happy with to save yourself some tiresome undoing and re-rendering.

■ Decisions made by the computer to re-render can be made for all sorts of obscure reasons—hiding, then viewing your shy tracks can be just one of them. Don't change your settings (codec, resolution, frame rate) and options halfway through a project: you risk losing your media altogether.

■ Use markers for specific video points for precision audio sync. They can sometimes be used, too, to indicate chapters when burning to DVD.

■ Gang your monitors to create a preview monitor of how your edit will look in place without actually undertaking it. This can be a very useful device, particularly with complicated edits.

■ Without trying to spoil your fun, monitor the progress of your edit on occasion through your print to video option. This full-screen version of your program in progress will give you an idea of where any problems lie.

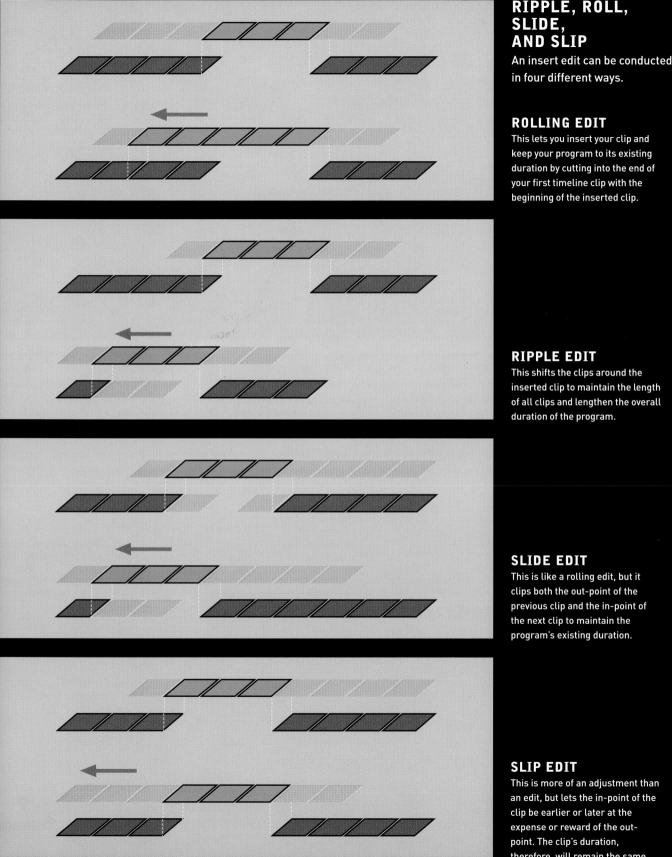

RIPPLE, ROLL, SLIDE, AND SLIP

An insert edit can be conducted in four different ways.

ROLLING EDIT

This lets you insert your clip and keep your program to its existing duration by cutting into the end of your first timeline clip with the beginning of the inserted clip.

RIPPLE EDIT

This shifts the clips around the inserted clip to maintain the length of all clips and lengthen the overall duration of the program.

SLIDE EDIT

This is like a rolling edit, but it clips both the out-point of the previous clip and the in-point of the next clip to maintain the program's existing duration.

SLIP EDIT

This is more of an adjustment than an edit, but lets the in-point of the clip be earlier or later at the expense or reward of the out-point. The clip's duration, therefore, will remain the same

FILM EFFECT Film Effect is a curious thing. You've shot on digital video, you're editing on a digital video NLE, yet you want your video to look like film. Film smacks of quality, of expense, of control of light and depth of focus. It implies money—and yet its analog, tactile image is subject to all sorts of imperfections.

This is where digital comes in. If the image from a digital video camera is as good a representation of reality as it gets with a high sample and frame-rate, turning it back into the "look" of film will keep the quality and the control while gaining all the implications of a production shot on film.

The "look" of film is based on three major factors: frame rate, light, and scanning. The film stock runs past the lens, sandwiched on the other side with a shutter that is letting light in 24 times every second. This exposes the film with 24 frames per second. It is, in effect, an animation of photographs. It is becoming more and more common for digital video cameras to have the option of running at 24fps. What this means digitally is that the shutter is allowing the light to reach the CCDs 24 times a second.

With regard to light, film has a wide dynamic range that allows detail in both black shadow and bright light—all within the same frame. Digital video, on the other hand, is optimized to lift light no matter what the cost to detail. New digital video cameras that have taken 24fps on board can now have gamma correction devices that digitally emulate a wider dynamic range.

The shutter speed of film, creating an animation of analog motion, is defeated digitally by interlaced scanning, which blurs the action. Progressive scanning, by taking each half of the image as a whole (rather than each other line), has the ability to create more of a filmic look.

FAKING IT
This film effect was created by applying a preset sixties color wash and a horizontal jitter, razoring the clips at random points and altering the speed slightly for each section, before finally rendering Quicktime's hair and noise lightly over it. The effect is not the classic old-time sepia look, but a smoother Super 8 film effect.

To create your own film effect and up your production values within your edit software without a 24fps camera is, ironically, a matter of corrupting your image. This concerns the addition of dust and scratches, sepia, or black-and-white tint, soft borders, and projector jitter through your effects palette. If you're feeling bold, you can create frame jumps with non-interpolated keyframing, luma up your dust and scratches to burn, and alpha key uneven light distribution.

Alternatively, if you want a cleaner look—and this works truer with PAL's 25fps—deinterlace your video in the edit to get your 50 fields down to 25. Your horrible picture now needs to be interpolated or have a single-pixel motion blur in a vertical direction. Resharpen your image with your effects tools and render up with any additional colorization that you might need.

INTERVIEW
Amrit Bharry, Editor

"Every decision I used to make in linear was pretty much final. Over the past six years, non-linear systems have completely changed my job creatively. A lot of shooting these days involves just catching what you can, working off the cuff, and non-linear lets me keep moving those blocks of captured footage around to try to give the director what they want. If they've got a narrative, it's very easy to put it into place in big chunks and then move them around to make it more interesting and to the satisfaction of the client.

I work like a kind of counselor and even if the director knows what they want to do, they don't necessarily know if the way they want to do it is a good way or a bad way. It's my job to help them achieve their goal and understand what they're trying to do. It may sound a bit bizarre, but I tend to study their body language and try to keep eye contact to an absolute minimum because I'm constantly listening to the tone of their voice to gauge how they're feeling toward the edit. I can change things with non-linear in a matter of seconds and give them something else, which is the beauty of the non-linear environment. Sensing the client's mood and understanding their personality dictates to me the right kind of shots to use.

What is useful is to look at what they might think would end up on the cutting room floor. Sometimes what they think is useless is something that I can combine with their edit to create tension and excitement and draw the viewer in rather than using the standard wide shots and close-ups. Non-linear also lets me use DVE effects so that I can blow up shots and cut in tighter, or create camera moves out of static shots. Transitions help to make things interesting, but sometimes a cut has more impact.

If a director comes in with static shots and wants something effective, I might turn to audio to create that effect. If they want excitement from their rigid footage, I might add jungle music for a violent feel—or create a completely different mood by adding classical music.

If they've got a script, I'll read it and work with it on paper and try to visualize it before I start. Again, understanding their ideas helps in such a forced, close environment and allows me to cut something that perhaps they didn't think of or didn't realise could be done."

STORAGE We're back to the facts: for every 4.4 minutes of DV captured, you're going to need 1Gb of hard disk space. Even if this doesn't sound like too much of a deal for your monster of a machine, get a few projects down the line and you might want to reconsider.

STICK WITH IT
Sony's 1Gb memory stick—a fraction of the size but with more memory than a conventional DVD.

Organization will help by deleting files hanging around that you don't want and compressing and burning off those that you want in the future. The problem will always be that these files are still relatively huge and, if you have a lot of them, you will also have a lot of CD-ROMs or DVDs gathering dust.

What you really want is some kind of storage dedicated to clips that you don't want to have to find again from your digital video rushes.

Consider, also, the inherent computer issues of the 2Gb clip limit. There are two versions of an AVI: 1.0 is at a 32-bit range of values and is limited to a 2Gb file size; 2.0 is at a 64-bit range of values and is "limited" to an 18 billion Gb file size. The file size is directly related to the length of your clip. If you are running with AVI 1.0, then you can expect your longest clip to be no longer than nine minutes before you are working with invisible edits.

What you need is a storage connection dedicated to capturing your lengthy clips.

External hard drives aren't a new invention. They are now just smaller in size, larger in capacity, are much more affordable, and have instant FireWire connections. The smaller

they are (without forsaking disk space), the more their potential can be realized. They can instantly play clips or a product back to a client on their computer, they can be taken to an edit suite to download your clips there and then, and you can tout your finished program around in it. What's more, they're also cross-platform. All the receiving computer will need is a FireWire (or USB2) connection.

If you are thinking of buying external storage, it is important to work out how much space you will need—and how many drives. The reason this can be significant is that it's all very well having one 120Gb external drive full of your favorite clips, but if there's a technical or criminal problem, or if you have lent it to an editor to pull off a few clips, you've got nothing to work with—clips or drive.

The alternative is to buy a number of smaller drives for your money. A RAID system (Redundant Array of Independent [or Inexpensive] Disks) lets you connect two or more external drives to operate as one separate and logical unit from your desktop's hard drive. The good thing about a RAID is that it is extremely resistant against data loss and can always be accessed if your hard drive should ever fail. It also increases your CPU's performance—something that only helps you in the edit.

If you do buy an external hard drive, shop around. As well as incompatibilities (LaCie won't work with Sony Vaio), you should be looking for healthy disk read and writing speeds.

External drives can also offer the service of recording directly from your camera on set or location at the same time as your tape. Memory sticks are beginning to do exactly the same job. They provide chewing gum stick-sized external storage geared more toward MPEG-senders than video-makers due to their lower storage capacity. Sony are flying the flag with better capacity and data speeds, but they are expensive and perhaps rather more suited for audio.

Archiving is an important part of digital video process and can save you in times of crisis. It's worth investing in.

Above: **The LaCie Databank.**
Left: **A LaCie RAID system.**
Below: **LaCie's USB connectable pocket hard drive.**

A RENDER-FREE WORLD
From really time-consuming, to a
consumer using realtime... The
NLE once astounded the industry
by trimming down the physical
layout of an edit suite. Now it's
downsizing again—in time.
Patience used to be a virtue, but
there is no time for virtue in this
industry...Welcome to the
realtime real world.

RENDERING AND REALTIME
Bigger, better, faster, shorter... Humans can be terrible creatures when it comes to wanting more. Now rendering is the bugbear of the NLE world, and realtime the buzzword *du jour*.

The actual procedure for rendering is for your CPU to calculate or recalculate any changes that you make to your clips on the timeline. Those clips are compressed, digital information stored in your hard drive. Every clip that you import is copied from this original source and location to your temporary scratch disk for preview. The clip, in effect, is as virtual as it gets.

The faster your CPU, the quicker it takes to process the clip, any effect, or transition on your timeline.

The speed that the CPU takes, though, is usually longer than it would take to simply play that clip through on the timeline, something that has generally become frustrating to editors. The introduction of realtime into NLE suites has speeded up this time while still using the same fast CPUs.

The time required by your system to respond to the changes in your clip is called latency. Realtime operates by speeding up the latency through the videocard. How it works is not by speeding up the CPU, but by applying the complex calculations of that effect or transition to your clip's digital information. This gives your clip new values on the timeline—i.e., the clip with the effect or transition.

Videocards, however clever, can contain only a certain amount of these pre-calculated calculations—especially the infinite combinations of the calculations together. For this reason most cards contain only a certain amount of the difficult math compared with the number of effects and transition algorithms that it wants to offer a user. The calculations that haven't been stored are handed over to the CPU for application onto the clip.

Videocards find new ways of storing more and more information, and more intricate sums—at a price. Matrox and Canopus are leading the market in quality realtime videocards that can put a lot of pleasure back into your edit, especially in effects-laden projects.

Still, these calculations are being applied to your virtual preview clips—not to your final exported program. When you do come to export, you will have to render your clips, effects,

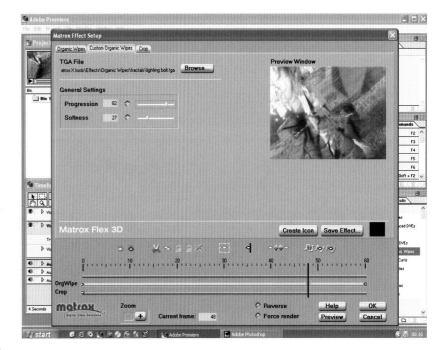

and transitions traditionally, and that usually means a lengthy latency—although, again, rendering is much quicker with a faster CPU.

Previews of changes to your clips, with effects and transitions are all-important, though, especially if you've got a client in the edit who can't see why you are taking so long, or hasn't the time to hang around themselves.

Some of the videocards also assist your edit software's standard effects and transitions in render-time, notably Matrox's RT.X100 Xtreme working with Premiere.

The question is whether rendering will eventually become a thing of the past. And the answer is...
...that'd be nice.

FLEXING MUSCLES
Matrox's RT.X100 Xtreme's customization of effects and transitions in realtime means experimentation at no cost of render time.

04.02

Just as you are concentrating on cutting and adding ornate transitions to your production, you realize that there's a whole load of strange audio coming through from beneath the timeline.

Your movie clips will be, by default, automatically linked to your audio WAV files. And the WAVs are quietly following everything that you do with your images down below in the audio tracks. This can cause all sorts of chaos if you are not monitoring those tracks properly.

Like your images, a right-click either on your audio file, or on the audio track, will give you all the options you need. And like images, your audio files can be dealt with using audio effects and transitions from your edit and videocard software menus. How you work with audio is not only a matter of choice, it also depends entirely on the nature of your production. The first, and most important, thing is to always make sure that you're

working at CD quality—that is, 16-bit 48KHz sound. If you're going to downsize your files, do it at your final mastering stage. Audio quality can always be reduced, not enhanced.

Audio in your NLE will usually exist in chunks of WAVs, or AIFFs for the Mac. If you expand your audio track, the sound linked to each of your AVIs will be visually represented as a wave (or as Rorschach ink blot tests if you find yourself thinking about sex during your edit). If you double-click on your audio, you will be able to see it represented in greater detail, letting you visually and sonically find any tiny part of your audio using your keyboard arrow keys.

Navigationally, you will most likely have an audio mixer that you can bring to the desktop. The information that this gives you is merely feedback from the audio settings that you opened your project with. Keep this in vision whenever you are tweaking your sound to your pictures. By default, your upper dynamic range is set to 0Db—keeping it under 0Db is one of your main tasks during editing. If you've got a weak sound, raise your gain up to 0Db, but never go over this or the distortion will ruin your production. If you've got a really weak sound from your shoot, try copying it to two different audio tracks and boost both.

PART 04. THE EDIT

CHAPTER TWO

AUDIO

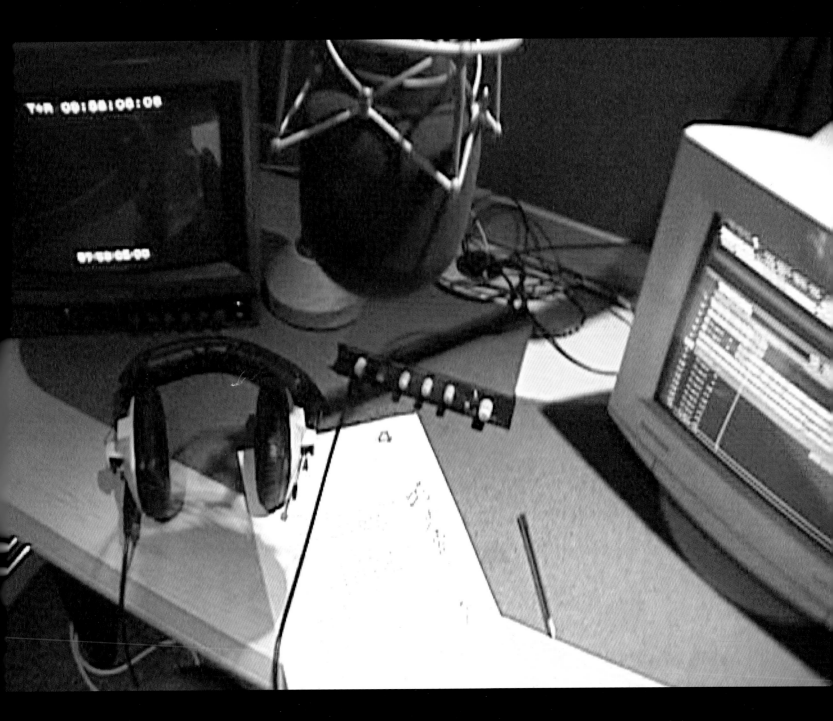

**EVERYTHING BUT THE GIRL
AND THE KITCHEN SINK**
An efficient and pared audio booth
with everything a voice-over could
ever need...but don't forget a glass
of water...

Any automated setting within your audio mixer lets you adjust the levels and balance of your audio signal, listen to it, and apply it to the clip while listening to it in realtime. This, however, will give you a level and balance for the whole of the clip. If you need to adjust within the clip itself, either cut it up and use the audio mixer to make separate part of the clip (if you're peaking in one section and low in the rest) or use your rubber band feature.

Rubber bands, while useful with tweaking your video effects, become nigh on essential with audio. Aside from using them with applied audio effects, their importance comes into their own when creating seamless video. Just as the eye notices changes in luminance more readily than chrominance, the ear is more attuned to changes in difference of sound rather than levels of sound. In fact, the human ear finds it difficult to measure level of sound because we make our own adjustments logarithmically. Changes in the difference of sound, though, are extremely relevant when cutting your program. While sharp cuts in scenes are part of cinematic language, in audio they can be noticeable to the point of distraction. Of course, this is often the effect you need to differentiate one scene from the next, but there will be many times when even that is simply too jarring and you might find that mixing your audio through over twelve frames or bringing it up slightly from the start of the scene will make it far more acceptable as an audio-visual experience.

Your edit software may well even incorporate logarithmic audio fades as an option. This refers to creating a more natural sound to the human ear instead of a point-click-and-drag controlled linear curve. On your timeline, this setting applies itself to preview and playback. If you require it

SOUND AS A POUND

Unless you're a sound-designer, the likelihood is that your main focus on your images. This is doing your audio somewhat of an injustice as it's perfectly willing and able to be played with just as much. If you're nice enough to invest in software for your visuals, do the same for your sounds.

incorporated into your program, you have to reselect it during export.

Most of the tools that you use for editing your pictures are equally applicable to your audio tracks. A cross fade will cross fade an audio transition, a rolling edit will make way for your audio clip, and so on. While this makes syncing your sound an easy companion to your pictures—and another reason why audio is very much stuck on the back-burner with edit software—it can also hinder the effect of your production.

Unlinking the synced audio from your images lets you be a little more creative and get the effect that you want from your WAVs and AIFFs. Working with sync sound as a separate entity can cause you unnecessary headaches, though, so find a way of working that is structured or you will either be leaving your audio or your video behind. Probably the best way is to lay a bed of your images with synced sound in place and then unlink each clip or clips in transition chronologically to work on individually.

This is the start of your audio deconstruction-construction process.

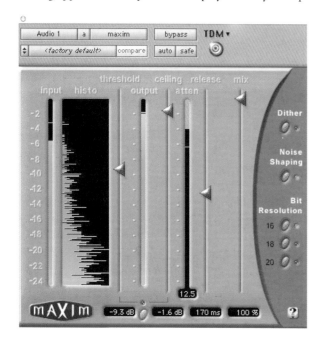

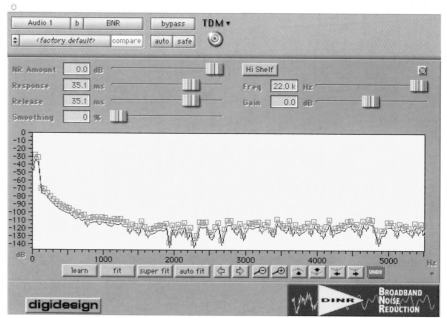

GET THEE TO AN AGENCY

Voice-overs are very particular and can be very trend-led. Many people think they can do one, but it's a sad fact that given an imposing mike and a script, most people can't. There are plenty of agencies out there that will be more than happy to send you demo CDs of their voice talents that can bring new life to your production at a price.

Breaking down your audio timeline sensibly depends, of course, on the nature of your production. In the worst-case scenario, though, you will have three different elements to your soundtrack: dialog, sound effects, and music. Whatever the combination of these in your program, always dedicate at least one separate audio track for each. Working off one preview monitor, though, can be a bit of a juggling act when there are pictures to consider as well, so try to maintain your good timeline housekeeping by expanding audio tracks when you are concentrating and not dedicating too many tracks for fear of ignoring them or losing them entirely. Like your video clips, lay your most important tracks from the timeline outward, so you can always see the crucial track that you're cutting with or—if it's music—to.

DIALOG

When you are working with dialog, you will hopefully have ensured that it was laid to your DV tape. Dialog is extremely noticeable when it is out of sync—even by a frame. The problem with timelines is that once one frame is out, there's a tendency for the problem to snowball. And this usually means that the frame rate for your audio doesn't correspond to the frame rate of your video.

If you are taking your dialog off DAT, confident that your method is tried-and-tested enough to sync properly, your problem is always going to be different takes and syncing to your clapper. But then, if you're bold enough to be doing it this way, you've probably learnt that lesson and written the book.

Because dialog is the central driving force to anyone's program—if they're using it—it has to be clear WHAT THE SUBJECTS ARE SAYING. If they are quiet, lift them with some gain. If there is hiss or hum getting in the way of your making them audible enough to hear, then you will have to think about putting them through an audio processor. As a general rule of thumb, hum is slightly more workable than hiss, particularly because, if you are really pushed, you can hide it under an audio effect to some degree. Hiss, on the other hand, is a closer frequency to the the human voice, something that we are programmed to notice rather more.

Your dialog doesn't have to be straight. An audience, with their subconscious understanding of cinematic language, understands voices off-camera. If you don't particularly like a shot with your subject in frame talking or you simply want to add a different rhythm to your program, lay their voice on your dialog track and use another shot as overlay. If you're going to do this, remember that you are then not limited to using a specific take. You may find that another version of the shot has better audio or a better delivery. Your audio software may let you pan the sound from one speaker to another. If it does deal with stereo sound this way, then dedicate a speaker to the direction of the voice in your chosen overlaid frame. This only adds depth to your audio.

Just like mixing sound or pictures from one scene to the next, dialog is also understood if it overlaps the last few frames from the previous shot. This is easy enough to do on the timeline by unlinking your audio and video and chopping off the top of your dialog shot, and leaving the audio long.

SOUND BET

The Fairlight Computer Music Instrument was the first commercially available digital sampling instrument—a classic. Today, Fairlight suites have developed to become an integral part of high-end audio postproduction with both their DREAM and FAME series.

Introducing your dialog shot from the last frames of the preceding one has the effect of giving the speaking character control over both scenes. This lends itself to either omniscience or soap-opera irony with a character talking about something that is going on behind their back.

Dialog isn't just about using these techniques for narrative. They work with documentaries too. While you might think about your interviews on one track and your voice-over on another, there are few times when either will interact unless using your interview for natural sound. Factual programs actually become more real with rougher sound—not that this is an excuse not to pay any attention to sound... But even though sharp cuts in sound from location to location may exaggerate reality, they are not too pleasant on the ear, so they may require slight fade-in/fade-out or mixing through from the previous shot.

Your dialog track is also where you would place your Voice Of God. There are two ways of working with a VOG: place it onto the timeline and work to it, or cut your video and write your VOG to the pictures. There are benefits and drawbacks to both: the former lets you talk about whatever you wish at the price of being forced into padding out certain scenes and cutting your favorite shots in others; the latter lets you work with your precious pictures to your esthetics, but corners you into talking at length about things that don't need much explanation or shutting you up when you've got a lot to say. If you opt for writing a script to your images, three words to one second is a very useful guideline. There are also client and budget implications in scriptwriting before you go to edit. They will be able to check it over for factual accuracy and general approval, and you won't be wasting money cutting and recutting your images to a constantly revised VOG. Having said this, they may start adding to your script with sentences that you haven't the pictures to use as wallpaper...

When recording a VOG, try not to do it live in the edit and into the machine. Your digital video camera is a perfectly good tool, records at exactly the same frame rate as your images, and is your required 16-bit 48KHz CD quality. It is also portable. If you're going to use your camera, rather than a professional audio suite, take it somewhere you won't be disturbed, somewhere dampened by furniture, and away from airconditioning or street noise. Test your equipment first and find the right distance from talent to mike without being a victim of popping, noises made by their pronunciation of p's and b's. This will mean that they are too close to the mike, but don't put them much farther away or you will end up competing their voice with the ambience of the room.

MUSIC

Music is something that can be very over-used by over-enthusiastic auteurs. Music is a bit like a special effect—it is special only if there is a reason for it to be there. Music is there to support your images and the only exceptions to this are when it's the music that you are promoting and not the images, in which case it's the other way around.

The ways to support your images, though, come in many different guises. Sometimes letting your images speak for themselves is absolutely the way to go. VOG can not only be tiresome if used top to tail in your video, it can be redundant. Instead of explaining the obvious, do away with VOG and bring up some music along with your natural sound as an interlude.

Likewise, scenes can often do with a little breathing space—not ponderous, aching hang-ons from the shot, but just enough to stop the video from being a downhill scramble of cuts to the end credits. Breathing space can often be lifted to the right side of cumbersome by a bar of music or a short, recurring theme or "sting."

If you haven't composed your soundtrack in a separate audio application or studio, don't be afraid to experiment either with an audio application or with royalty-free music CDs. Such CDs are widely available and are, in the main, horrible corporate affairs. In a litigious world, steer away from using your favorite band's track—even if you are planning only on domestic use. The reason for this is that if you do eventually decide to put your project into the public domain (on the Internet, say), you'll have a hard time getting the copyrighted music off,

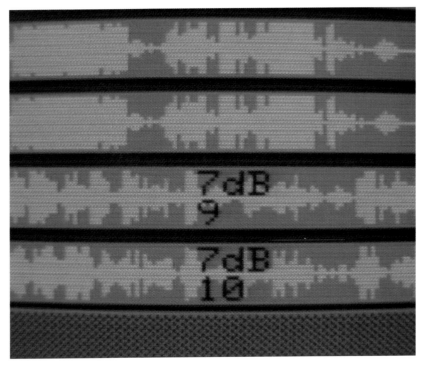

AUDIBLE RHYTHM
Above: Keeping your audio tracks as waveforms can really help to gauge a rhythm to your visuals. Left: Copyright-free CDs can be useful when you just want to fill in a few gaps in the background of your audio. Unfortunately, the genres of music or effects tend to be so generic that they can be heard by keen ears a mile off. Keep them low and use them sparingly if you have to at all.

unless you saved off your project and clips at the time to remake it.

Music can invoke a place—great for travelogs or low-budget movies where the Gobi Desert is actually your sandpit. It can be ironic—a jolly 1920s Charleston always goes well with teen slaughter. It can be predictive—informing of impending disaster. Use music for a reason—the exception that proves the rule being a high-kicking song and dance number in a construction corporate.

SFX Sound effects are a crucial part of any narrative; not so any other genre. If you're using sound effects, use a separate audio track. Sound effects are to be used if any part of your live sound doesn't supplement the action sufficiently and there's little that you can do with it in the edit, or for where the sound is absent.

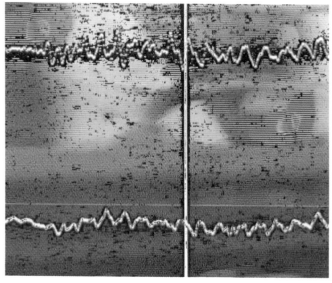

The danger of sound effects is quite apparent with ludicrous embellishment in any TV home video show (no one makes a sound that loud when they hit their head against a window) and on many dubbed foreign movies. Amplification is one thing; exaggeration is another—especially if you are trying to suspend belief.

Aside from sound level, there are enough critics (and Charlton Heston) out there to tell you that the gunshot you sampled is not the Beretta of your clip, but a double-barrelled twelve-gauge. Choose your effect wisely. Sometimes (in defiance of Charlton), the most inappropriate effect is the most effective when put through an audio production tool. It might not even be a sample of a gun: some of the best stabbing sounds have become part of the cinematic audio language by using knives and cabbages. Why the odd producer wasn't used to sample the real sound is part of audio's mystique…

Sourcing audio samples can be done on the Internet, but often a low sample rate means that they need converting. An 8-bit 11KHz WAV can be imported into a sequencer or worked up with tools, but this is only really to disguise the sound's quality. WAVs are, by nature, uncompressed. Lower-end audio software will often have a converter, but some of the more expensive ones don't. Logic won't lower itself to use MP3 as a format, for example.

Aside from the Internet, CDs provide a stock answer. Audio effect CDs are rife and you automatically get CD quality of whatever the sampled sound is. CDs tend to come in

AUDIO VISUAL
The audio track for this pop promo has been dragged in sync to the visuals, providing constantly moving lines to track matte images behind. Clever, effective, interesting—and above all, simple.

themes and most are copyright-free—which is why if you watch enough media, you will often hear the most popular samples in completely different programs.

Your sound effects, used sparingly, will take up only a few tiny blocks on your timeline. They are very easy to lose if you're not careful. For this reason, your SFX track is made wide open for your atmos to be brought in. This is where your ten minutes of standing round in a herd of cows pays off. Atmos—natural ambient sound recorded at your scene's location—can be annoying to the hearer if too quiet or too loud. It's just one of those things. If you find the right level, you can quickly raise your production value with the richness of audio within the scene: it really works to place your subjects within their surroundings.

Again, atmos can be found on the Internet or on CDs and is merely a bed laid for the rest of your audio to lie on. Because it runs from the beginning of a scene to the end, you always have to think about this audio track in terms of subtly mixing your audio from one scene to another. Certainly, if you're doing it with your pictures, don't forget to do it to your SFX track with atmos.

THE MIX Mastering audio is not to do with writing audio as such; it's working with the dynamics of your audio in relation to your video. By using your audio software to finish off the audio to your video, you really can deliver 50% of the production deal.

If you have two sounds with similar frequencies, they'll be fighting for the same space. These are the types of issues if you've got a loud kick drum and a loud bass drum where their frequencies are such that one masks the other. It's more of a hazard for an auteur when dialog is being pushed out of the way for a soundtrack or a sound effect. There will always be an annoyance or a redundancy of sound if you simply treat a conflict of frequency with volume. The way to get around it is by eliminating the same frequencies out of, say, the kick drum or the sound effect. This is EQing—equalization.

Gating will let any background hiss be silenced, which is excellent for cleaning up dialog tracks. Using gating, silence itself can be reduced to nothing to make room for more sounds to fill the space should you want them.

Dialog tracks or voice-overs can also be compressed to temper massive contrasts in peaks and troughs of volume. Compressing it reduces the dynamic range, bringing up the quieter parts of your soundtrack within easy reach of the lowered peaks.

Your dialog tracks are the most important thing you have, so be sensitive with them. Master the dialog track from your video separately from the rest of the audio to enable the relationships between the two to be easily controlled. Don't let them get drowned out by loud music—but then don't let them take over or the rest of the soundtrack becomes a mere annoyance. It's worth recalling the one exception that doesn't prove any rule here: a nightclub scene in David Lynch's *Fire, Walk With Me*, where the music is so loud that there are subtitles for the incoherent dialog. Indeed, in some versions of the film, it's interesting to note that there aren't subtitles…

BOOM BASS MIX
Non-linear desktop editing has replaced the conventional mixing desk with a digital screen interface. Audio suites and purists, though, still rely on the sensitivity that manual, programmable sliders provide and the sound that they deliver to your soundtrack.

Mastering your audio also means you can make use of any panning or direction effects that you might have in your edit or audio software. Don't go too far with it or you'll drive yourself and your audience mad. Even one well-placed pan on an effect can really raise the production values of your video.

You can control the relationship between one track and another to a comfortable balance—again, bring another pair of ears in to listen to the finished audio. See if they can put images to it in their mind before watching the masterpiece with the mastered sound. Does it all make sense? If it does, it's time to mix it down, save it off and import it as your master audio track.

The array of video effects and transitions available in an NLE can be quite overwhelming as a playground. Worse still, the ability to both customize them and multi-layer them turns the possibilities of two simple shots into Disneyland.

Don't be overwhelmed—and don't let them overwhelm your production. As an auteur, you followed your instincts and creativity, and designed your program beautifully. You called the shots. And you didn't call them to be teased and tweaked, distressed and deconstructed by an effects palette.

Well, you might have done. And as they're there, it would be a mortal sin not to use them.

Trends with effects come and go. When wipe buses and mattes became a broadcast reality in the 1970s, pop video makers went crazy, matting their wipes and wiping their mattes until the world cried "stop". In the 1990s, there were a good five years when nothing could be seen around the border of a frame because of the digital Vaseline smears. Effects and transitions can date a program, though—like all good trends—they eventually come around again.

This is still an inherent feature of effects and transitions in edit software, or as plug-ins. They still insist on providing blasts-from-the-past, maybe just in case they come into fashion once more. Or maybe some people just like to show off their A to B push-offs.

Effects and transitions can add or subtract from your production values. The use of color and black-and-white is a typical example. A richness of color doesn't just throw back to overcompensation when color televisions came in, but when Technicolor turned the cinema upside-down. On the other hand, black-and-white's retro-yet-always-contemporary look tends to beautify subjects and scenes by highlighting tone and form. Used in tandem with a slight flare and contrast, and cut hard against a colorized shot, it can work wonders for your production.

PART 04. THE EDIT

CHAPTER THREE

FX, TRANSITIONS, AND TITLING

WAVE MACHINE

Trends in effects come and go, but if you can find something that works with your imagery, it'll never be out of style. This is a ripple effect in full flow punctuating a beat and accompanying a clip of a musician on a beach. Thematically it makes sense to a viewer and thereby becomes visually easy, not just cheesy.

BREATHING SPACE
Using long mixes can create
entirely new images between your
clips. Using high contrast on this
mix lets the second image live
through the heavy blacks of the
first image throughout the
duration of the transition.

A lot of the plug-in transition and effect applications that are available talk about "incredible" transitions and "cool" effects. Funnily enough, though, add a few of them and there's very little that's incredibly cool about your production. It'll just look as though you've been playing around in your playground, and essentially lower your production values. Corporate videos are notoriously the worst offender for this. They have a tendency to cover up the fact that it's a company's vanity project with a whole load of outdated effects and transitions. See that box in the corner with the blonde fleshpuppet spouting her lines? Watch her bounce against the edge of the frame with the two hard-hatted men pointing at a blueprint. Sometimes, learning from watching tripe can help you no end.

COURSE OF EFFECT

The root map that Combustion displays is a useful device to see the chronology of effects throughout this mini-timeline of image compositing. From this window, effect paths can be moved or individual layers selected for tweaking.

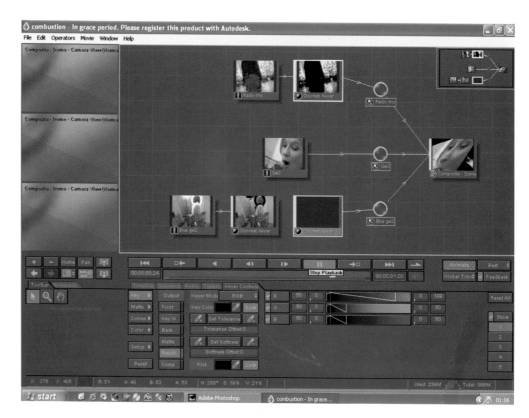

Practically, there are a few rules with placing effects and transitions on timelines. While effects are dragged onto the clips themselves, transitions have to be dragged onto your transition line and overlap between the clips above and below for the duration of the transition. Every kind of edit software has its own quirks: in Premiere, a clip has to be in video track 2 or higher in order to be eligible for right-click > transparency.

Always question the real realtime ability of your effects. As said, all the effects on a good videocard can't be realtime—there are too many of them and too many algorithmic permutations. Often there are a good handful, and these will only be realtime if they exist in one layer. Drag one more effect or even another realtime effect on top and you are probably forced to render.

Remember the rules of transitions and their relation to time. With narrative, a dissolve marks time passing; a hard cut tends to infer a passage within immediate time; and a fade to black is the end of an era or cinematic chapter. In fact, these three devices are the only transitions normally used within broadcast and cinema. Anything more and you are into the realms of music, children, kitsch, and the televisual delights of light entertainment.

The bottom line is that effects are great if used simply for correcting and enhancing your image to raise your production value, but fancy transitions are best left to demonstrate your videocard's realtime potential. They are fun to play with, though.

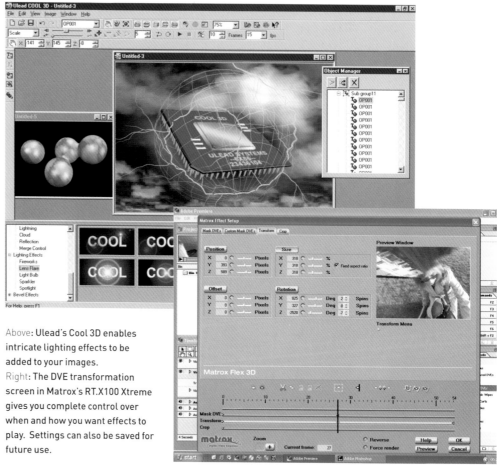

Above: Ulead's Cool 3D enables intricate lighting effects to be added to your images.

Right: The DVE transformation screen in Matrox's RT.X100 Xtreme gives you complete control over when and how you want effects to play. Settings can also be saved for future use.

TITLING Titling is a strange thing. It turns your program into A Production. It makes an audience aware that you, the auteur, think that it is worthy of watching and that you are proud of your product. Conversely, if you don't have titles, your program becomes undefined (without the knowing awareness of a painter using the title *Untitled*) and perhaps unfinished. This is not necessarily a bad thing.

As an example, more and more Hollywood movies are doing away with titles in order to represent their production as a "reality." This is usually an edit decision, as traditional start titles can be quite apparently seen at the end of the movie.

Traditional titles are such that Hollywood lists, in order, the distributor, the production company, the name of the movie, the actors, the body of significant crew, and then the director of photography, writer, producer, and lastly director. Television, on the other hand, keeps things minimal and can just have the name of the program and the writer.

Decide what kind of genre your production fits into and whether you want to follow a trend or buck the system. You can often lead the audience into believing that they're about to watch one thing and then pull the rug with something else. If you try this, make it deliberate—if it's ironic, be subtle. The last thing you want is to annoy or bore your audience before your opus begins. They'll sit through the rest of it, arms folded with an "amuse me" neon sign over their heads.

By not boring the audience, it doesn't mean to say that you have to have the flashiest titles ever. Indeed, the flashiest titles tend to overwork your processor and the results, when compressed, can make flashy simply look cheap. The most important thing about titles is that they are legible. If you have something to say and you want an audience to read it, use the same rule that you should for captions: they require at least three seconds in view. That means that if you're mixing up and down, place the mixes outside the three seconds.

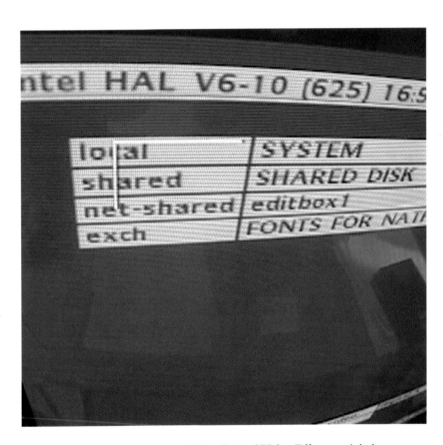

ENTITLED TO BENEFIT
Working within screen-safety is vital for broadcast and pretty essential elsewhere. While screen ratios vary, so do different types of monitors or televisions. Work out how you intend to play your program before you begin titling or you may find out that you're missing pixels, letters, or words.

Using Digital Video Effect won't help your legibility or quality either. The more effects you use, the greater the loss of resolution—and on titles, aliasing becomes unforgiveable, especially if you're bringing the titles up to the front of the screen. If you are thinking about doing this, create the titles large and reverse the effect, not the other way around. "Steppiness" is all too obvious with white or colored titles matted onto any background (although less so on export).

TEXT EFFECTS

Once you've created your title and moved it onto your timeline, your work with it doesn't have to end there. Transitions and effects can be applied to your text just as much as they can to your pictures, which creates some unique results.

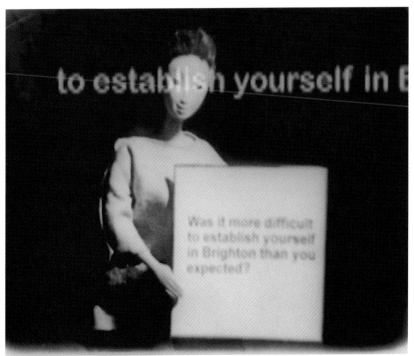

Think thematically for dramatic effect: remember the titles sliding away like forgotten memories in *Total Recall* or the titles that become part of New York's architecture in *Panic Room*. And yet, even if your software doesn't have the capabilities of 3-D or motion control titling, remember that some of the starkest, most radical, and even menacing titling can be straight black on white or white on black.

The real way to manipulate a title without using anything remotely fancy is by your background and your soundtrack—similarly to how this can be used as a pay-off into your credit roll. Abel Ferrara's *Dangerous Game* uses the black on white/white on black to great gritty effect with a silent soundtrack, while *Evil Dead* plays its credit roll out to a comedy gramophone track for sinister release. And of course, no introduction to titling would be complete without mention of Saul Bass, designer of the titles for Hitchcock's movies. The simplicity of horizontally dividing titles to invoke the schizophrenic themes within *Psycho* are obvious, effective, and now much easier to create within an NLE environment.

Use sound effects with your titles as an alternative. The screeching of tires as the titles speed on and off in Bass' *Goodfellas* sequence is, again, easy and effective—especially if you're opening with a car scene. It's almost de rigueur to let your titles follow your opening critical scene in many genres, so find a way of relating the two. If you have chosen to superimpose the titles onto a montage, don't cover up what you're trying to show. And if your opening contains dialog, don't let the titles interfere with it for fear of losing the concentration of your audience. For this reason alone, titles are often used over broadspread landscape establishers or a significant fragmentation montage.

TITLE-TATTLE

While you might have all the digital titling and captioning capabilities under the sun on your NLE, there's no reason why you should always use it. If your production calls for something more quirky, more hands-on, do it—or use both.

Titles are a good way to experiment in your edit, if you have the time or budget. If you haven't the time, they are also a good challenge for someone else with fresh eyes on your project. When you start to add titles, open up a few more video tracks to work with. Make sure you are working with screen safety on, and work critically within it.

Technically, the other two major points involve those of opacity and motion or mixing through. Video 1A or 1B will create an opaque title, whereas it is only in Video 2 or higher that complete superimposure can take place. Your title software may have roll or crawl options to bring the title into and out of frame, but if you are mixing them through into vision, use your elastic bands, accessing them by expanding your video track.

Mattes are useful tools for your titles, not only allowing them to be resolved properly onto your background images, but to add effects. And, of course, effects and transitions themselves can be added, bearing in mind that the more effects, the more loss of resolution, something that titles will show vividly. Feathering or blurring, even through another layer, can help out here.

All of this is applicable to captions and credits, although titlers do tend to keep these a little more simple for instant legibility.

PUT IT IN THE MIX

Top: Mixing media can create some truly distinctive effects. This is a mixture of telecine and digital text compositing.

Below: Final Cut Pro's LiveType application uses keyframes to let you animate titles and wireframes and to enable you to monitor any work that you do in realtime.

GRADING AND LEGAL COLORS Color correction is one of the most important tools in your effects box, not just for wielding willy-nilly over your clips, but to keep them legal. If you are thinking about broadcast as the perfect porthole for your video, you'll have to abide by a few rules that broadcast media sets out.

Legal broadcast colors are measured in IRE—to you, the Institute of Radio Engineers. Broadcast television has different tolerance limits for both luminance and chrominance, which vary depending on whether the source is digital or analog. A standard digital system uses a luminance range from 0 (black) to 255 (white).

With digital video, the luminance range permitted for broadcast is 16 for black and 235 for white, keeping it well within the limits—black is 6% brightness and white 92% brightness. This relates to your color values as 16 for each R, G and B at the darkest limit, and 235 for each R, G and B at the brightest limit.

If you are exporting to an analog format for broadcast, the IRE values change. While white is universally 100 IRE, black is 0 IRE with PAL, SECAM, and Japanese NTSC, but 7.5 IRE with American NTSC. Make your adjustments to suit and don't ask why…

The way that edit software will deal with the adjustments you make to get your pictures legal are to change a pixel's brightness (luminance) or move the pixel's color saturation towards a gray of equal brightness (chrominance).

BROADCAST VIEWS
While high contrast (within legal limits) works with the production value of monochromatic images, it can make color "shriek" badly—and illegally.

To actually apply broadcast colors to your program depends on the facilities that either your edit software or your videocard software have to offer. If your video effects palette doesn't have a broadcast or legal color option, then try your videocard settings when exporting. If you see any mention of IRE, you might be halfway there.

If you are playing out to NTSC analog, make sure you are ticking the 7.5 IRE box. The other things to watch out for are your titles, graphics, and credits. If you're creating these in a different application, make sure that you're putting them through legal color correction at the time. If you do it once they're on the timeline, your (usually) vivid colors will change dramatically.

SAVING YOUR EDIT FROM DISASTER
All is not lost. Okay, so you can't quite hear what your lead is saying, and she's out of sync anyway—but you can only just tell because the shot's so dark (except for the bit with the silvery dropout). There's always another way.

RESHOOTS AND OUTTAKES

Impractical, inconvenient, expensive, and sometimes impossible, a reshoot of a scene in whole or in part can be pretty disheartening for all concerned. On the plus side, you will have learnt what's wrong with your scene and you'll be overcompensating to make sure that it doesn't happen again. A reshoot also gives your talent a chance to better their performances, and it gives you a chance to fix anything else that wasn't quite perfect in your scene. It's expensive not only because you're shooting again, but because of the edit that you are missing out on.

If it is just a bit of dialog that you've lost or is incoherent, consider ADR (Additional Dialog Recording). Professionally, this is cue-based in an audio suite with your talent. Unprofessionally (not that anyone ever is in this game), it's sitting with your talent and a hot-plugged or video camera mike and watching the clip on repeat until the repeated dialog hits the mark.

If you're just missing a cutaway, you've got brief dropout or you just need something to paper over a small bit of audio, find an outtake—even if it's just an abstract blur. If it looks like nonsense even if you tart it up with effects, find a shot and DVE in (digital zoom as an effect) to get rid of the continuity context. Use that close-up of her eyes that you shot while she was having her make-up applied or, if it still isn't working, aim your camera in the edit and capture a tight of something else in your surroundings: your hand holding a pen, your keyboard, a passer-by out of the window…

AUDIO

If you've got audio hum or hiss, or you can hear the airconditioning or some other distraction, invest in an audio processing tool—it's absolutely the best thing you can do rather than reshooting. And while cleaning up your audio is your first stop, if it doesn't work, try some similar frequency ambience in the back of the shot to explain (and disguise) the distracting audio.

If you're out of sync with your audio at 24fps and your video at 25fps and this is snowballing, it's the video frame rate that needs adjusting, even if that means remaking the entire project. The change in frame rate of video by a frame is far less noticeable than with audio. If there's too much done or not enough time to start remaking, use long shots, long mixes, blur-outs—whatever it takes at the end of a scene to disguise the sync slip.

USE THE COMPUTER

Color correction, contrast, and brightness, gain—all of these filters and more will assist you in cleaning up your pictures and audio. As effects, they will lower your resolution to some degree but that's just NLE's nature.

If you've made a mistake with your actual editing, Edit > Undo Edit is the key to most problems, especially if you have set your project to save at regular intervals. Use your history and effects trashcans to get rid of regrettable edit and effects decisions and revert to get rid of all your rash decisions since you last saved. The best advice with saving is to give your project a different sequential number every time you're closing it down, giving you a few versions of the same project on different edit days. Better still, save them off onto an external hard drive as you go to avoid confusion between each of them, and in case your computer decides to act up.

CLEANING UP

Good cleaning tools show you the result of what filters are actually doing to your production before you apply them. Canopus' ProCoder not only does this, but allows for editing and stitching of clips as well as encoding entirely different types of files at the same time.

CUT CUT CUT

If it's dull, cut it. The problem with inexperienced auteurs is that they think that anyone and everyone is interested in what they have to say. Just because a shot took an inordinately long time to set up or the limo for the sequence was incredibly expensive to rent doesn't mean that it's got anything more to say than any other shot.

When your narrative or the point to your documentary isn't clear or has no rhythm, it's probably not doing its job. Find someone who is objective and represents the kind of audience you are playing to, to come into the edit and watch it. Shorter is usually better and the more dismissive you are with shots, the more you can raise your production values.

Be ruthless, not precious.

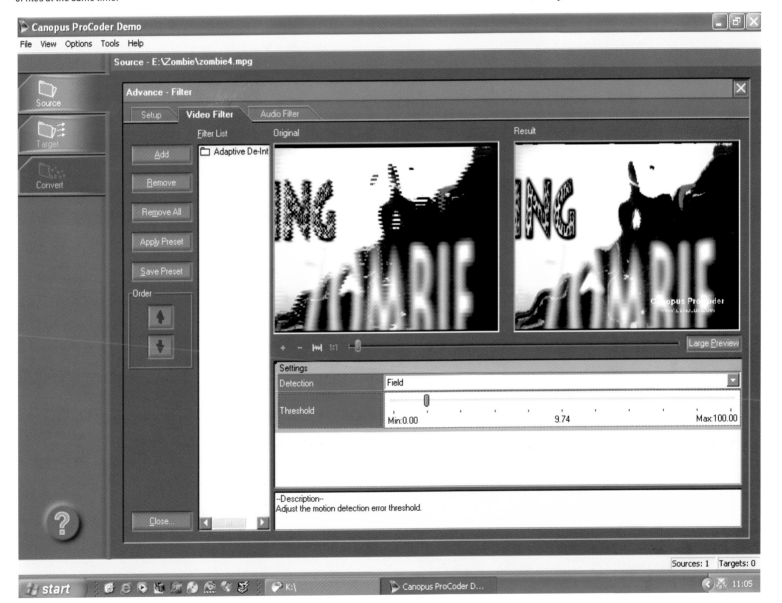

EXPORTING

EXPORTING Exporting your program can be one of the most time-consuming and frustrating experiences in your project. You are eager to see how your finished production will play away from the preview confines of your edit software, and all it seems to be doing is making your picture look worse.

Here's a thing: sometimes, it will look worse.

Your project exists as a preview, even including your final render. In order for you to do anything physical with it, the project has to be converted from the virtual into the real world. Exporting has to be based on your original project settings to function, or you may just find all of your precious clips erased. The only change that you are making is the format of how you want your program encoded. With a change in format, you might want to alter the settings for export, such as the resolution that you want, the bitrate, your audio preferences.

When you are encoding to anything other than AVI, which is most probably how your media has been reading your files, bear in

EXPORT CONTROL

Below left: Encoding and exporting programs to MPEG as a professional DVD requires intricate monitoring to check that all images and audio are within legal limits.
Below right: Make sure that you're previewing your production during conversion. It can be a time-consuming process—and a time-wasting one if an evident problem with your movie or your settings becomes obvious only when you play back your encoded effort.

mind your distribution. If you are exporting to stream, always consider the user viewing it and their lowest possible quality workstation. Your CPU will work faster the cooler it is.

As well as tweaking your export settings, the most important consideration for export is in which format you want to contain your video. The opposite page shows a breakdown of this.

Your other alternative is to export back to DV via FireWire to your digital video camera. This is the best way to archive if you want to keep the resolution and quality of your program. Use some black leader, bars, or a clock at the top of the tape for the first thirty seconds to get past the more easily damaged part of your tape.

With certain videocards, the dream prospect of realtime export is now becoming more common. This means that instead of your project taking forever to export, it will export one minute for one minute… within limits…

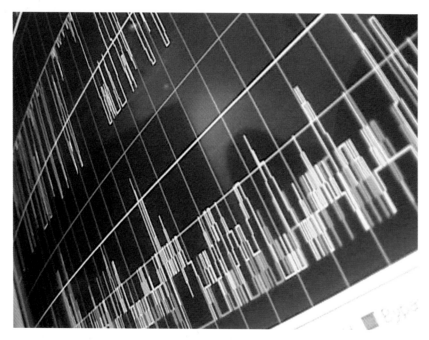

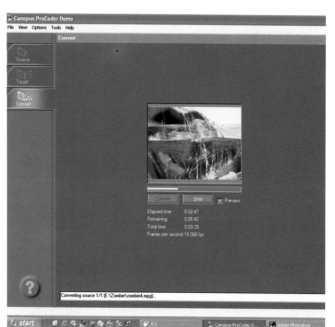

FILE FORMAT	EXPORT TARGET	PIXEL RESOLUTION	FRAMES PER SECOND	COMPRESSION	VIDEO BITRATE	AUDIO
Mov	CD-R Quicktime	4000 x 4000 max		Cinepak, JPEG MPEG-1		22KHz
MPEG-1 NTSC	CD-R VCD	352 x 240	29.97	MPEG up to 100:1 but is lossy from about 10-20:1	Max 1.7Mbps	44.1KHz
MPEG-1 PAL	CD-R VCD	352 x 240	30	MPEG up to 100:1 but is lossy from about 10-20:1	Max 1.7Mbps	44.1KHz
MPEG-2 NTSC	DVD-R CD-R	720 x 576	60	MPEG	Max 8Mbps	44.1KHz
MPEG-2 PAL	DVD-R CD-R	720 x 480 1280 x 720	60	MPEG	Max 8Mbps	44.1KHz
AVI NTSC	Windows Media Player Quicktime CD-R	720 x 480	29.97	RLE, DivX, Indeo Cinepak Sorenson et al: low compression		48KHz
AVI PAL	Windows Media Player Quicktime CD-R	320 x 240 720 x 576	25	RLE, DivX, Indeo Cinepak Sorenson et al: low compression		48KHz
VCD NTSC	Windows Media Player MacVCD DVD-R, CD-R DivX	352 x 240	29.97	MPEG-1	Max 1.15Mbps	
VCD PAL	Windows Media Player Mac VCD DVD-R, CD-R DivX	352 x 288	25	MPEG-1	Max 1.15Mbps	
SVCD NTSC	Windows Media Player Videolan (Mac) DVD CD-R	480 x 480	29.97	MPEG-2	Max 2.6Mbps	
SVCD PAL	Windows Media Player Videolan (Mac) DVD, CD-R	480 x 576	25	MPEG-2	Max 2.6Mbps	

MPEG-4 The latest standard defined by the Motion Picture Expert Group is MPEG-4. If you ever see this as an export or save option, it's a standard that allows compression for streaming media.

The standard that MPEG-4 can offer is potentially MPEG-2 quality with lower data rates (5Kbps to 10Mbps) as a video and audio stream. An MPEG-4 codec provides a variable bit rate controller that can be adjusted between high quality and high speed (may they never meet…). The compression is based on Quicktime technology, but the files are a lot smaller and are able to be delivered by a much narrower bandwidth.

There are versions of MPEG-4 suitable for different jobs. These nine video and four audio profiles allow specifications for different tasks from mobile phone video or audio compression to HDTV. Alongside this versatility is its interactive capacity. MPEG-4 standard permits interaction with video itself, bringing up menus and other features at the touch of a button. This makes it of particular interest to websites and DVD—indeed, it's touted as an MPEG-2 replacement.

The good and bad sides of MPEG-4 are where it comes to digital video. While DV is plagued with incompatibility problems, MPEG-4 has been embraced by most companies as the way to go. The bad side of it, as ever, is that DV is still the best quality to edit with, so carry on as you were. Indeed, any audio expert will tell you that if its destiny is to become a video MP3, we're all in trouble…

VIDEO CONTAINER FORMATS

.mov
Apple's QuickTime Audio/Video Container. Sports a variety of features such as multiple audio/video streams, sprite tracks, header information at the beginning of the file, Annotations, Text Tracks, and support for hundreds of codecs. This is the basis for the MP4 file format.

.avi - Audio Video Interleaved
Microsoft's first video format. Header information is placed at the end of the file. Limited codec support. Spec has been hacked too many times, and is not fully supported.

.mp4
ISO MPEG-4 file format, based on the QuickTime .mov file format.

.m2v - MPEG-2 Video
Raw MPEG-2 video. Often found multiplexed in .vob or .mpg files

.m1v - MPEG-1 Video
Raw MPEG-1 video. Usually found multiplexed in .mpg files or .dat files on VCDs.

.mpg
Container for MPEG-1 or MPEG-2 video. Usually multiplexed with an audio track. MPEG-1s can be found on VCDs.

.asf - Advanced Streaming Format
Microsoft's second video format, principally designed for streaming.

.vob - Video OBject file
Main video container on DVDs and SVCDs. Can contain audio, video, subtitles, etc., all multiplexed in.

3ivx
High compression, high quality, low bitrate. Variation of MPEG-4. Very good results, usually found in QuickTime .movs; can be in .mp4's combined usually with .mp3 or .aac audio.

DivX
High compression, high quality, low bitrate. Variation of MPEG-4. Good results, usually found in .avis combined with .mp3 or .ac3 sound.

XviD
High compression, high quality, low bitrate. Variation of MPEG-4. Very good results, usually found in .avis, .mp4s, and possibly .xvid).

MPEG-1
Moderate compression, found on VCDs and many web downloads. Can be high quality. Usually contains MPEG-1 Audio.

MPEG-2
Moderately compressed. Usually high bitrate, high quality, found on DVDs and SVCDs. Usually combined with .ac3/.dts audio (DVDs) or MPEG-2 audio (SVCDs, some DVDs).

Sorenson 3
Moderate compression, can be high quality. Found in QuickTime .movs. Common for web downloads (e.g. Apple's Movie Trailer Site).

DV
Low compression. Found on video form DV camcorders, used in iMovie.

Animation
Usually found in .movs. Nearly uncompressed, used for exporting to a high-quality source (such as animation) from QuickTime.

MJPEG
Low compression. Usually found in QuickTime movies. Basically, just a lot of JPEG pictures in a movie (Hence the name Motion JPEG).

Component Video
Packed YUV4:2:2 format.

YV12
Planar YUV4:2:0 format.

ENCODING, BURNING, AUTHORING, AND COPYRIGHT The Digital Versatile Disc uses MPEG-2 standards to compress information. It can store between seven and thirteen times the amount of information that a CD offers, and it can use dual layers on both sides of the disk. Therefore, the amount of data that can be stored on a double-sided dual-layer DVD-ROM would be nearly eight hours of MPEG-2 compressed audio and video.

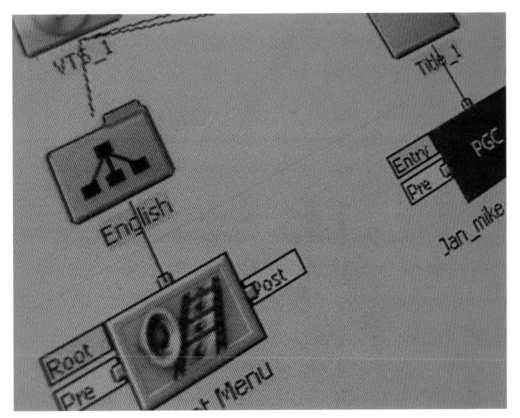

A DVD-ROM, however, is read only, and can be read by any DVD recorder. A writeable DVD-ROM, though, comes in different formats with compatibility issues:
DVD-RAM can be rewritten but is not compatible with most DVD-ROM drives or DVD players. It's more like a removable hard disk.
DVD-R and DVD+R can be written only once.
DVD-RW and DVD+RW can be rewritten many times.

AUTHOR! AUTHOR!
Because of the nature of menus and sub-menus within DVD authoring, it's useful to have a root map to show exactly how they branch. Any problem areas can quite easily be seen from this logical screen.

The dash formats are supported by the DVD Forum and the plus formats by the DVD+RW Alliance in an effort to explain the confusion, but writeable DVD drives are getting better at understanding the difference. If you are having problems reading a disk between two drives, format support is your first stop. Disks that are writeable are able to store 4.7Gb of data each side—a single-sided disk is called DVD-5, and a double-sided disk DVD-10.

Manufacturers' preferences aside, there are two main uses for recordable DVD. The first is as an archive for files. This will give you 4.7Gb to simply transfer files onto your writeable DVD-ROM. The second way—and perhaps the most appropriate for digital video users—is for playout of your finished production. This doesn't simply require copying the file over if you want it to automatically play on any DVD player.

There are three steps to this becoming a reality, encoding, authoring, and burning:

ENCODING
Your digital video footage has already been compressed, but the bitrate is still too high for DVD. For this reason, you need to encode your program again to be within DVD's maximum rate of 9.8Mbps.

Export your production using MPEG-2, making sure that your frame-rate is compatible for PAL or NTSC. For your audio options, opt for Dolby Digital if you can, or otherwise your selected 48KHz. Your videocard will either let you make these

BURN, HOLLYWOOD, BURN
Right: Sony's dual rewriteable DVD/CD drive records over 2 hours of high quality MPEG2 video on either DVD+RW/+R or DVD-RW/-R.
Below right: Roxio's Easy CD & DVD Creator doesn't just stop at burning DVDs. It captures, edits, and manages photos, videos, and music. DVD Builder is the authoring and burning application within the software and provides a friendly interface for quality production.

decisions or default to its own MPEG-2 settings. If so, go with the flow and hope for the best (quality). If you can't directly export using MPEG-2 encoding from your capture card, export your project as an AVI and use an encoder or authoring software to transcode from there. MPEG-2 is a plug-in encoder for applications such as Premiere, although you may find your videocard doesn't like to be ignored during export.

AUTHORING

To author your MPEG-2 file, you can create chapter stops, menus, and links using a dedicated application. There is some great authoring software out there that makes this very easy, so it seems a shame not to use it. As it's made easy, don't worry about creating chapter stops in your edit software. It's also something that can't be undone once you've exported it anyway, which doesn't give you much room to maneuver once you are working with your app.

A lot of the DVD authoring software is pretty cookie-cutter, but that shouldn't stop you from being able to import menu and button designs or using other fonts from desktop graphics applications. The actual process of authoring requires the building of data architecture and file management information based on DVDs specifications.

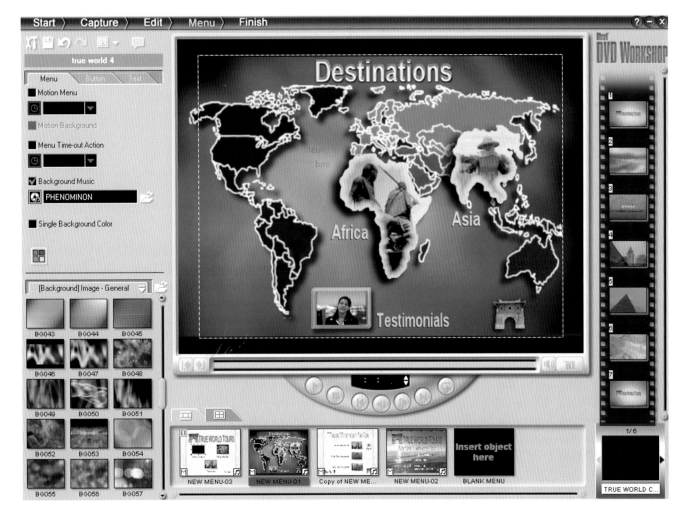

BURNING

Storing your authored video data onto DVD is the easy part of the whole process because your authoring software will be keen to do everything for you. Your only real problems will be the application's support of your DVD drive.

If you have skipped both previous steps, you are probably just burning data files to disc. If this is the case—even if your file is encoded as MPEG-2—without authoring software that will convert your information, you will most likely be burning to CD-R. Platforms that house Windows XP simplify dragging and dropping your files into your drive, by asking what you want to do with them when you single-click on them. Burning operates by copying the file, not transferring it, so if you are cleaning up your system for archive, don't forget to go back to the original files to zip them up for storage elsewhere on your computer or—eek—delete them. If you're deleting them, make sure you check your burnt files on the CD first and label it immediately.

FLEXIBLE FRIEND

Versatility is becoming the trend for DVD burning software. Ulead's DVD Workshop contains facilities for editing as well as building slideshows and introducing menu soundtracks. Its strength, though, is in graphics and text, something appealing to all those who want their productions finished on DVD with finesse.

COPYRIGHT

The copyright belongs to you unless:
• It belongs to your employer if you have created your video during the course of employment.
• It has been purchased by another business or individual.
• You've signed a work-for-hire agreement.

Official registration for copyright isn't obligatory—all it does is support you financially in a lawsuit. If you are putting your video on the Internet, you can encode it with information that is embedded in the video itself that refers the copyright back to yourself. It's a big bad Internet world out there and monitoring the use of your video is close to impossible. But what you don't know probably won't harm you…

WEBCASTING AND STREAMING Putting your production on the web may seem like a glamorous idea: a potential audience of six billion, and the chance to be talent-spotted by a rich media mogul… In reality, the current limits of the Internet impose limits on your personal production. While your video might be of the highest digital quality, it won't be once it is on the Internet. This is largely to do with a server's available bandwidth and tailoring your production to the lowest common denominator user.

Exporting your project as an Internet multimedia extravaganza is an option that you will probably have once you've finished your production. Making the choices that suit you and your server from there is another option.

There are two fundamental ways of delivering your production to an end user:

DOWNLOADABLE MEDIA

This is your video placed on a web server made available to a user for download to a drive. The entire video has to be downloaded and opened before the user can view it. The most popular formats for these are Quicktime, MPEG-1, and AVI.

PROGRESSIVE DOWNLOAD

This is your video placed on a media server. Playout from the server will begin before the whole of the video has been downloaded, relieving the computer's hard drive of storing the video before the viewer can play it. Depending on how fast the user's connection is, the video will begin streaming only a few seconds into download.

While downloadable media can be stored on your web server in its existing exported format, streaming media (progressive download) has to be encoded through a specific streaming architecture. The three main architectures around are Windows Media Player, Quicktime, and RealMedia.

If you have decided that you do want your video to stream from your site, you need to check that your service provider supports streaming media. If you are using a web server, the data stream going to the user is a simple file transfer—the video information is sent to the user and it is left up to the appropriate architecture on their machine to work out the bitrate used when the file is played out. This is because the file is actually being transferred to one of the user's cache files, but is played during transfer once enough information has been buffered in the application.

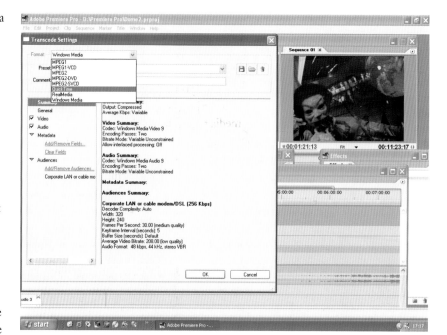

If you're using a media server, the server will detect the limits of the user's ability to accept streamed information and deliver the file in three-second increments to the user's cache to let the file be played continuously.

Delivering the video from the server can be engineered in three different ways. Unicast is one data stream that is copied and sent to anyone who wants to view your video on demand. Multicast is one data stream that is accessible by multiple viewers at the same time. Reflected multicast is either a unicast or multicast stream that is detoured via another server to become multicast.

Progressive download has become known as pseudostreaming due to the arrival of true streaming. True streaming is now an option with all three of the main architectures

QUICKLY DOES IT
Exporting your movie to be downloaded or stream is becoming easier and easier. Now that everyone is a director, everyone's got something to show to the world. Software like Premiere and Final Cut Pro very much hold your hand and offer options that make exporting as Quicktime, MPEG, or AVI simply a matter of ticking the right boxes.

and may be available to you when exporting your project. The reason that it is "true" is that the stream plays straight into the user's machine in realtime—that is, there is no storage in that cache file at all. It does this by means of a specialized server compensating for available bandwidth by adjusting the rate of transmission.

Your video and audio together are huge files and your problem is either going to be with the user's impatience to download or with your server's capabilities. The settings you apply to your project when exporting make crucial differences to the way that your masterpiece is viewed and who is going to view it. Multiple bitrate files, ensuring that the stream bitrate is adjusted to available bandwidth and smoothing the audience's viewing experience, are only available from a streaming server. Each of the three main architectures have their own technologies for this: Quicktime's uses Hinting; Windows Media Player uses Intelligent Streaming; and Real uses SureStream.

Think again about your audience when you configure your settings. Are they likely to be the kind of people with Broadband (businesses, home offices, media types), or are they stuck with a 56K modem (families, occasional users, the locationally unfortunate)? The one thing that you don't have to worry about is that all the main architectures are cross-platform.

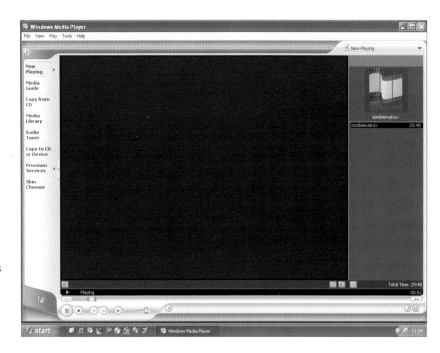

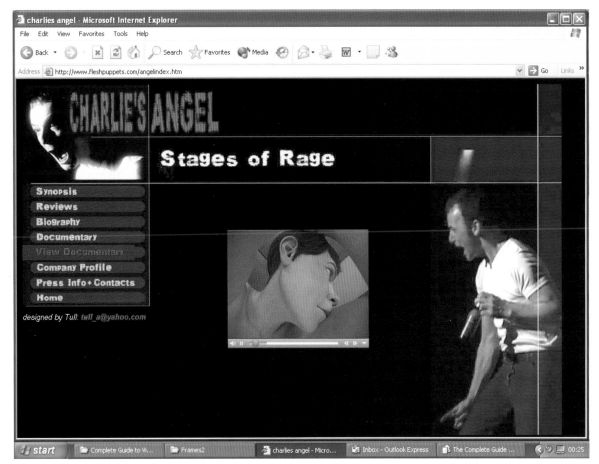

STREAMING THROUGH

Above: **Windows Media Player** opens as a new application and displays a multipurpose streaming screen that invites more than just the playout of your download. It's diverting—and might even divert viewers away from your site onto one of Microsoft's own.

Left: Alternatively, a Quicktime download can be placed as an incorporation of your webpage, giving viewers a sense of your own branding and offering text around the moving image that can supplement it.

GLOSSARY

A/B roll A term derived from film editing in which two picture tracks are laid side by side in sync with each other. Desktop video editing programs like Adobe Premiere and Ulead Media Studio Pro use a system of parallel video tracks, Video A and Video B—between which transitions are applied. More advanced programs like Final Cut Pro now offer a much looser method of track assembly, but the principle is the same.

ADC Analog-to-Digital Converter. A digital video camcorder employs two ADCs—one to process luminance and the other chrominance. Given that the human eye is more sensitive to brightness than it is to changes in color, luminance is sampled at four times the rate of chromance.

ADR Additional Dialog Recording. A system employed in professional audio dubbing studios that enables artists to replace dialog recorded on location with new, clean dialog in the controlled conditions of a recording studio.

AGC Automatic Gain Control. Circuits designed to increase a signal in order to bring it within acceptable parameters, such as light or audio. Used in a camcorder's automatic video audio level control circuits.

AIFF Audio Interchange File Format, the native audio format on Apple Macintosh computers.

anamorphic Normally associated with widescreen recording and playback, anamorphic lenses or attachments produce a true 16:9 widescreen picture, as opposed to the pseudo widescreen effect offered on many DV cams, in which a standard 4:3 picture is cropped top and bottom to give a letterbox

effect. Some recent camcorders use a "wide" CCD to achieve this.

aspect ratio The ratio of the width of a picture to its height. The conventional video and TV aspect ratio is 4:3 (4 units of width measurement to every 3 units of height). Widescreen video has a standard aspect ratio of 16:9.

audio sampling Sound entering the video camcorder via a mono or stereo microphone needs to be converted from analog to digital before it can be stored on tape. On entry, it is sampled at a frequency equivalent to twice its highest pitch—most commonly sampling at 48, 44.1 and 32kHz. (See also Nyquist Theorem).

authoring The process of combining all of the media assets into one file prior to the execution of a DVD or CD video project. Results in the creation of a .VOB file containing compressed video, menu graphics, and chapter marking data.

autofocus A circuit provided in all consumer format camcorders and many professional ones, in which the optical system will focus on the predominant object within the visible image.

AVI Audio Video Interleaved. A Microsoft media file format for use within Windows, and the default file format for captured video files on Windows-based systems due to its high-quality compression. Also used as an internet streaming and nonstreaming format.

Betacam-SP The system of recording broadcast-quality analog component video signals to half-inch video cassette, developed by Sony Broadcast, and commonly used in TV and video production worldwide—especially in news and

current affairs programming. Though still in use, it has largely been replaced by Digital Betacam and Betacam SX, as well as DVCAM, DVCPro, and Mini-DV portable digital production formats.

bidirectional The field of sensitivity possessed by a microphone which gives it a figure-eight sensitivity pattern. Useful for picking up conversation between two people.

bit A commonly used acronym for binary digit, the smallest piece of information a computer can use. Each alphabet character requires eight bits (called a byte) to store it. (See also byte.)

BITC Burnt-in-Timecode. After being read from a tape's timecode track, the timecode data is inserted into (and over) the relevant video frames. This can be copied to a logging tape, such as VHS, without subjecting the master to wear and tear.

breakout box A connection box designed to connect to a computer's FireWire (or other serial digital connection) in order to convert incoming analog (composite, s-video, and audio) signals to IEEE1394 standard digital using the computer's FireWire port. Breakout boxes will normally facilitate digital-to-analog conversion, too.

byte A single group of computer data made up of eight bits (0s and 1s), which is processed as one unit. It is possible to configure eight 0s and 1s in only 256 different permutations. A byte can therefore represent any value between 0 and 255. Multiples are commonly measured in thousands (kilobyte), millions (megabyte) and billions (migabyte).

call sheet The form containing details of a forthcoming shooting location, in addition to timings and lists of who and what is required and by what means they are to get there. Issued to all artistes, crew, and other personnel by the production office or Production Assistant.

capture card Unless preinstalled, a capture card occupies a spare PCI slot in a computer and contains the input sockets required to capture sound and vision into a computer prior to editing. Video capture cards will contain one or more IEEE1394 FireWire sockets to enable the connection of a DV or Digital-8 camcorder. (See also i.Link.)

cardioid A term applied to the heart-shaped field of sensitivity of many popular microhones, with the larger area being in front of the microphone's pickup head.

CCD Charge Coupled Device. A critical component of a digital video camcorder, the CCD has a photo-sensitive surface containing an array of semiconductors, each collecting data for a single pixel. The CCD converts the information into an electrical charge that is proportional to each pixel's color (chrominance) and saturation (luminance). As a general rule, the larger the CCD, the more pixels it is capable of generating, which in turn leads to higher-quality images.

chromakey The process of electronically substituting an alternative image or sequence into an area of continuous color within a video picture. This is commonly identified with TV weather broadcasts where a presenter, actually standing in front of a blue or green screen, appears in front of a computer-generated weather map. The overlaid image is keyed to a specified color—or chroma reference. Also known as Color Separation Overlay (CSO).

chrominance The technical name for the color component of a video signal.

codec An abbreviation for Compression / Decompression. The result of mathematical algorithms applied to dispense with redundant data in an image or sound file in order to save space without perceptible loss of quality when decompressed and displayed.

color temperature
See Kelvin scale.

composite video An analog video signal in which the luminance and chrominance signals are combined into a composite signal, which uses a single connection for transfer of data between devices.

compression The 8-bit ADC generates too great a stream of binary numbers for an average camcorder's circuitry to handle, so the data has to prioritize the information into what it needs and what it can dispense with. After two filter stages, the resulting compressed datastream is written to tape. The DV codec, as used by MiniDV and Digital-8, is the result of a 5:1 compression ratio.

CRT Cathode Ray Tube. The technology behind standard TV sets. A cathode ray tube uses electron guns to project RGB (red, green, blue) beams of light at a phosphorous lining on the inner face of the screen.

data transfer rate The speed of data transmitted across a communications network, measured in bits per second (bps).

dichroic filter A filter designed to permit certain wavelengths of light to pass through whilst filtering others.

DigiBeta The near-standard professional film and television production format favored by broadcasters around the world.

DVCAM, DVCPRO Higher-specification variations of the MiniDV standard used by broadcasters. Sony produces DVCAM, whereas DVCPRO is the product of Matsushita (Panasonic).

DVD Digital Versatile Disk. High-capacity development of the Compact Disk, allowing storage of up to 4.7Gbytes of data, including MPEG-2 files for playback on domestic players.

EDL Edit Decision List. The list of decisions that have been made during the use of an editing program. The EDL contains specific references to timecode in/out points and all the events connected with the assembly of the final master program in order that the project might be later reassembled using the list as a blueprint. An EDL is used to convert an offline edit to an online master edit.

fields A conventional television picture comprises of sequences of frames, each of which is made up of two interlaced fields. PAL video uses 25 frames per second, which are displayed at 50 Hz. NTSC is displayed using 525 lines at 30 fps (actually 29.97 fps) at 60Hz. Each field represents one pass—odd scanning lines followed by even lines. This interlacing reduces the effect of flicker.

FireWire A standard of high-speed digital data transfer employing a single cable connection, which was developed and patented by Apple Computer Inc. Now the standard means of connecting digital camcorders to suitably equipped computers and other devices.

fishpole A precision-engineered telescopic pole—often wrongly called a "mic boom"—designed to support a microphone during filming or recording. The fishpole will often be handheld by a boom-swinger or a sound-recordist in a position close to the sound source but out of camera shot.

f-stop A measurement of the aperture, or opening, of a lens and measured in f-numbers. Each f-stop represents a doubling of the amount of light entering the lens over the preceding higher number. Eg: f2 passes twice the light level than f2.8 does.

FX (Effects) A general film and TV production term for effects that can be applied to either sound (SFX) or video (VFX). In desktop video, FX are normally associated with the digital transitions that are applied to two or more video tracks—the FX track being the one containing the transition between the primary and secondary video tracks. In audio, an FX track is one containing spot effects of dogs barking, gunshots, and so on.

helical scan Videotape wraps around a head-drum during recording, enabling the minute recording and playback heads to write and read tracks at an angle across the tape. This helical scanning system was further developed by IBM in 1995, resulting in no physical contact between the heads and the moving tape. This system is employed by DV systems in which the heads rotate at 9,000 revolutions per minute.

Hz Hertz, or cycles per second. Sound sampling frequencies are measured in kHz (kiloHertz). DV camcorders typically sample and digitize audio at 48kHz 16-bit stereo.

12-bit audio (as available on camcorder with an audio dub facility) is sampled at 32mHz, 12-bit rates.

i.Link The Sony registered brand name for a digital connection that conforms to the IEEE1394 standard for high-speed data transmission (commonly known as FireWire).

IEEE1394 The technical specification for the FireWire data transfer standard.

image stabilization Optical Image Stabilization (OIS) and Electronic Image Stabilization (EIS). The former uses optical elements to compensate for camera shake, producing marginally more steady images. The latter processes incoming data digitally to achieve a similar effect. The advantages are minimal in low-cost camcorders.

Kelvin scale A scale for measuring the color (or "temperature") of light, and universally used by film and videomakers as well as stills photographers. Average daylight is measured as 6,500 degrees Kelvin in Europe and 5,000 degrees Kelvin in North America. Blue colors radiate high temperatures, whereas red colors radiate lower temperatures. Artificial tungsten light has a red bias.

Li-Ion Lithium Ion. A compact rechargeable battery system for use with camcorders and other portable devices. The battery's initial charge will be seen to drop quickly during initial use, but will then stabilize.

luminance The technical name for the saturation, or brightness, of a video signal.

macro A lens, or lens attachment, designed to provide pin-sharp images of objects situated in very close proximity to the front lens element.

GLOSSARY

matte A matte is so-called due to its roots in early cinema production, where a "travelling matte" (as flown by the mythical Ali Baba) was inserted into a sequence of film using hand-painted luminance reference and optical printing. Today, electronic blue and green screen techniques have long since replaced hand-painted mattes. See also Chromakey.

Memory Stick Flash memory storage card developed by Sony. Memory Stick PRO allows 1 gigabyte of storage with a theoretical capability of 32 gigabytes. A rival format to the older SmartMedia and Compact Flash cards, and the newer SD Memory Card (Panasonic).

MICROMV Sony digital video format that encodes a variant of MPEG-2 to videocassettes that are 30% smaller that MiniDV.

minijack The standard means of input and output for microphones and headphones on consumer-format digital camcorders, mobile audio players, etc.

MOV The file extension applied to Quicktime media files. The default video capture file format as used by Apple Mac-based video capture and editing applications.

MPEG Motion Picture Expert Group, responsible for the MPEG-1, MPEG-2, MP3, and MPEG-4 formats.

Ni-Cad Nickel Cadmium. A type of rechargeable battery cell commonly found on professional camcorder systems and some consumer formats. It discharges at a steady, even rate.

NLE Nonlinear Editing. The use of computer systems to digitally capture and arrange video, audio, and associated media clips using appropriate editing software. Evolved from the use of linear, tape-based editing in which sequences and shots had to be assembled one after the other, making rearrangement difficult.

NTSC National Television Standards Committee. This is the TV standard employed in the USA, Canada, Japan, other countries in South America, and many nations in the Pacific. NTSC uses 525 lines made up of two interlaced fields scanning at 29.97 frames per second or 59.94 fields per second. SECAM recordings will often play in monochrome on PAL TV receivers.

Nyquist Theorem Henry Nyquist, who joined Bell Labs (USA) as an R&D engineer in 1917, developed a theory that the sample rate of an analog frequency must be at least twice the rate of the source's analog frequency for perfect digital coding and decoding. According to his Theorem (1924), it would take 8,000 samples (2 x 4,000) to capture a 4,000Hz signal perfectly.

offline A term applied to a process of producing a lower-resolution cut of the edited program whilst preserving the quality and security of the original master tapes. Today, offline editing is undertaken using low-resolution digitized rushes into a computer video application like Avid, though the practice has its roots in the use of low-quality video-cassette copies made with burned-in timecode.

online Online editing follows the process of offline editing, in which the Edit Decision List is used to produce a master conform of the original rushes in the assembly of a final edited master tape. (See also EDL, offline.)

PAL Phase Alternation Line. The standard TV display format for the UK, most other European countries (with the exception of France), Australia, New Zealand, and several African nations including South Africa. PAL is made up of 625 lines, using 25 frames made up of two interlaced fields, this producing 50 fields per second.

postproduction This is the process that takes place once production footage has been acquired, and encompasses everything from the first offline cut to computer graphics, edit mastering, compositing, and audio track-laying and dubbing. It's common to talk of a production going into "post."

POV Point-of-View shot. A commonly employed cinematic device designed to represent the viewpoint of a character in a sequence. A cylcist, for instance, might be proceeding along a street when a car crosses his or her path. The camera assumes the position of the cyclist as contact with the car is made, offering the viewer the cyclist's "point of view."

progressive download A method of receiving a media resource from a remote web server without having to wait for a complete download prior to viewing or listening to the file. In the case of audio and video, the early portion of the file will be viewable whilst the remainder downloads in the background.

progressive scan A process of combining interlaced fields (see PAL, NTSC) into a sequence of single "progressive" frames at rates of 1/50th sec (PAL) and 1/60th sec (NTSC). This reduces the effect of flicker, and benefits the recording and playback of sequences where sharp individual frames are required. Several DV camcorders now support Progressive Mode shooting.

quantization The human eye is able to distinguish approximately 2 million colors, and an 8-bit camera CCD using 8 bytes (one each for red, green, blue) per pixel can represent 16.7 million colors (256 x 256 x 256). However, visual interference (noise) can result, and this is referred to as quantizing noise.

Quicktime Media compression and streaming playback format developed initially for use on Apple Mac computers, and now also available for use with Windows PCs.

real time The ability to set up and view often complex video effects and composites immediately at full resolution. Real Time (RT) video cards boost the computer's ability to perform these tasks without the editor having to wait for rendering to take place.

render The process of producing a composite file from a number of source files—such as video clips, audio clips, titles, graphics, etc., on a desktop video program timeline. A render will also take place in order that the result of applying a transition between two video clips may be viewed. On fast computers, renders will take place in real time. On other systems, rendering might be undertaken as a background activity. A "final render" is the effect of preparing the completed project in a format appropriate to a particular use, such as compressing as MPEG-2 for DVD playback.

RGB Red, Green, Blue. The three primary colors employed and processed by all analog and video systems. Analog data is converted to a digital data stream by an Analog to Digital Converter (See ADC.)

SECAM Sequential Couleur avec Memoire. TV system developed in Russia and adopted by France. It is similar to PAL 625, but employs a modified system of color encoding.

Steadicam A portable gyroscopic film and TV camera mounting system designed to provide a high level of stability for cameras when worn by a trained operator. Steadicam is an equipment brand that has earned generic status, though Glidecam is an alternative brand designed to achieve the same effect.

streaming A method of making a media file (audio, video) available to a user's web browser without requiring a download in order to hear or see it. Commonly used for live web-casting.

S-Video A process of transferring and recording standard composite video in which the chrominance (color) and luminance (saturation) are handled separately in order to reduce picture noise. Used by Hi-8 and S-VHS format devices.

telecine The process of electronically scanning each frame of movie film negative or positive and converting the image using an array of CCD imaging devices into digital information, which can then be transmitted or recorded as digital video.

telephoto Term applied to a lens with a high level of magnification. A zoom lens' telephoto setting is considered to be its maximum magnification factor.

timecode A system of uniquely identifying a frame within a video recording, whether analog or digital. The timecode is made up of four sets of two digits, representing hours, minutes, seconds, and frames, which are generated internally within the camcorder (or, in the case of other recording systems, by a standalone timecode generator) and electronically embedded into the recording. Timecodes can be used to identify the location of a shot within a recording on tape, providing that the codes are unique—DV camcorders have a habit of resetting the code to zero if a blank section of tape is detected.

timeline The visualization of a video or film project in time. Desktop video applications emply a timeline as a means of constructing the clips that make up a project, starting with the first clip at the zero point and proceeding to the end in a left to right direction. Some desktop video editing tools offer an alternative method of viewing clips on a timeline, commonly referred to as the Storyboard viewing mode.

transition The means by which the viewer is transported from one part of the story to another using a wide range of visual tools. The most common transition is a dissolve (also known as a mix or crossfade). Other transitions includes wipes (linear, rectangular, and circular) and DVEs (more complex digital video effects in which sequences are assigned motion paths relative to each other).

turnkey A system that has been designed and built to be switched on and operated without the user having to make additional modifications or settings. Many professional desktop video editing and compositing workstations are designed as turnkey systems.

USB Universal Serial Bus. A standard port on most modern computers for the connection of peripheral devices. USB has two versions: USB 1 offers transfer speeds of 12 Mbps, whereas USB 2 can transfer data at 480 Mbps.

video capture card The video capture card is used to connect the camcorder to the computer being used to edit a video production. Typically, the capture card will contain one or more FireWire ports enabling the transfer of data from the camcorder to the computer and back. Such cards will often occupy a PCI slot in the computer, although they are increasingly built-in to modern systems as standard.

VNR Video News Release. The video equivalent of a printed press release in which corporate bodies, charities, and other organizations employ video cassette or disk as a means of disseminating a message that might incorporate interviews, key footage and other supporting information.

VOG Voice of God, also known as commentary or narration. The narrator is not seen but is omnipresent, hence the term. Commonly referred to as a Voice-Over, the commentary, narration, or VOG track will be added to the edited production by a voice artist using a V/O booth at an audio dubbing facility.

VTR Video Tape Recorder—a generic term for all systems that record video to physical tape, though commonly used to describe open reel-to-reel systems like 2" Helical, Quad, 1" B, 1" C and half-inch helical recording systems. VTRs are now rarely seen outside specialist archiving and transfer facilities.

WAV Derived from "wave" or "waveform." The native audio file format as used by Windows-based computer systems.

white balance The process of referencing a camera or camcorder to either daylight or artificial (indoor) light in order that white objects (e.g.: paper) appear their correct color on camera. (See also Kelvin scale, color temperature.)

wide-angle converter Optical lens attachment designed to reduce the minimum focal length of the lens and therefore increase the field of view. Will also have the effect of increasing the depth of focus of a shot. Typically, a wide-angle lens converter will offer a factor of 0.5x to the cam's focal length.

wide chip A CCD imaging chip employed by manufacturers, such as Sony, to enable the resolving of true 16:9 widescreen images without the need to crop a standard 4:3 image by the use of black bands at the top and bottom of the screen.

XLR A standard 3-pin connection most commonly used with microphones and high-quality audio sources feeding a camcorder, recorder, or mixer with a balanced audio signal.

Y/C A video signal in which the two main components—the luminance (Y) and the chrominance (C)—remain separate throughout the signal chain. If the Y and C components remain separate, the resulting image display will not suffer from the same cross-luminance and cross-chrominance artifacts as composite video. (See also composite video.)

Zoom A zoom lens is used to vary the focal length of a lens by altering the relationship of the optical elements within the lens. Zooming in and out can also be achieved by digital signal processing within the camcorder—called Digital Zoom—though high zoom ratios are to be avoid due to the resulting heavy pixelation.

INDEX

index

ACKNOWLEDGMENTS

DIGITAL DISCOURSE AND EXPERTISE

Professor Mike Bird
Colin Barrett, http://www.simplydv.co.uk/
DVC, Brighton

SPECIAL ASSISTANCE AND IMAGERY

Asdis Petursdottir and Matrox
Daniel Loshak and Discreet UK
Sarah Bell and Sarah Browne and Sony (Europe)
Hayley Buery and Canon
Lesley Vernon and Canopus UK
Jeffrey Hyland and JVC UK
Adobe images courtesy of Adobe Systems
AVID images copyrighted to AVID
Dazzle images courtesy of Dazzle
IBM images courtesy of IBM
Intel images courtesy of Intel
LaCie images courtesy of LaCie
Mac images courtesy of Apple
Roxio images courtesy of Roxio
Sennheiser images courtesy of Sennheiser
Sonic Solutions images courtesy of Sonic Solutions
Soundblaster images courtesy of Soundblaster
Ulead images courtesy of Ulead
VisioWave images courtesy of VisioWave

IMAGE SUBMISSIONS

Sarah Baker
Elisabeth Bayliffe, BBC
Katie Bond
Jane Couldrey, Picnic Productions
Kathryn Fleet
Fleshpuppets
Gary Miller, Akira Films
Sean Moody
Eduardo Sanchez

TIME AND TOLERANCE

Amrit, Eduardo, George, Kath, Mark, Martyn and Maxim
Jennie Jones, Bill Cullen and M2 Post Production, London
Oasis Television, London
Louisa dePrey
Barrie Dunn
Thomas Hanover
Clea Smith

SPECIAL THANKS

The cast and crew of G-Gnome, the internet, and all those
tearing their hair out in video forums